# A SHADOW ON THE HOUSEHOLD

# A SHADOW
# ON THE
# HOUSEHOLD

ONE ENSLAVED FAMILY'S
INCREDIBLE STRUGGLE FOR FREEDOM

BRYAN PRINCE

McClelland & Stewart

LIBRARY AND ARCHIVES CANADA CATALOGUING IN PUBLICATION

Prince, Bryan, 1951-
A shadow on the household : one enslaved family's incredible
struggle for freedom / Bryan Prince.

ISBN 978-0-7710-7125-6 (bound)

1. Weems, John – Family. 2. Weems family. 3. Freedmen – United
States – Biography. 4. Slaves – United States – Biography. 5. Freedmen –
Canada – Biography. 6. Slavery – United States – History. I. Title.

E444.P75 2009          306.3'62092          C2008-904191-7

We acknowledge the financial support of the Government of Canada through the Book Publishing Industry Development Program and that of the Government of Ontario through the Ontario Media Development Corporation's Ontario Book Initiative. We further acknowledge the support of the Canada Council for the Arts and the Ontario Arts Council for our publishing program.

Typeset in Fournier by M&S, Toronto
Printed and bound in Canada

This book is printed on acid-free paper that is 100% recycled,
ancient-forest friendly (100% post-consumer recycled).

McClelland & Stewart Ltd.
75 Sherbourne Street
Toronto, Ontario
M5A 2P9
www.mcclelland.com

2  3  4  5      13  12  11  10  09

To John and Arabella

# SLAVE FAMILY

CECILIA TALBOT

ARABELLA MARGARET

M.

JOHN WEEMS

MARY JANE (*free name* STELLA)

CATHARINE ANN

WILLIAM AUGUSTUS

THOMAS RICHARD (DICK)

CHARLES ADAM (ADDISON)

ANN MARIA

JOSEPH

JOHN LEWIS

SYLVESTER

MARY

ANN MARIA (ANNIE)

M.

ABRAHAM YOUNG (*slave name*)

WILLIAM HENRY BRADLEY (*free name*)

MARY MAGDELINE

CATHARINE ELIZABETH

# SLAVE OWNER FAMILY

ADAM ROBB

JANE NEAL     JOHN     ALEXANDER     CATHARINE ANN

M.                                       M.

UPTON BEALL                      HENRY HARDING

JANE ELIZABETH          CATHARINE JANE

MARGARET                 ELIZABETH ANN

MATILDA                    CHARLES ADAM

                               WILLIAM R.

                               MARY ANNA

                               M.

ROBERT W. CARTER

ELIZABETH ANN "NANNIE" CARTER-DOVE

When John returned to Washington, he learned the heartbreaking news: the Hardings — attracted by the prospect of sudden wealth or at least a loosening of their financial bindings — had sold his wife and children to the slave traders for the goodly sum of $3,300. Arabella and their sons had been transferred to a slave pen in Washington, D.C., where they would be sold and sent to the South forever. Meanwhile, their remaining daughters had been sold to slave traders and were now held in the nearby town of Unity, Maryland. In an act filled with venom, the Hardings had stipulated that the Weems family not be sold to anyone in the vicinity of Washington.

Fuelled by desperation and love, John used his best powers of negotiation to save his family. A noble man in Washington pledged to loan him $1,600, but only if John could raise the remaining $1,700. This proved impossible to do in a short period of time and the pledge was lost. Such was the peculiar nature of the pledge — it was to be all or nothing, perhaps because if the entire family were purchased, they could all work to repay it.

Time was running out. It was becoming clear that John's children would be lost to the South and probably his beloved Arabella as well.

CHAPTER I

JOHN AND ARABELLA WEEMS LIVED near the town of Rockville in Montgomery County, Maryland, just outside of Washington City, the capital of a country that claimed to embrace the ideals of independence and equality. In its infancy the United States was divided into the North and the South. Although it was halfway down the map and bordered on the free state of Pennsylvania, there was no mistaking that Maryland was in the South; everywhere, it seemed, was gentility and hospitality – and slavery.

John Williams Weems and Arabella Margaret Talbot received the sacrament of marriage from St. Mary's Roman Catholic Church on March 1, 1829, an uncommon privilege for the majority of slaves throughout the South, who consecrated their marriage by "jumping the broom" or other less formal rituals, if there was any ceremony at all. (In the fifteenth century, the Catholic church had ordered slaves to be baptized throughout the western hemisphere, including in Maryland, a largely Catholic state. Once baptized, these slaves became eligible for the sacrament of marriage and for a Christian burial.) The priest who married John and Arabella carefully noted in his ledger all of the ceremonies that he performed, for both slaves and their owners, occasionally recording unique details such as a Protestant husband's promise that any children born to the marriage would be baptized by a Catholic

*St. Mary's Church in Rockville, Maryland, where John and Arabella Weems were married and had their children baptized* (courtesy Peerless Rockville)

minister and that he would never hinder his wife from observing her faith.[1] He also noted special dispensations granted by the archbishop, such as for cousins marrying or for grooms who were minors.[2] In one case of a "presumed impediment of *honestas publica*" – the couple was suspected of having prematurely consummated their relationship – he listed the consent of the bride's mother and sister.[3] Entries in this priest's ledger usually designated race whenever blacks were involved, with "col'd" in the margin, or "free black" or "property of" beside a name. Later entries indicated that the masters had given written permission for their slaves to marry, as was required by a papal decree. Another entry suggested a double cause for celebration, one immediate and one in the near future: the marriage of Ann to "Henry Edmonson, yet for a little while property of Edward Daws."[4] The record of John and Arabella's marriage simply said: "John, a free man, to Airy, property of

Mr. Robb. Witnesses, William, property of the same Mr. Robb, & Susan, property of B. Curran."[5]

As the nineteenth century reached its midway point, the Weemses had become the parents of a large family, and by law, the offspring of black couples took the mother's status, so the Weems children were born slaves. John had purchased his own freedom before marrying. He worked as a labourer on the modest Rockville farm of George Huddington, struggling to support his family and to set aside a few dollars in the hope of eventually buying his wife and children.[6] He was "a peaceable, unoffending, industrious citizen, who had always supported his family in comfort and respectability."[7] "Airy," as Arabella was affectionately called, was "a slave-woman of superior culture and endowments."[8] She was devout and very well respected from an early age, having, from the time she was fifteen, frequently been chosen to be godmother to neighbourhood children.[9] Depending on the whim of her master, Arabella was occasionally allowed to share a home with John, and each year they paid him a large sum in exchange for the privilege. With the income from their labour going to their owner and to feed their large family, it was difficult to save money. They tried their best because both Arabella's master and his daughters had promised John that he could buy his family's freedom at a bargain price. But like so many slavery-related transactions, it eventually turned out to be a deal made with the Devil. In the meantime, the family went on about their lives as best that they could.

Being devout Catholics, they took each of the children in turn to St. Mary's church in Rockville to be baptized: first Mary Jane, then Augustus, then Catharine, then Richard, followed by Adam, then Joseph. John Jr. and Ann Maria were baptized on the same day.[10] John and Arabella's extended families witnessed each baptism from the upper loft where the "Negro pews" were situated. In attendance were Arabella's mother, Cecilia Talbot; her younger sister Ann Maria; Mary Jones, who was probably her older sister; close friends (or possibly relatives)

Charlotte Brannum (Branham) and Hester Diggs and their families; as well as the Butlers, Tylers, Proctors, Watkins, Cooks, Gants, Brogdens, Halls, and Hattons – all part of a large slave community in Montgomery County whose members were often related by blood. Their community was also a part of a much larger society that consisted of the county's labourers, builders, domestics, farmers, waiters, and launderers. Theirs were the hands that harnessed the horses, stoked the home fires, cobbled the shoes, and rocked the cradles for the social order enforced by their masters. The slave families witnessed one another's sacred rites and shared in one another's joys and sorrows. Everyone knew that none of John and Arabella's children really belonged to them – they belonged to Master Adam Robb and, in the language of legal documents of the day, "to his heirs and assigns forever."

Relationships between master and chattel were complex, ranging from well-earned hatred to genuine affection and everything in between. The Weems family appears to have been treated relatively well by Adam Robb and they were granted a degree of autonomy. Presumably they were favourites, because while Robb ripped apart the families of other slaves, Arabella, her children, her mother, Cecilia Talbot, and her sister Annie Young remained together. Perhaps there was something to Annie's baptismal record, in which someone later crossed out the father's name, leaving legible the priest's original entry: "Adam Robb." Whatever the

*Annie Young's baptismal record suggests her owner, Adam Robb, may have been her father.* (Montgomery County, Maryland Historical Society Library)

reason, the family existed under what was termed "the mild form of slavery." Whether "mild" or not, slavery was a horror nonetheless.

From Robb's household they regularly witnessed their friends' devastation when loved ones were sold away. They could recall the vigilance of the patrollers and bounty hunters seeking the fifty-dollar reward offered for the capture of the twenty-three-year-old runaway slave Basil from neighbouring Prince George's County, who was presumed to have run to Rockville, where his mother was enslaved by Robb.[1] The fact that the Weemses were still together may also have meant that they felt they had nowhere else to run to. This was their home – at least for now.

❧

Maryland had gone through many changes since 1632, when Charles I of England granted Lord Baltimore the territory by royal charter for a paltry rent of "two Indian arrowheads" per year, to be paid during the week of Easter. In return, Lord Baltimore and his successors would grow wealthy from the sale of tobacco to the British Isles. At first, most

## FIFTY DOLLARS REWARD.

RAN AWAY from the subscriber, living in Prince George's County, Md. on the 14th of August, a negro man named BASIL; he is about 23 years of age, 5 feet 6 or 7 inches high, of a dark copper color, and has a down look when spoken to; his mother lives at Rockville, in Montgomery, and was owned by Mr. Robb. I will pay 20 dollars, if taken in Maryland or the District of Columbia, and the above reward if taken elsewhere and secured so that I get him again.

    aug 19—          BENJAMIN B. MACKALL.

*A runaway slave ad for Basil, whose mother was owned by Adam Robb. Ads frequently noted where the slave's family lived, in case he or she tried to hide with them.* (Maryland State Archives) of the intensive labour required to grow and harvest the crop was supplied by indentured white servants, many of whom had leapt at the chance to leave England, with the hope of one day becoming prosperous landowners or merchants themselves. In exchange for their ship's passage, these labourers committed to work for their sponsors for a period of time, often seven years. During their servitude they cleared forests, built homes and outbuildings, and tended crops.

Africans (considered by many of European ancestry to be a lesser species who could rightfully be enslaved for life) gradually replaced the indentured servants. Blacks were seen as being able to withstand the climate, the diseases, and the work better than either Caucasians or Native Americans. Their skin colour made it difficult for them to flee and to remain inconspicuous among whites. Nor could they easily disappear and survive in the wilderness, as Indians could. Blacks could be relied upon – albeit under the threat of painful repercussions for non-compliance – to provide the consistent labour needed for a myriad of New World tasks, including the cultivation of the vast and lucrative tobacco crop.

When the constant planting of tobacco began to exhaust the fertility of the soil, the economic base of Maryland began to shift to smaller mixed crops and more industry, which reduced the demand for slave labour. Conversely, crops such as cotton and sugar cane, which required a huge workforce, became popular further inland and to the south, in Louisiana, Alabama, Mississippi, and Georgia. The invention of the cotton gin in 1794, which more easily separated the seeds from the cotton fibre, led to the establishment of large plantations in those states and to the explosion of their need for slave labour. While slavery became less essential to the financial well-being of Maryland's overall economy, owning slaves remained a status symbol and a continuing source of potential wealth. If work was scarce at home, owners like Adam Robb could rent out their slaves to others and collect their wages.

As was the case in the northern states and in Canada, where owners possessed fewer slaves and often had more personal relationships with them, manumissions were not uncommon in Maryland. A considerable number of blacks were also able to purchase their own freedom, or that of loved ones, with pay received – a few coins at a time – from extra work done during stolen moments. Women might take in laundry, men might fish or trap animals, or families might sell the surplus vegetables grown in small garden patches. In addition, slaves who had been "let out" were occasionally allowed to keep the money that remained after the master had received the agreed-upon rental fee.

As a result, over time the free black population increased in Maryland and the rest of the Upper South, giving rise to currents of unease in the white countryside. Although free blacks enjoyed a measure of rights, by and large they were certainly not welcomed and were often barely tolerated by whites. These "freedmen" competed with slaves and poor white immigrants for the lowest-paying jobs. Even worse in the eyes of many, they served as a constant and unsettling reminder to the enslaved that perhaps their condition was not permanent and that perhaps, despite their owners' arguments, it was not decreed by God.

Legislative measures were taken to prevent misconceptions that free blacks were entitled to any measure of equality under the law. In 1805, the General Assembly of Maryland passed a law decreeing that any blacks who were born free and who wished to travel outside the county in which they had been born had to get a certificate from the county clerk, stating how they came to be free and including a physical description. The clerk was to keep a register of their names, just as he did for blacks who had been manumitted or who had purchased their freedom.[12]

On March 12, 1832, in the early years of John and Arabella's marriage, the Assembly passed another controversial act, which called for the newly incorporated Maryland State Colonization Society to appoint a board of managers "to remove from the State the people of color then free, and such as should thereafter become so, to the Colony of Liberia in Africa, or such other place out of the limits of Maryland as they should consent to go to."[13] This move caused deep divisions throughout all segments of society – both white and black.

The whites had a variety of reasons for supporting or opposing the plan. On the pro side, some Marylanders wanted to be rid of free blacks by any means possible. The recent Nat Turner Rebellion, an uprising of slaves and free blacks, had left shudders throughout the South. After seeing visions and hearing voices that led him to believe he was on a mission from God, Turner and an estimated forty other blacks had killed about sixty whites, using axes, clubs, swords, muskets, and a fence rail, near Southampton, Virginia, before being captured and hanged. Turner himself was hanged and skinned. The aftermath of this revolt was a pervasive fear among whites that they might be murdered by angry slaves who were inspired, assisted, or organized by freedmen. Those of a more sympathetic vein felt that blacks could never be a part of American society and that independence and progress could be theirs only if they were resettled in their own colony. Years later, even the great emancipator Abraham Lincoln would share that philosophy, as his country reeled from the devastation caused by civil war. Other whites were against the act because they worried that it would remove a source of cheap labour and cut into their own livelihoods.

The black community was likewise torn by the Liberia plan. Many felt that because they had been born on American soil, they were entitled to stay in their own homeland, rather than in what they were being told was their ancestral continent. No matter how humble their possessions or oppressive their lot, there was a certain comfort to be found in familiar surroundings. A black waiter in a Washington hotel remarked to a travelling British writer that the establishment of the Colonization Society had hurt all blacks because what little interest whites had previously displayed in their plight had lessened and the desire to be rid of them had increased.[14] For a freedman like John Weems, whose family was enslaved, immigrating to Liberia would mean leaving his wife, children, and other relatives and friends behind – separated no less painfully than if they had been sold and sent away to another state. Mercifully, there was a clause to allow freedmen such as himself to apply for a special dispensation to remain in Maryland – or at least it was merciful if the request was granted.

In 1838, a law was passed in Maryland dictating that anyone caught escaping from the state with the intention of freeing himself was to be sold by the sheriff at a properly advertised public auction and then removed from the state. As assurance that the slave would indeed be taken from Maryland, the buyer had to place a bond, which doubled the purchase price. If these terms were not met, the bond was forfeited and the slave put up for sale again.[15]

The next year another law was passed stating that any "free negro or negroes, mulatto or mulattoes" who did not have visible means of financial support or "good and industrial habits" would be arrested and, if a magistrate agreed, sold into slavery at public auction for the remainder of that calendar year. At the end of that term of enslavement, if that person did not either leave the state, or "hire him or herself to some respectable white person, to serve as a slave for the following year, then he or she shall be again sold and disposed of." In an additional demonstration of cruelty, the act went on to say that that person's sons under the age of twenty-one or daughters under the age of eighteen would be "bound out as apprentices to good masters" until they reached the age of majority.[16]

A chilling example of this is recorded in the land records in the county where John and Arabella Weems lived: "Maryland, Montgomery County to wit: The Orphans' Court of said County by virtue of the act of Assembly of December session 1839 Chap. 35, bind as an apprentice, Negro boy Otho Beall (the child of Mary Beall a free woman) four years old the 6th day of Augst next, and to serve until he arrives to the age of twenty one years, to Samuel N.S. Williams farmer. The said Negro boy to serve his said master faithfully in all respects . . ." On the same day

Otho's sister, ten-year-old Isha, was also apprenticed to the same master.[17] The word *apprentice*, like the frequently used term *servant*, had a softer connotation than *slave* but any difference was purely illusory.

Washington also controlled the black population through a series of punitive laws. Each free black had to have a "certificate of freedom" stamped by the city's registrar. The initial cost was two dollars plus a one-dollar annual renewal fee.[18] Any black who could not establish his or her title to freedom could be arrested and committed to the county jail as a runaway. Furthermore, all free blacks had to post a bond signed by five white men who could guarantee his or her good character and that he or she would not become a charge on the public purse. These five "sureties" would be fined one thousand dollars if the black fell upon hard times. Blacks had to renew their assurances annually or pay a crushing twenty-dollar fine and be expelled from the city. Failure to pay the fine meant commitment to the workhouse for either six months or until they could prove to the mayor that they, along with any family and dependants, would "forthwith depart from the city."

Some of these laws were the result of a disturbing activity that began to flourish as the eighteenth century ended and the nineteenth began: the domestic slave trade. The transatlantic slave trade had been greatly curtailed in the first decade of the nineteenth century after Britain and the United States abolished the practice. Because Maryland and other states, including neighbouring Virginia, had a growing slave population and a diminishing need for them, more and more local slave dealers surfaced, hoping to profit from selling this human "commodity" to the newly opened settlements further south, where cotton was becoming king. In the next half-century, the area in and around the District of Columbia became the heart of this burgeoning domestic trade. Whereas it had been common in Maryland for slaves to be held for a fixed term prior to their release, the interstate trade allowed them to be sold to other states that did not honour such stipulations. The young and strong were most at risk, as were the most physically attractive.

In a letter to President John Adams, a Quaker from Delaware named Warner Mifflin shared his horror of passing through Maryland and witnessing "the abominable Trade carried on through that part of the Country, by Negroe-Drovers, buying Drove after Drove of the poor afflicted Blacks, like droves of Cattel for Market; carrying them into the Southern States for Speculation; regardless of the separation of nearest Connections & natural ties." Mifflin even feared that a yellow fever epidemic was being visited on the country by God to punish it for this abomination. He questioned how the new republic could justify this contradiction to the grandiose language contained in the Declaration of Independence: "We hold these truths to be self-evident, that all men are created equal . . ."[19]

Several slaves bearing the surname Weems were among the victims of this trade. While the records do not reveal if they were related to John and Arabella, it is not unreasonable to assume that they may have been. On December 23, 1843, seventeen-year-old Fanny Weems and twenty-year-old Robert Weems were placed on the *Kirkwood* (which was specially outfitted with chains in its cargo holds) by the trader Joseph S. Donovan for the voyage from Maryland to the New Orleans slave market. So many miles from home and too far south for slaves ever to visit loved ones or to attempt escape, New Orleans, the largest slave port in the South, was the destination where hope was left behind. Donovan's sixteen-year-old slave Charity Weems, also on the *Kirkwood*, and Hope Hull Slatter's twenty-year-old Augustus Weems, aboard the *Victorine*, followed in spring 1845. Another John Weems was sent on the *Elizabeth* in 1848, at age twenty-three. Twenty-year-old Martha Weems said her final goodbyes to her home and loved ones in autumn 1852 as she, along with 114 others, boarded the *Helen A. Miller* under the order of slave trader Bernard M. Campbell. The trip was extraordinarily swift, taking only eleven days, and for Martha Weems, the end no doubt came far too soon.[20]

In addition to those who were "legitimately" enslaved, free blacks were also at risk of being kidnapped and sold into the domestic slave trade. John and Arabella would have shuddered had they learned of the case involving Solomon Northup, a free man who had travelled to Washington from his home in New York State. After arriving in the District, he was drugged to unconsciousness. He awoke to find himself in a cell in a slave jail owned by William H. Williams. He was handcuffed and his ankle was fettered with a chain secured to a large ring in the floor. His money and, more importantly, his "free papers" were missing from his pocket. Three hours after panic began to sink in, his cell door swung open and two men entered. Years later, Northup could still vividly recall the details of the meeting: "One of them was a large, powerful man, forty years of age, perhaps, with dark, chestnut-colored hair, slightly interspersed with gray. His face was full, his complexion flush, his features grossly coarse, expressive of nothing but cruelty and cunning. He was about five feet ten inches high, of full habit, and without prejudice. His name was James H. Burch [Birch], as I learned afterwards – a well-known slave-dealer in Washington."

The daylight that shone through the open door allowed Northup to observe his otherwise dark cell. The single tiny window was crossed with iron bars and covered with a firmly secured outside shutter. The floor of the twelve-square-foot room was made of heavy planks. The furniture consisted of a wooden bench and a small stove. There was neither bed nor blanket. Beyond the iron-covered door was a small, windowless passageway that Northup later learned turned into a stairway that led to a yard enclosed with a ten- to twelve-foot-high brick wall. A small sloping roof offered little shelter from the sun or rain. The jail's exterior was neat and had the appearance of a home, and the nation's Capitol building could be seen down the street.

Birch informed the incredulous Northup that he had purchased him and intended to sell him to New Orleans. Northup forcefully pleaded his case – that a mistake had been made, that he was a free man. After directing several oaths at Northup, who would not be silenced, Birch went into a rage. The slave trader ordered his assistant to bring a "cat-o-nine-tails" and a hardwood paddle that had several small holes drilled through it. The victim later described what followed:

As soon as these formidable whips appeared, I was seized by both of them, and roughly divested of my clothing. My feet, as has been stated, were fastened to the floor. Drawing me over the bench, face downwards, Radburn placed his heavy foot upon the fetters, between my wrists, holding them painfully to the floor. With the paddle, Burch commenced beating me. Blow after blow was inflicted upon my naked body. When his unrelenting arm grew tired, he stopped and asked if I still insisted I was a free man. I did insist upon it, and then the blows were renewed, faster and more energetically, if possible, than before. When again tired, he would repeat the same question, and receiving the same answer, continued his cruel labor. All this time, the incarnate devil was uttering most fiendish oaths. At length the paddle broke, leaving the useless handle in his hand. Still I would not yield. All his brutal blows could not force from my lips the foul lie that I was a slave. Casting madly on the floor the handle of the broken paddle, he seized the rope. This was far more painful than the other. I struggled with all my power, but it was in vain. I prayed for mercy, but my prayer was only answered with imprecations and with stripes. I thought I must die beneath the lashes of the accursed brute. Even now the flesh crawls upon my bones, as I recall the scene. I was all on fire. My sufferings I can compare to nothing else than the agonies of hell![21]

Northup was indeed shipped to New Orleans, where he was housed in a slave pen until he was sold. His case was by no means unique; countless others were similarly kidnapped and transported south. Luckier than most, Northup was finally liberated with the help of

*The freedman Solomon Northup being beaten in a Washington slave jail*
(New York Public Library image 1167919)

sympathizers who learned of his story and who knew that he was legally free.

Twelve years after being sent to the South he returned to Washington and faced an unrepentant James H. Birch in court. The slave trader suffered no punishment for his crimes. Things had changed little since Northup had first been kidnapped. Despite a law passed by Congress in 1850 that forbade slaves being brought into the District of Columbia for the purpose of being sold "or placed in a depot to be subsequently transferred to another state to be sold," the slave-dealing business continued and the dealers prospered.

Such was the world in which John and Arabella Weems lived. Members of their family would soon become more intimately acquainted with the horrors of the slave pen.

CHAPTER 2

ADAM ROBB WAS A NATIVE of Ayr, Scotland, who had come to the United States around the time of the nation's birth. After living for a while in Alexandria, Virginia, and in Prince George's County, Maryland, he moved to nearby "Montgomery Court House," as it was then known, soon to be renamed Rockville, Maryland. In early 1797, after working in a public house, he and his wife of eight years, Elizabeth Ann Lansdale, and their family moved into their own home and eagerly advertised for friends and former customers to patronize their new establishment for "Private Entertainment."[1]

Two years later, he and his family moved from this home into a brick house in the centre of Rockville that was "large and commodious, with good stables and a carriage house." In an advertisement in the March 5, 1799 issue of *Centinel of Liberty, and George-Town and Washington Advertiser*, he thanked all of those who had done business with him previously and assured them that his new "HOUSE OF ENTER-TAINMENT" was "well provided with all necessities for the accommodation of travellers and others," including a line of stagecoaches and horses for hire. He christened his new tavern the Fountain Inn.

Robb's Tavern, as it was generally called, quickly became a community gathering place. On one occasion the area men met there to nominate a candidate for Congress. It was also a busy centre of commerce, being

## FOUNTAIN-INN.

THE Subscriber, having removed from the house he lately occupied in this place, hereby gives notice, that he has opened a HOUSE OF ENTERTAIN-MENT, near the centre of the Town. The house is large and commodious, with good stables and a carriage house.

He takes this opportunity of returning his thanks to his friends and the public in general for the encouragement he has hitherto met with, and being well provided with all necessaries for the accommodation of travellers and others, solicits a continuance of their favors, which he hopes to merit by his attention.

ADAM ROBB.

Montgomery Court House, Maryland, March 15th, 179~. 85~-84.

*Adam Robb, owner of the Weems family, advertised the opening of his new tavern, the Fountain Inn. (Centinel of Liberty, and George-Town and Washington Advertiser)*

the regular midpoint stop between Georgetown in the District of Columbia and Frederick, Maryland.[2] Other entrepreneurs took advantage of the tavern's location by scheduling stops for their coaches there. Messrs. Semmes, Brish, Scott, and Hallar advertised their "Accomodation Line, now in compleat order and inferior to no line of Stages on the continent – passing through a beautiful country and for good and cheap accommodations to the Traveller exceeded by none." After departing Frederick at four in the morning on any Monday, Wednesday, or Friday, the weary travellers would stop for lunch at Robb's Tavern, before continuing on to Georgetown. For the return journey on alternate days, Robb's Tavern would serve them breakfast. The tavern was part of a pleasurable experience, complemented by "careful drivers, excellent horses, compleat, new and easy stages." With an eye for every detail, the owners expected the trip to be "most agreeable and convenient to passengers, and superior to any other on the road."[3] Not to be outdone, stage operator Henry Winemiller, whose drivers were "sober" and "obliging," had a similar route that also stopped at Robb's.[4]

Robb's Tavern was also chosen by the General Assembly of Maryland as a collection station to raise ten thousand dollars, from five hundred shares valued at twenty dollars each, for a proposed turnpike road to join the District of Columbia to the town of Frederick. This was part of a larger effort to raise $120,000 for the entire project, which after being interrupted by the War of 1812 increased to three hundred thousand dollars.[5] Adam Robb was one of those appointed as a commissioner to collect the money and later as a manager for the Rockville and Washington Turnpike Road Company.[6] His standing in the community was further demonstrated by his role in administering the estates of deceased men of local importance.[7]

Public sales and auctions were regularly held at Robb's Tavern by a wide variety of sellers. On one occasion, the chancellor of Maryland decreed that it be the venue for the sale of lands to satisfy a legal judgment.[8] It was likewise a regular setting for the sale of large pieces of property that were either wooded or suitable for the cultivation of corn, wheat, and tobacco.[9] When an Edward Willet decided to join the westward exodus from Maryland to the newly opened lands of Kentucky, he chose to sell his modest farm of two hundred acres at Robb's.[10] Following the death of a neighbour, William Williams, whose family was long on land but short on imagination when it came to naming

## Public Sale.

The Subscriber will offer at Public Sale, on Thursday the eighth day of March next, between the hours of ten o'clock in the forenoon and one o'clock in the afternoon, at the house of Mr. Adam Robb, at Montgomery Court house, about fifteen Negroes, consisting of Men, Women and Children. Six months credit will be given, the purchasers giving bond and security bearing interest from the day of sale.

THOMAS PETER,
Acting Executor of
ROBERT PETER jr.

Feb. 10.                    d18m.

*Public sales of land and slaves were frequently held at Adam Robb's tavern. (Independent American, March 6, 1810)* their children, Robb's Tavern was the logical location for his estate sale. During his lifetime, Williams owned between eight hundred and one thousand acres, including the jail and part of the courthouse square; much of present-day Rockville occupies land that once belonged to him.[11]

Real estate was not the only thing put up for auction at the inn. Slaves were as well. One wonders the lasting effects on Robb's children – Jane, Catharine Ann, John, and Alexander – as they saw the crowds gathered to witness or to bid. The children of slave owners often mimicked the behaviour of their elders and lorded their power over the slave children with whom they had once played as equals. The poet John Greenleaf Whittier wistfully quoted remarks that a slave-state representative made about slavery's negative effects: "The youth of the country are growing up with a contempt of steady industry as a low and servile thing, which contempt induces idleness and all its attendant effeminancy, vice, and worthlessness."[12]

To run his flourishing business and his farms, Adam Robb employed many slaves of his own. He started off slowly, purchasing a woman named Grace and her child in 1790 before leaving Prince George's County.[13] Ten years later, after settling in Montgomery County, he owned seven, and over the years he gradually added to that number.[14] One of them, a young Josiah Henson who had recently been separated from his mother, sisters, and brothers at an auction, later related stories about the horror of Robb's slave quarters. Henson described being placed along "with about forty others, of all ages, colours, and conditions, all strangers to me. Of course nobody cared for me. The slaves were brutalised by this degradation, and had no sympathy for me. I soon fell sick, and lay for some days almost dead on the ground. Sometimes a slave would give me a piece of corn-bread, or a bit of herring. Finally I became so feeble, I could not move." The slaves were forced out to work at daylight, and were too exhausted at day's end to give a thought to their fellow-sufferers. In the words of one, the slaves worked from "can't see to can't see." They slept on rags on a dirt floor until morning, when they would rise to relive the day before.[15]

Robb's slaves who worked at the tavern were in a different position, and perhaps had better living conditions. Compared with those who worked in the fields, they had more contact with the outside world. To better accommodate the guests, the cooks, housekeepers, and those who tended to the horses and stables were expected to have a degree of sophistication and some social skills. Their world was much enlarged by hearing the news and stories of the tavern's various guests. By listening to and interacting with travellers who came from northern cities such as Philadelphia en route to the nation's capital, they probably became aware that there was a different life just outside the border of Maryland.

During the War of 1812, the buzz that normally consumed everyone around the tavern grew louder, with all of the slaves straining to overhear conversations about the war. On the evening of August 24, 1814, the excitement got a little stronger following the disappearance from outside the tavern of a nine- or ten-year-old sorrel horse that had been sent by its Georgetown owner to the American camp to keep it out of the hands of British soldiers. He claimed that it was usually a very fine horse but "having used him severely of late, he is thin and his back is hurt." The U.S. army captain who had received the horse had left it at Adam Robb's stable under the care of two dragoons. It was suspected that a former soldier had pressed the horse into duty that night and had taken it.[16]

The slaves heard alarming stories during the war from soldiers and militia men who retreated to Rockville as the British torched the White House and the Capitol building in retaliation for the Americans having burned the Parliament Buildings in York, the capital of Upper Canada.[17] They could easily see the glow from the fire, which was visible for fifty miles. The slaves must have wondered what their future would hold if there was a British victory. Would freedom be theirs? As she nursed the infant Arabella, Cecilia Talbot must have thought about what possibilities

*The White House and Capitol building burn during the War of 1812* (Library of Congress image cph3c17176)

there might be for her child. Thirteen-year-old John Weems must have tried to make sense of it all.

The American Revolution was still fresh in the minds of many. During that conflict, the British had promised freedom to any slaves who joined in to put down the rebellion. Many did. Following the American victory, many accompanied the "United Empire Loyalists" who wished to remain under British rule to the refuge of Canada. Some accompanied their masters but still others went as free people in their own right. During the War of 1812, the British made a similar offer of freedom to runaways. The coastal areas of Maryland and Virginia were particularly affected by this offer, as slaves seized boats and canoes and paddled their way out to British warships. Others fled by land and followed the invading army. Slave patrols along the Chesapeake Bay shot suspected runaways on sight. Further south, thousands of slaves from the Carolinas and Georgia escaped to the enemy.[18]

In Washington, with the militia otherwise engaged, the slave patrols worked extra duty. It was no secret that slaves in the area were becoming emboldened as they optimistically waited for their liberators. Some refused to work, declaring that they would soon be free. One of the patrollers confided to his diary that there would be a slave uprising should the British attack.[19] Some wary masters sent their slaves across the mountains for "safekeeping." However, during the invasion of Washington in 1814, the final year of the war, any hope for freedom evaporated within days as the British evacuated the countryside, leaving most of the slaves, if not the Capitol, as they had found them. Adam Robb's slaves returned to business as usual.

Robb was a shrewd businessman who steadily added to his property and wealth. He was also sensitive to helping his children. On June 18, 1821, "in consideration of the natural love and affection which he the said Adam Robb hath for his daughter Jane Neale Beall," he gave her a 188-acre farm known by the alluring name of Locust Thickett.[20] After his daughter's husband, Upton Beall, died Robb helped by purchasing three slaves for her farm: Mariah, about twenty-three, and two young girls, Louisa and Sarah, ages four and one respectively.[21]

As Robb's prosperity grew, neighbouring planters sought him out as a moneylender. To diminish his risk, he occasionally required that the slaves of the borrower be put up as collateral and the transaction recorded at the county courthouse. Although slaves usually had a surname that they had chosen, their owners often identified them simply by first name and approximate age, as in the case of James Offutt, who borrowed $891.87 using his slaves as security: one negro man, Hanson, twenty-two years old; one negro boy, Albert or Elbert, seventeen years old; Lawson, fourteen; Henry, sixteen; Richard, nine; and one negro girl, Susan, eleven.[22] On another occasion, Adam Robb and his son-in-law Henry Harding accepted four-year-old Cronin and two-year-old Nora as security on a loan.[23] If the borrower defaulted on the loan, the children would be theirs.

On at least one occasion, Robb also had dealings with one of the most infamous slave dealers in the area, George Kephart, from whom Robb bought a slave named William for nine hundred dollars.[24] Kephart was reported to have roamed throughout Montgomery and Frederick counties, frequenting taverns to conduct his business and familiarizing himself with the backroads and the financial situations of all who lived on them. By so combing the landscape and keeping his ear to the ground, he knew where to look for his next opportunity for quick profits. He regularly advertised in the Rockville newspaper, *Maryland Journal and True American*, for "likely young negroes" of either sex who were between the ages of ten and thirty.

In addition to buying and reselling slaves, Kephart was in the business of tracking runaways. As early as 1831, he and a partner were "determined to go the whole hog for any negro" who had absented himself from his owner. Distance presented no obstacle to their ambition. Neither did uncertainty that a black was truly a fugitive – mere suspicion would do.[25] Many years later, a former slave recalled, "Ever'body in Frederick knowed Kephart, an' was afeerd of 'im too. When it was reported that he was about, they trembled."[26] The Weems family and all of the others belonging to Adam Robb would have shared those feelings, but would have been powerless to do anything about their lot in life.

However, occasionally some of Adam Robb's slaves would strike back, with whatever means they could. For example Charity, Kitty, Mary, and her infant child took their fight to the nearby Montgomery County Courthouse, where they declared that they were entitled to their freedom because their original owner had agreed that any offspring of their parents were to be freed upon reaching the age of twenty-five years. Before that happened, their owner had transferred the slaves to Charles Lansdale, who negotiated to raise the age of manumission to thirty-one. When Charles Lansdale died – incidentally, without ever having paid for the slaves – his son-in-law, Adam Robb, inherited them.

Robb then gave Kitty to his son Alexander. Alexander, who had the nickname Sandy, carried Kitty away in 1817 to New Orleans when he decided to move to Louisiana. In that distant southern state, it was quite certain that Kitty would not be manumitted at thirty-one and that she would have no redress.

The other sisters feared that they too were about to be sold and carried out of the state. They alleged that both of Adam Robb's married daughters, Jane Beall and Catharine Harding, were perfectly aware that the slaves were entitled to their manumission, as they had been present, along with both their mother and father, during conversations on the subject. In his court statement, Adam Robb denied that any of this was true. Besides, Alexander Robb had advised his father in a letter that both Kitty and her baby had died in Louisiana during childbirth. The case of these complainants, as of many other slaves, looked hopeless.[27]

Like his father, Alexander continued to rip families apart, from the Upper South of Maryland to the bowels of the Deep South. On March 2, 1819, the slave ship *Missouri* departed from the port of Baltimore for New Orleans. Among the many slaves on board were three belonging to Alexander: nineteen-year-old Hannah and her infant child, Henson, as well as thirteen-year-old Adam. Robb kept Hannah and Henson, then twenty months old, for over a year before selling them as a package, along with a twenty-five-year old mulatto male named Leve, for seventeen hundred dollars. On October 26 of that year, the brigantine *Agent* sailed from Alexandria, Virginia, the cargo hold containing two more slaves belonging to Alexander. Two years later, on October 17, eight more of his slaves left Alexandria en route to Opelousas, Louisiana, where his slave-trading business was based.[28]

Alexander Robb had been busy making purchases in Montgomery County and the surrounding area in the time leading up to the *Agent*'s departure. On October 1, 1821, he bought nineteen-year-old George for $380 and two days later recorded the purchase of nine-year-old Mary for $175.[29] In April of the next year, he bought twelve-year-old Milly, "of yellow complexion," for $230 and ten days later bought from his father his "negro boy Sam" for $300.[30] During that same month Alexander travelled to neighbouring Prince George's County to purchase twenty-two-year-old Kenny.[31] The business was lucrative, and despite his youth Robb's social status soon increased, along with his wealth. As early as 1825 he, along with five other men, pledged a bond to Louisiana Governor Henry Johnson as security that the district sheriff and his deputies would "faithfully collect and account for all taxes of the State within the Said Parish of St. Landry." Robb was confident enough in the district officials to make this very public display of his political connections and his wealth. The amount was a staggering eight thousand nine hundred and forty-five dollars and forty-two and one-half cents.[32] Although Alexander Robb was half a continent away from the rest of his family in the deepest part of the South, his activities would leave a lasting impact on many Maryland slaves.

Alexander's brother, John N. Robb, lived much closer to their father's home in nearby Georgetown. On February 2, 1817, he and his former business partner, Samuel Childs, ran a notice in the *Daily National Intelligencer* that Childs & Robb had dissolved by mutual agreement. However, by April their differences had become public knowledge as Childs's new partnership with John Osbourn, Osbourn & Childs, went to the newspapers with accusations that John and Adam Robb had signed bonds promising to pay them a very large amount of money "to certain people for goods bought." Those "goods" presumably included items such as silk, cloth, furniture, and carpeting, but they may well have also included those of the animate, two-legged variety.[33] Whatever the items were, Osbourn and Childs made it very clear that they would not be responsible for payment of Robbs's debts. In response, John Robb took out his own ad, demanding payment from anyone who owed him money. The front-page notice had a postscript: "N.B. The subscriber has a family of negroes for sale."[34]

It appears that John Robb, too, dealt in slaves, judging from the frequent and rapid changes of his slaves' names and ages. On March 23, 1816, he had purchased George, age forty-five; Betty, thirty-five; Middleton, nine; and Mason, seven.[35] The following year, the tax assessment rolls reveal that he owned nine slaves, consisting of four male children, two women ages sixty and thirty, and three men in their prime of whom two were ages thirty-five and forty.[36] A year later, John sold his father three horses, a cart, two cows, all of his household furnishings, his land, and his leather-tanning business for twenty thousand dollars. Included in the sale were seven slaves, including fourteen-year-old Charles, who had been sold to John Robb by his maternal grandmother when he was only four or five years old.[37]

Despite that lucrative sale, John's finances continued to deteriorate, and by February 1820 he was thrown into Washington County prison for non-payment of debts.[38] Three rooms on the upper floor were reserved for debtors, and the main floor held not only criminals but also those accused of crimes, witnesses for trials, and "lunatics" awaiting transport to the asylum in Baltimore. The brick building was overcrowded, with inadequate sanitation and poor ventilation. At times, as many as sixty to seventy inmates were crammed into sixteen cells.[39]

In 1823, John, now out of prison, and Adam ran an advertisement in the local newspaper offering John's tanning business for sale or rent.[40] At about the same time, the *Republican Star and General Advertiser* included Adam Robb's name in a list of people who owed back taxes on his land in Allegany County.[41] Given the turbulent economic circumstances in which they lived and the disregard for family ties that Adam Robb and his sons had shown, freedom appealed strongly to their slaves.

Slaves belonging to Adam Robb's daughters, Jane and Catharine, no doubt felt the same. Both daughters were well established and married to important men – Catharine in 1812 to Henry Harding, who had been the county sheriff, road commissioner, registrar of wills, justice of the peace, tax collector, and a seven-term legislative representative to

*Washington County Prison, where John Robb served time for not paying his debts*
(Library of Congress image ppmsca 12611)

the Maryland House of Delegates; and Jane in 1815 to Upton Beall, who had been the clerk for the county of Montgomery, as well as a friend to President Adams and to the Marquis de Lafayette.[42] Like most prominent people from that time and place, both the Bealls and the Hardings owned a considerable number of slaves. John and Arabella Weems could only stand by as powerless witnesses to a family that controlled their lives.

The Weems family felt the first troubling rumbles of a distant thunder in 1847, when their by now long-widowed master, Adam Robb, died. Up until then Arabella, her children, her mother, sister, and other family members had been held together and hired out or had laboured on Robb's farms, which had such exotic and curious names as "Oatry's," "The Resurvey on St. Mary's," "Coup de Main," "Wickham's Chance," "Spittlefields," "Smoch Ally," "The Resurvey of the Wheel of Fortune," and "The Resurvey on Valentines Garden Enlarged." Now, the very real possibility existed that they might be forcibly removed from the fields and meadows to which they had become attached.

On May 15 of that year, Adam Robb's estate was listed and evaluated. Despite his advanced age, Robb had avoided facing the inevitable and had died without having prepared a last will and testament. It therefore fell to his then widowed daughter, Jane Beall, and to his son-in-law, Henry Harding, to put a price on all of his belongings. At that time, Robb's daughters, Jane and Catharine, were the only two legal heirs acknowledged; John had died several years before, and curiously Alexander was not named.[43] Robb's assets included a herd of cattle, a flock of ewes and lambs, numerous pigs and horses, a team of oxen, and a large quantity of farm and blacksmith equipment that had been needed on Robb's huge plantations. Household goods were included – a weaving loom worth five dollars, an old butter churn worth a quarter of a dollar, a bowl and pitcher worth twelve cents, and even a "lot of broken spoons" inexplicably rated at $1.50. Two old muskets worth fifty cents and three leg chains valued at $1.25 each conjure up more ominous images.

Then appeared the long list of "negroes," male and female, adult and child. Fifty-year-old Mary Jones was worth $75. Fifty-five-year-old John Henson was evaluated at $150. Arabella's sister, twenty-seven-year-old Annie Maria (hereafter called Annie), $450. Their aging mother, Cecilia, at $15, was worth exactly the same value as a roan cow and only three dollars more than six silver tablespoons. Arabella's children were also listed: Mary Jane, 16, $500; Catharine, 13, $400; William (Augustus) 12, $375; Adam, 7, $175; Ann Maria, 5, $125; eighteen-month-old Joe was listed along with his thirty-five-year-old mother, Airy, at $325. The age of Richard, who was considered "infirm" and therefore worthless, was not deemed significant enough to list. By comparison, a grey horse named Charley was worth $50, a water bucket 16¼ cents, and the Muscovy ducks in the barnyard 37 cents each.[44]

In the following winter, on February 10, 1848, the estate sale was held and the financial ledgers balanced. A few deductions were made to the earlier property evaluation, such as $57.27 for Adam Robb's funeral as well as $7.50 for taxes paid for his "negroes in George Town." Another $450 was removed because of the untimely death of the slave Ninian while still in his mid-thirties.[45] His passing denied him the opportunity to be united with his wife, Sarah Ann, and his two daughters, who were already the property of Henry Harding.[46] Although neighbours bought many of the items, most were bought by Adam Robb's daughter, Jane Beall, and by his grandson, Charles Adam Harding. Thankfully none of the slaves were sold at that day's auction.

In fact, rather than being sold, some of them actually purchased items from their late master's estate with pennies saved over the years. Hester Diggs bought a flax wheel and Mary Jones bought several items, including a tea canister, two ovens, bottles, a pitcher, and a set of brass candlesticks. Among Arabella Weems's purchases were a coffee mill, an iron pot, a walnut table, and chairs. Her bill came to $1.91. The recorder of the transactions was careful to note all of the purchases the slaves made on a separate page.[47] As they gathered these reminders of their former lives, the slaves nervously tried to comfort themselves that perhaps life would not change too much.

Adam Robb's daughter Jane died on August 2, 1848, at age fifty-six, and her death before Robb's estate could be settled between her and her sister, Catharine, made the entire process more complicated and more painful. Jane's share would go to her daughters – Jane, Matilda and Margaret, all destined to be lifelong spinsters. The legal disposition of the estate was initiated on December 11, 1849, at the Orphans' Court of Montgomery County, and although the slaves had been appraised in 1847, Catharine's husband, Henry Harding, made a request to reassess them.[48] Ironically, Henry was by this time registrar of the county court and recorded the proceedings. William Viers Bouic, a lawyer, and Michael H. Letton, a Rockville butcher, were called upon to give their learned opinion on the value of the human flesh.

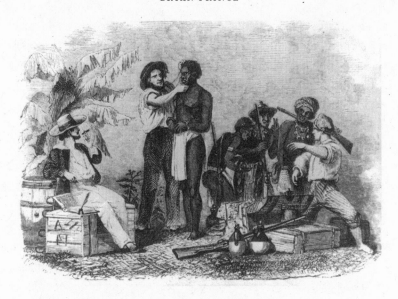

*An African man being inspected and valued before being sold into slavery while a white man talks with African slave traders* (Library of Congress image cph 3a17639)

A gentle snow fell during the week that Bouic and Letton went about their work. The *Baltimore Sun* painted a romantic picture of Rockville covered in white. "The sleigh bells are sounding and the beaus, wrapped in their furs, are enjoying themselves to their heart's content. When the sleighing time passes the priest and the parson will be called upon to finish the frolic."[49] Adam Robb's slaves, who were being examined like livestock, did not share in the frivolity.

Two weeks later, on Christmas Eve, Bouic and Letton's official status as appraisers was reconfirmed by George R. Braddock, Montgomery County's justice of the peace. They made an "oath on the Holy Evangely of Almighty God that they will well and truly appraise the negroes belong to the estate of Adam Robb late of the said county deceased and to the best of their skill & Judgement perform the duty imposed upon them."[50] They had accomplished their ghoulish task, not only appraising the slaves but also dividing them. Thirteen went to Jane's estate, including an aging

John Henson, Josiah's brother, as well as Arabella's elderly mother, Cecilia, often called Cicely, then estimated to be in her seventies and valued at ten dollars. Along with them went Arabella's sister, Annie, and Annie's two infant daughters, who were valued as a unit at $525. The remaining fifteen slaves went to Catharine Harding, including:

- Mary Jones (the godmother of some of the Weems children), fifty, $80
- Hester Diggs, fifty-five, $20
- Gus (Augustus) Weems, fourteen, $425
- Catharine Weems, fifteen, $550
- Ann Maria Weems, six, $200
- Adam Weems, nine, $250
- (Mary) Jane Weems, sixteen, $550
- Airy (Arabella) Weems and her youngest children Joseph, four, and John, two, $500
- Dick Weems, eleven and "infirm," was valued at only $25.

To ensure that the division was equitable, Jane Beall's orphaned daughters were ordered to pay $32.50 to their aunt, Catharine Harding.[51]

Attributing worth to humans was always an inexact science. Much depended upon sex, age, and physical attributes. At thirteen, Catharine Weems had been evaluated at four hundred dollars. Two years later, as her body developed and her beauty blossomed, another $150 was added to her value. Six-year-old Ann Maria and her fourteen-year-old brother Augustus had increased by $75 each. Nine-year-old Dick's physical disabilities had rendered him worthless in 1847, and in 1849 his value had increased only slightly to a still insignificant amount. Thirty-seven-year-old Arabella, who always seemed to have an infant at her breast and another in her womb, had declined in value in contrast to that of her younger sister, Annie, and even to her eldest daughters.[52] At this time, Arabella was five months pregnant, expecting her ninth child, another

31

son, whom she would name Sylvester when he was born the following April.[53] But by enriching her own life with the joy of motherhood, she inadvertently enriched her owner's net worth.

The signs were ominous for the Weems family and for all of the other slaves whose lot fell to Catharine Harding. For years leading up to Adam Robb's death, she and her husband had been constantly plagued with financial troubles, despite their family's prosperous background and their standing in the community. On the second Monday of November 1843 a judgment had been passed against Henry Harding and a neighbour for non-payment of a $431.32 debt, plus $1006.933 in damages and court costs. The sheriff who was ordered to collect the money seized one of the Harding farms, known as Hermitage, and offered it up at auction. Perhaps intimidated, no buyer surfaced at the sale. Well over a year passed with no further action taken until January 20, 1845, when the Montgomery County Court again issued a writ demanding payment.

*The Montgomery County Courthouse, circa 1870, where, among other things, locals registered their ownership of slaves* (Charles Brewer collection, courtesy of Peerless Rockville)

Again, the Hardings did not comply and continued to occupy the land until another court ruling on January 26, 1848 once more ordered the sheriff to place the land up for public sale. On this occasion Henry and Catharine's son, Charles A. Harding, was the highest bidder, at $230 – more than twelve hundred dollars less than had been demanded to settle the court ruling – thereby retaining within the family the land that had once belonged to his great-great-grandfather and to every succeeding generation.[54]

This was not the first time that the son was forced to help pull his parents out of financial quicksand. On November 11, 1844, Charles and his brother-in-law, Robert W. Carter, again bailed Henry Harding out of his difficulties. A record at the county courthouse lists part of Henry and Catharine's extensive list of creditors and debts from this time in approximate amounts: to William Braddock, seven dollars; Matilda Holland, two hundred dollars; Edward Harding, two hundred dollars; Otho Magruder, forty dollars; Charles A. Burnett, fifty dollars; William Grooms, executor of James Grooms, fifty dollars; Surby and Duvall, thirty dollars; Joshua Davis, twenty dollars; Bradley and Estess, one hundred and fifty dollars; William Willson, forty dollars; Lewis Shots, fifty dollars; Adam Robb, twenty dollars; Samuel Clements, one hundred and twenty dollars; Gassaway Martin, seventy-five dollars; Ruben Summer, trustee of Anna Willson, four hundred dollars, and Samuel Viers, twenty-five dollars. Clearly Henry and Catharine Harding had been drowning in debt and threatening to take her father, Adam Robb, and his sister and brother-in-law, the Carters, with them. These relatives had made the error of signing their names as guarantors to Harding.

In order to prevent this looming financial and familial disaster, the Hardings signed over to Robert Carter and to Charles A. Harding their livestock, crops, farming equipment, and all of their household and kitchen goods and furniture. Several slaves were also included in the transfer and were listed with their approximate ages: Enos, 55; Charles, 50; Ause, 30; Ned (Branham), 46; Ned (Branham) the younger, 18;

Charlotte (Branham), 45; Harriet, 21; Fanny, 14; and Lewis two and a half. Should the need arise, Carter and Harding were to sell at public or private sale whatever was deemed necessary to pay the outstanding debts. For their trouble and expense, the trustees were to receive a 6 percent commission on the sales. They were to hold any remaining proceeds in trust in case anyone further challenged Adam Robb and Robert Carter to make good on the bond they had pledged on behalf of Henry Harding.[55]

Thanks to their troubled financial history, the Hardings were only too aware that Catharine could lose her share of the inheritance following her father's death. Creditors would salivate at the opportunity to get the money due to them from Henry, who had already experienced a contentious battle with his brother, Edward, over the estate of his own father. Ultimately the Orphans' Court had stepped in and appointed an independent party to help settle the conflict. A guardian was also appointed to look after the best interests of their half-brother Josiah Harding, who was still a minor at that time.[56]

Crafty with their business dealings, Henry and Catharine again turned to their son Charles to employ a legal loophole. By law, creditors could seize property owned by a spouse but not that owned by the debtor's children. On February 4, 1848, before Adam Robb's estate was divided, Henry and Catharine Harding registered a document at the county courthouse to ensure that Henry's creditors could not lay a hand on Catharine's inheritance. It stated that they "do give, grant, bargain, sell, assign, transfer and set over to the said Charles A. Harding, his heirs and assigns, all the right, title, claim, interest and demand whether legal or equitable of her the said Catharine Ann Harding both an heir at law and distributee of the said Adam Robb." Therefore all of Catharine's share of the estate – including the Weems family – would go directly to her son, who would "invest, manage, use and employ in such way or manner as the said Catharine Ann Harding shall from time to time direct." The annual profit derived from the estate would also "from time to time" be given to the mother. The shrewd family left nothing to chance: Charles, in his mid-twenties and still unmarried, had already prepared his last will and testament on July 14, 1847, bequeathing all of his goods and property to his mother, and upon her death to his sisters.[57] Creditors would find no easy route to collect debts from the Hardings.

Catharine also wisely included a clause that she would "have full power and authority without the lot, hindrance or control of her said husband to direct the sale, exchange, investment, reinvestment or other distribution or disposal" of the properties involved. However, Charles would still have the right to make business decisions and to sign any legal documents. With an eye to the inevitabilities of life and out of fairness to all three of their children, the Hardings also made provisions for their daughters to receive a share of the estate after their mother's death. In the document, the Hardings expressed the wish that Catharine's sister, Jane N. Beall, be approached to divide their father's estate as soon as possible.[58] Those slaves who would eventually go to the Beall family would face a more stable and brighter future than those who would be claimed by the Hardings.

The only slave who had any reason to be somewhat pleased to be owned by the Hardings was Hester Diggs. She and her husband, George Diggs, had belonged to Adam Robb, but their children, including David, who was the property of Josiah Harding, had remained the property of other members of the Harding family.[59]

The issue of the estate would soon become even more complicated following the death of Jane N. Beall, who left as heirs three unmarried daughters. Suddenly the Bealls and Hardings had three separate estates to divide – those of Jane Beall, and of her husband Upton, and that of Adam Robb, who had been the executor of Upton Beall's estate but had died himself before settling it. It became a nightmare to sort it all out, made even worse because tattered emotions were mixed with the money. The complexities of the estates combined with a financially troubled in-law, Henry Harding (whose official position as registrar of wills gave

## COMPLETE LIST OF SLAVES IN ADAM ROBB'S ESTATE

| NAME | SURNAME | SEX | AGE 1847 | VALUE MAY, 1847 | VALUE DEC. 1849 | GIVEN TO |
|------|---------|-----|----------|-----------------|-----------------|----------|
| Hilliary/Henry | Tyler | m | 26 | $600 | $725 | Beall |
| John | Ninian | m | 25 | 600 | 600 | Beall |
| Frank | | m | 24 | 600 | 725 | Beall |
| Ninian | | m | 35 | 450 | dead | |
| Pat | | m | 30 | 400 | 550 | Harding |
| Dick | | m | 55 | 50 | 25 | Harding |
| Hester/Hasty | Diggs nee Butler | f | 55 | 25 | inc'd with George | Harding |
| Catharine | Weems | f | 13 | 400 | 550 | Harding |
| Charlotte | Plowden | f | 29 | 400 | 500 | Beall |
| Henny | Tyler nee Diggs? | f | 28 | 450 | 500 | Beall |
| Rose | | f | 55 | 35 | inc'd with Romeo | Beall |
| William | Hatton | m | 35 | 350 | 450 | Beall |
| Henry | | m | 22 | 600 | disappeared | |
| George | | m | 30 | 300 | 400 | Harding |
| Edward/Edmond | | m | 16 | 450 | 600 | Harding |
| John | Henson | m | 55 | 150 | 150 | Beall |
| William (Augustus) | Weems | m | 12 | 375 | 425 | Harding |
| (Annie) Maria | Talbot-Young | f | 27 | 450 | 525 | Beall |
| Margaret | Young | f | not born | | inc'd with Maria | Beall |
| Catharine | Young | f | not born | | inc'd with Maria | Beall |
| Mary Jane (Stella) | Weems | f | 16 | 500 | 550 | Harding |
| Mary | Jones | f | 50 | 75 | 80 | Harding |
| Airy (Arabella) | Talbot-Weems | f | 35 | 325 | 500 | Harding |
| Joe | Weems | m | 18 mo. | inc'd with Airy | inc'd with Airy | Harding |
| John Jr. | Weems | m | not born | | inc'd with Airy | Harding |
| Richard/Dick | Weems | m | infirm | inc'd with Airy | 50 | Harding |
| Adam | Weems | m | 7 | 175 | 250 | Harding |
| (Ann) Maria | Weems | f | 5 | 125 | 200 | Harding |
| George | Diggs | m | 55 | 25 | 50 | Harding |
| Romeo | | m | 65 | 25 | 60 | Beall |
| Cicely (Cecilia) | Talbot | f | not given | 15 | 10 | Beall |

him the power to be involved with the final distribution of estates), made conflict inevitable.[60] Henry Harding proposed that in order to begin to untangle the mess and to settle the claims between the various heirs, a partition be made "of the negroes of the late Adam Robb."[61]

✦

With the distribution of Adam Robb's estate, the Weems family went to Henry and Catharine Harding, who were described by Mary Jones, one of their slaves, as "bad enough." The Hardings' adult children – daughters Elizabeth and Catharine and their physician son, Charles A. Harding – all of whom were unmarried and still living at their Rockville area home in 1850, were even worse, so as to be unbearable.[62] The Hardings were one of the county's more prominent and wealthy families and traditionally owned large numbers of slaves. Many of these displayed their lack of affection for their owners by taking a trip on the Underground Railroad. The Weems family would have had a deep personal attachment to all those who escaped, connected as they were by circumstance and probably by blood. But in a fragile attempt to remain together, they stood by and watched and stored away intelligence for the future.

Catharine Harding Sr. occasionally allowed her slaves to hire themselves out for wages and to live in neighbouring Washington and Georgetown in return for her receiving a large portion of their pay. But even that hint of generosity belied the truth. Twenty-eight-year-old Ned Brannum (possibly Arabella's nephew), described in his runaway ad as a bright mulatto with straight black hair and grey eyes who was "quite intelligent and has a fine address," found life under her control to be intolerable. It was assumed that he was aided in his escape by abolitionists in Washington and that he had likely stowed away on a ship loaded with coal.[63] On June 25, 1849, Henry Harding's "negro" Frederick was committed to the District of Columbia jail for running away. After five days in custody, he was delivered to his master, who had to pay the confinement fee of $1.18.[64] George Diggs made his escape nearly a year later but was captured and returned to Henry Harding on May 24, 1850.[65]

Robert White was more successful a few years later. He had been hired out by Henry Harding to work in Norfolk, Virginia, for nine dollars per month. By age thirty-five his master had received a cool three thousand dollars for renting out his services, but Harding wanted even more of his earnings, which the slave refused to give. By the end of September 1854 White, along with a companion, successfully reached the free city of Philadelphia, where they were concealed for two and a half days, then smuggled away with the help of Underground Railroad agents.[66]

Mary Jones, the godmother of George Diggs, complained that "in nine years, I have not even as much as received an apron from them." She showed her disdain for the Harding family with an escape attempt but was caught by the slave hunters John H. Goddard, who was captain of the Auxiliary Guard, and one of his deputies, James F. Wollard, who scoured the District of Columbia at night in search of runaways and delivered them to the Washington slave jail.[67] Supported by government funds, the jail had partially replaced the private pens owned by slave dealers.[68] Members of the Guard, some of whom were slave dealers, were infamous for concealing themselves near meeting houses where blacks would congregate, in the hope of catching some of them out after their ten o'clock curfew.[69] The slave patrols were naturally despised by the black residents of the District. One recalled that slaves would "stretch clothes lines across the street high enough to let the horse pass, but not the rider; then the boys would run, and the patrols in full chase would be thrown off by running against the lines. The patrols are poor white men, who live by plundering and stealing, getting rewards for runaways, and setting up little shops on the public roads."[70]

A quivering Mary Jones must have been terrified by her captor, who "may be known by the official cockade on his hat, and a knavish, treacherous smile on his face, [and] is a cold-blooded cunning, crawling creature,

*John H. Goddard, the dreaded
captain of the Auxiliary Guard,
which patrolled the District of
Columbia at nighttime in search of
runaway slaves* (from the book
*District of Columbia Police* by
Richard Sylvester, 1894, courtesy
Library of Congress)

exactly the Uriah Heep of Dickens' *David Copperfield*." According to an
observer he

> was bred a shoemaker, but finding honest handicraft industry not
> respectable in a slaveholding community, he contrived to get himself
> employed as a bum-baliff and watchman, and by dint of a persevering
> spirit of servility, has risen to be captain of the night-watch, and one
> of the police magistrates. We wish to warn all Northern men who may
> visit Washington against this very dangerous person, who has consti-
> tuted himself chief slave-catcher and conservator of the slave prop-
> erty of the District, and who, in that capacity, whenever any chance of
> currying favour or making money may occur, would not scruple, at
> any time, to snap up any man or woman suspected of humanity, confi-
> dent of being upheld by the authorities of the District, however illegal
> or ungrounded the arrest might be.[71]

It would be another tortuous week before Goddard released Mary back into the custody of Henry Harding on August 15.[72] A similar fate befell Dorsey, a slave who was caught while trying to escape in July 1857, and forced to spend three weeks in the Washington jail before being returned to the Hardings' youngest daughter, Catharine.[73]

Henry's half-brother, Dr. Josiah Harding, eventually felt the sting of one of his slaves escaping. Thirty-seven-year-old David Diggs, the brother of George, whose unsuccessful escape ended in his return to Henry, was "dark, tall, and rather of a slender nature, possessing very large hopes."[74] His life had been spent separated from loved ones, not only his parents, who had once belonged to Adam Robb, but also his wife and child, who belonged to other owners.[75] In slavery, he was hired out to do various jobs and at times he was a farm labourer, a carriage driver, a cook, and a waiter for six judges on the Supreme Court. Of course his wages went to the doctor, whom he begrudgingly (and somewhat confusingly) acknowledged "was clever, but a Catholic."

In a similar vein, David thought that his mistress, Mary Valdenar Harding, was "tolerable clever," but he had not been around her enough to learn of any "bad habits" that she might have. Perhaps it was well that he had not. Her father, Francis Valdenar, became forever infamous in anti-slavery lore as the person who sold six members of the Edmonson family, who were among the more than seventy slaves who fled from the Washington wharf aboard the schooner *Pearl*. Captured and returned to Washington the next day, many of the slaves were sold to traders by their incensed owners, including Francis Valdenar, who received $4,500.

Josiah and Mary Harding had agreed that David could buy his own freedom by annually giving his master and mistress eighty-five dollars for twelve years. David worked diligently to earn the money and with the help of some friends was about to make his final payment, when Dr. Harding had a change of heart and pretended anger at some insignificant thing. In this feigned fit of rage he told his slave that there were already too many "free niggers" around and that David would do far better if he remained a slave. David disagreed, and along with eight others who were in similar circumstances, eventually concocted an escape plan that ultimately led them to Canada.[76]

John and Arabella Weems nervously observed all of these episodes involving their kinsmen and friends. On occasion they even helped in planning the escapes, despite the danger of repercussions for them and the others left behind. Their angry owners would certainly be more vigilant and further restrict the movements and activities of blacks, whether enslaved or free. Whatever small liberties they may have had would be curtailed. The threat of beatings or being sold hung over the heads of anyone suspected of knowing about or assisting with an escape. But the Weems family would have found some pleasure in having thwarted both the increasingly despised Hardings as well as the hated slave patrollers. They rejoiced whenever someone successfully found freedom, but they also felt pangs for the lost companionship. Reuniting their entire community in Canada became the stuff of dreams.

## CHAPTER 3

JOHN AND ARABELLA WEEMS BECAME intimately acquainted with painful goodbyes. When the new year dawned in 1850, they had eight children, with a ninth on the way, but soon they were reduced to seven. Richard, the Weemses' fourth child, who had been burdened with a physical infirmity, disappears from all subsequent records. No doubt he passed away. The eldest, Mary Jane, had a happier fate. She, along with her mother's sister Annie Talbot Young and Annie's husband, Abraham Young, and their two small children, took no chances on being sold to the cotton or cane fields of the Deep South. Early that same year, the five fled from Maryland into the free northern state of New York.[1]

The Youngs, each of whom belonged to a different master, had been married for only a couple of years. In 1847, they had received permission from their masters, he from William C. Pearce and she from the executors of Adam Robb's estate, to go the short distance to Washington to have a Catholic wedding. The ceremony was in late September on a Sunday, the one day when even slaves could occasionally enjoy a respite from their duties. Their first two children, both daughters, came quickly thereafter; first Mary Magdalene, followed within two years by Catharine Elizabeth. Just as Cecilia Talbot had done on September 20, 1820, with Annie when she was two months old, the young couple had the girls baptized.[2] In a wistful gesture, Annie Young asked her niece Catharine

Weems and her mother, Cecilia, to serve as sponsors.[3] But would they be able to fulfill their promises as godparents? When families belonged to two different owners, their chance of remaining together – uncertain at the best of times – was exceedingly precarious. Compounding the threat even further was the uncertainty hovering around the disposition of Adam Robb's estate. In May of the same year as Annie's wedding, Robb's executors had placed a value of $450 on the young bride. At age twenty-seven, in the prime of her life, she could fetch even more at auction.

Abraham and Annie were only too aware of the dangers associated with attempting to escape. In 1845, forty runaways had tried to make their way to Canada but were discovered and surrounded by a Rockville volunteer slave-hunting patrol. When one of the slaves resisted, the volunteers opened fire. Their well-aimed shots were intended to kill. A witness stated that one runaway received a musket ball to the neck that likely would prove fatal, while another was shot in the back and probably crippled for life. Another who was shot in the neck and the side also had his cheek blown away. One had his arm shattered. Several others were shot in the face, neck, and back, and some were expected to die for want of medical attention. All were arrested and marched through Washington bound with ox chains and handcuffs, "more like a drove of hogs than human beings." Those who survived were sent to the cotton fields of Louisiana. Some of the party that made the arrest lamented that not all of the slaves had resisted, thereby depriving them of "the pleasure of shooting them all down."[4]

But the Youngs also knew about the Underground Railroad through people like William Lawrence Chaplin, a fearless agent whom a local minister described as having "one of the noblest, most self-sacrificing, unselfish hearts that ever beat in human bosom."[5] Although Chaplin was white and free and Abraham and Annie were black and enslaved, they shared a hatred of slavery and all three fought back in their own way.

Chaplin, the son of a Congregational minister, came from Massachusetts, a state with a strong abolitionist tradition. Formerly editor of the New York state newspaper *American Citizen* and later of the *Albany Patriot*, the Harvard-educated Chaplin devoted the pages of both papers to the anti-slavery cause. His moral standing on the issue being well known, he was often approached to put his words into action. Examples of his work are plentiful, including his arranging the purchase of a slave so she might be freed before getting lost in the fields of Virginia, or his arranging passage on the *Pearl* for a group that had reached seventy-five people and that, in his words, was "increasing on my hands daily."[6]

One minister who disagreed with Chaplin's anti-slavery tactics nevertheless admired the man: "We have no doubt but he honestly conscientiously and fearlessly, thinks he is acting on the principles which a God of mercy and of justice will sanction . . . We give him the credit of being honest, sincere, unselfish, generous, devoted to the good of humanity, and one who would not value his life a straw, if by it he might alleviate the sorrows of the slave."[7] He lived up to that praise, and blacks sought him out "all Winter – by night & day, at all hours they have thronged my room & have listened to their tales of sorrow & outrage till my heart sickened."[8] As he had done with so many others, Chaplin appeared to have clandestinely helped Mary Jane Weems and the Young family to leave slavery behind. A cryptic reference in an anti-slavery newspaper that Abraham Young "well knew Wm. L Chaplin" and that "it would do Chaplin's heart good now to see this man" suggests that Chaplin played a role in their escape.[9]

Shortly after helping Mary Jane and the Youngs escape, William Chaplin fell under intense scrutiny by slave catchers. He had been involved with numerous courageous slave rescues, including the mass escape aboard the *Pearl*. But he had pushed his luck too far when he had agreed to help with the escape of two slaves, Allen and Garland, who belonged to two congressmen who represented the state of Georgia. Both owners were powerful and influential politicians. One of them, Alexander Hamilton Stephens, would later become vice-president of the Confederate States of America. While they were in Washington, both slaves had seized the opportunity to escape to the nearby free state of Pennsylvania. For some time they were hidden by the servants of the prominent District of Columbia resident General Walter Jones.

The enraged congressmen secured the services of John H. Goddard, an avowed proponent of slavery who held the official positions of police magistrate and captain of the night guard. The congressmen's reward of five hundred dollars for each of the fugitives only strengthened Goddard's resolve to find the two young men. Chaplin made it his mission to foil that resolve.

On the starless night of August 8, 1850, an enclosed, four-passenger carriage drawn by two horses arrived at an appointed place and time and the two fugitives climbed inside. However, Goddard had been tipped off by a worker at the stable where the carriage and horses had been housed and waited for them with a posse, near the Maryland–Pennsylvania border.

In the darkness, the first sign of the ambush was the dragging of the carriage wheels, resulting from a rail being thrown into the spokes. This was quickly followed by a blow from a club that knocked Chaplin to the ground. He was pinned by the assailants, who were armed with Bowie knives and pistols, which they fired into the carriage. Inside they found Congressman Stephens's slave, Allen, badly wounded but spared from certain death by his large pocket watch, which stopped one of the bullets. Allen was taken away to the District of Columbia slave jail, and three days later he was delivered into a nightmarish future at the hands of the slave trader John C. Cook. The day of Allen's committal he was accompanied into custody by another runaway, Mary Jones, who more fortunately was released to her master, Henry Harding.[10] Garland, who belonged to Congressman Toombs, had made his escape but, suffering a wound to his shoulder, surrendered himself within days.

Chaplin was jailed under the charges of having "abducted, stolen, taken, and carried out of and from the city of Washington" the two slaves. A fine of two hundred dollars was the usual penalty for this offence, but the congressmen were outraged and felt themselves personally affronted, which no doubt came into play. The *New York Express* bemoaned the fact that the slaves brought to Washington by southern members of Congress "have been so seduced, abducted and ran away with," and that the owners of the few who remained quickly sent them back south. Representative Colbrook of South Carolina lost most of his slaves and Mr. Toombs lost his entire household. The paper warned that soon there would be no more slaves left, leaving only the Irish and free blacks to take on jobs as servants.[11]

Chaplin was little fazed by his prison experience at first. In a letter he wrote from his Washington jail cell to his friend Gerrit Smith, Chaplin said that he was comfortable and "treated with perfect respect." He thought this experience would be invaluable for him once he was released. He was overcome with the "floods of sympathy & such rich consolation" that he had received. Feeling that he was in God's hands, he had "not at any moment indulged in disquietude."[12] This tranquility would come to an abrupt end when his case was transferred from the nation's capital to the nearby courthouse at Rockville, Maryland.

Moving the case to the neighbouring slave state of Maryland allowed the addition of charges, however unsupported by the facts, of assault and attempted murder. Public opinion was demonstrated by the gathered mob that wanted at best to verbally torment the abolitionist and at worst to lynch him. Some citizens of Montgomery County pooled their money to hire J. H. Tuck, Esquire to act as co-prosecuting attorney at the trial. The lawyer made an impassioned appeal to the court about the "enormity of the offence attempted by the accused." His comments were met with vehement applause from the onlookers, and despite the judge's warning to desist, the applause was repeated.[13] Feeling the temper of the town, the defence lawyers argued for a change in venue, as there could be no fair trial in Rockville. The magistrate agreed and it was determined that the trial would be moved yet again, to the neighbouring county courthouse, but not until the spring term. It was by then mid-November and Chaplin had been in custody since early August. Justice dictated that the prisoner be allowed to post bond.[14]

Bail was set at the astronomically high figure of nineteen thousand dollars. Twelve thousand was raised from wealthy abolitionists in the North, but fear prevented many others from contributing. In a series of ironic twists, a wealthy slave dealer from Baltimore, in an attempt to polish the tarnished reputation that accompanied his occupation, agreed to pay the extra money, provided that there was enough security to ensure his profiting from interest. Slave traders – the very antithesis of supposed southern gentility – were so despised that "the odium descended upon his children and his children's children."[15] The person who offered to pay Chaplin's bail could very well have been Hope Hull Slatter, one of the country's major traders, who retired about that time and hoped finally to be accepted into decent society following his retirement. Despite this gesture, he remained vilified.[16] A reporter on the Chaplin case made the wicked observation that "Satan, no doubt, would eagerly avail himself of any opportunity that might offer to go bail for the archangel Michael, especially if it so happened that all the priests, deacons and church-members, had first been asked and had declined." In the end, three other Maryland slave owners gave the needed money and Chaplin was released. Chaplin's days of actively helping slaves thus came to an end.

◆

Once freed, Abraham Young left behind not only his slave tasks as a body-servant and a field-hand to his owner, William C. Pearce, but also his name, a common practice for runaways who hoped to avoid being tracked down.[17] Abraham would now be referred to by some as "Brown," but this name change would be temporary. Soon he would choose the name William Henry Bradley, which he would carry for the rest of his days. His wife's name change was much less dramatic.

Christened Ann Maria, she had been called Maria by her owner. In freedom she became known simply as Annie. Mary Jane Weems, their niece, became Stella.

The newly renamed group passed through New York City before settling temporarily in the small town of Geneva in the western part of New York State. Stella separated from the rest of the family at some point after arriving in that city, probably to make the fiendish work of slave catchers and bounty hunters more difficult. The parting became permanent when the Bradleys took their family to the Dawn Settlement near Dresden, in Canada West, now known as Ontario.

A new law passed that year, the Fugitive Slave Act, made it unsafe for any black, particularly a runaway slave, to feel secure even in the free states of the North.[18] This law was designed to pacify the southern slave owners by making it illegal for anyone to assist in the escape or conceal-ment of runaway slaves. The penalty was a fine of one thousand dollars or six months in jail. Under this law, U.S. marshals or special commis-sioners could also order any citizen to assist in the capture of any runaway or be tried for treason. Once arrested, the accused fugitive was to appear before a judge or justice of the peace, who was paid five dollars if he ruled the black to be a free person or ten dollars if a fugitive. Clearly there was an incentive to come down against the blacks regardless of their true status. Blacks were not allowed to testify in their own defence. As a result, they were sometimes kidnapped from the streets or from their own homes – even when their ancestors had been free for several gener-ations. In the resulting panic, the steady flow of refugees into Canadian communities such as the Dawn Settlement became a torrent.

Dawn was established in 1841, several years prior to the passage of the Fugitive Slave Act. It was founded and sustained with the assistance of British anti-slavery sympathizers who donated money to two of the settlement's founders: Hiram Wilson, a missionary to Canadian blacks, and Quaker philanthropist James Cannings Fuller, from Skaneateles, New York. Ironically, Hiram Wilson had chosen the site of the Dawn

*Free blacks in the United States were sometimes kidnapped and sold into slavery.*
(New York Public Library image 1129922)

Settlement along with Josiah Henson, who was "much esteemed for his piety & general character" and who in his youth had belonged to Adam Robb. Although the Bradleys did not know it then, some of those same donors would continue to play an important role in the future of their family members who had been left behind in Maryland.

Six trustees of Dawn were appointed and charged with the expenditure of the original contributions, to be used "for the alone purpose of education, mental, moral and physical, of the coloured inhabitants of Canada, not excluding white persons and Indians." They purchased two hundred acres of fertile land as the base to build "the British-American Institute of Science and Industry," a manual labour institution that would complement the common school in the district. Students over the age of fifteen were to receive a free education and their room and board in exchange for working on the land.[19]

By the time the Bradleys arrived in Dawn there were few signs that the considerable donations had been well spent in the decade since its establishment. A steam-operated sawmill to produce lumber had been erected but turned out to be a costly failure because there were no qualified managers to run it. There had been repeated difficulties in keeping the manual labour school open due to lack of regular funds. There were constant arguments among the various managers of the settlement, and charges of misrepresentation and misappropriation of funds were common.[20] Over the years Dawn's representatives would repeatedly appeal to British and New England donors for financial support for the settlement. To this the donors readily consented, demonstrating their continuous commitment to the anti-slavery cause.

But despite the problems surrounding the British-American Institute, there was no denying that Dawn afforded a safe haven and previously unknown opportunities to fugitive slaves who established a home on its adjoining lands. Hiram Wilson and his wife worked to keep the industrial school open during the winter months, he with fifteen to twenty male students, and she with twenty-five females. In the township's common school, the children as well as several adults of both sexes were taught to "read, write and cypher." John Scoble, the secretary for the British and Foreign Anti-Slavery Society, who would himself move to Dawn to help with its administration a few months after the Bradleys, believed that "in this settlement is found a larger amount of intelligence, a more elevated moral tone, and broader views of what the refugees should be and should do than in any other part of Canada."[21]

This description aptly fit William and his family, who quickly prospered as farmers. On December 22, 1851, the couple somehow found the means to pay 125 pounds to acquire a farm. They proudly signed the document with an X. The widow they purchased it from carried an additional mortgage for sixty-two pounds, ten shillings.[22] Within five years as a free man, William owned fifty acres of land, two horses, twelve head of hogs, six sheep and two milk cows, which he proudly stated that he bought and paid for with his own effort. His situation was so different from what it was in Maryland, where despite all

*William and Annie Bradley's farm in Dresden, Canada West (formerly the Dawn Settlement)* (Historical Atlas of Essex and Kent Counties, Ontario)

his work he had had no possessions to call his own. In 1855, a Boston editor named Benjamin Drew interviewed William Bradley for a book called *The Refugee, or the Narratives of Fugitive Slaves in Canada*. In it, Bradley reflected on slavery, escape, and his new life:

> I look at slavery as the most horrid thing on earth. It is awful to think of the poor slaves panting for a place of refuge, and so few able to find it. There is not a day or night that I don't think about them, and wish that slavery might be abolished, and every man have his God-given rights.
>
> I have prospered well in freedom. I thank the Lord for my success here . . .
>
> There is a great deal of prejudice here. Statements have been made that colored people wished for separate schools; some did ask for them, and so these have been established, although many colored people have prayed against them as an infringement of their rights. Still, we have more freedom here than in the United States, as far as the government law guarantees. In consequence of the ignorance of the colored men, who come here unlearned out of slavery, the white people have an overpowering chance. There are many respectable

colored people moving in, but I have not much hope of a better state of things. Public sentiment will move mountains of laws.

Steam engines don't work harder than a man's heart when he starts from his master, and fears being overtaken. I don't understand how an honest man can partake of any principle to carry him back.

If a man could make slaves of mud or block, and have them work for him, it would be wrong, – all men came of the hand of the Almighty; every man ought to have life, and his own method of pursuing happiness.[23]

William and his wife no doubt would have preferred to remain in their birthplace in Maryland surrounded by loved ones and familiar surroundings. The northern climate was harsher and the hardships of pioneer life were made more acute by the sharp pains of separation, particularly because they had an intimate knowledge of what Mrs. Bradley's sister and her family continued to endure. They longed to hear that some of the Weems family had also made their escape and would join them, but for that they needed patience.[24]

While her aunt and uncle braved the unknown in Canada, Stella Weems tried to build her new life in Geneva. She found a certain comfort in living in a town where two-thirds of the black community were other fugitive slaves who thought that they had reached a safe refuge.[25] However, Geneva would prove to be a treacherous place to attempt to put down new roots. Of the total population of 8,503 in 1850, only 203 were black and, judging by articles that appeared in the *Geneva Gazette*, there was a great strain between the races. The editor wrote unconvincingly of slavery that "we most sincerely and devoutly wish that it had no existence among us." Still, he felt that "slavery in itself is not sinful." He argued that the North and the South were bound together in a brotherhood and that disagreement between the two should be avoided. Abolitionists who thought otherwise were "our malignant foes," and their opinions "were of little or no importance to anybody" and "any intelligent and sound minded person" would realize that.[26]

It was under this pervasive cloud of intolerance that Stella was betrayed by a doctor in Geneva, identified only by the initials R.S.[27] Although details of this betrayal do not survive, the doctor may have been motivated by the offer of a considerable reward. An attractive female who was entering womanhood, Stella would have been particularly prized and the reward for her return substantial. If Stella were captured, she would face unimaginable terror. A return to her original master would be the minimum punishment – at least in that scenario she would be reunited with her own family. But it was not likely to be that benign. She might be beaten with a paddle or whipped. Prospective buyers sometimes shied away from those who carried the telltale scars borne by runaways or recalcitrant slaves, so whippings were often carefully done to avoid damaging the skin. Other means of torture might also be administered; her being sold to the cotton, rice, or cane fields of the South was a real possibility.

Newspapers regularly carried stories that would have sent shivers down Stella's spine. One such notice the same year that Stella escaped said:

> For sale, a coloured girl, of very superior qualifications . . . She is
> what speculators call a fancy girl – a bright mulatto, fine figure,
> straight black hair, and very black eyes; remarkably neat and cleanly in
> her person . . . Any lady or gentleman in Norfolk or Portsmouth, who
> may wish to purchase a girl of this description (whom I consider the
> most valuable in Virginia) may take her and try her a month or more
> at my risk, and if she does not suit and answer the description here
> given, may return her . . . The cause of offense for which I intend
> (though reluctantly) to sell her, is, that she has been recently induced,

by some colored persons, to make her escape with them to the north, in which she failed, and is now offered for sale.[28]

Fortunately Stella did not suffer that fate, as the doctor's treachery to have her captured was discovered. Sometime in 1850, she was whisked away at midnight and hidden by the family of a black minister named Henry Highland Garnet, also a fugitive slave from Maryland, who was then stationed at a church in Geneva. Reverend Garnet and his wife, Julia, soon adopted the seventeen-year-old Stella, making her the big sister of five-year-old Mary and three-year-old James.[29] The reverend was a prodigious writer but even years later he was guarded about details surrounding Stella's escape or about her eluding the mysterious doctor who would have returned her to slavery.

Henry Garnet knew only too well the terror of being hunted by slave catchers. His great-grandfather, a warrior and the young son of an African chieftain, had been taken prisoner following a tribal war and sold to slave traders who placed him aboard a ship and took him across the nightmare known as the Middle Passage. Various first-hand accounts survive of those trips, each more horrifying than the other. Bound together by chains, the males and females were led separately into the ship's hold. To prevent the infestation of vermin, all of their clothing was removed. Tightly packed together, sometimes stacked in layered perches, they lay in each

*Reverend Henry Highland Garnet, the fugitive slave turned abolitionist and renowned orator who adopted Stella Weems* (New York Public Library image 485488)

54

others' bodily waste. Many died of disease and despair. Upon being allowed above-deck to get some air, some took advantage of the opportunity to jump overboard, preferring death. Garnet's great-grandfather was one of those who survived and was delivered to the American colonies and sold on the shores of Maryland.

His descendants remained enslaved until Garnet's parents resolved to escape in 1822, taking their daughter and eight-year-old Henry with them. They had belonged to Colonel William Spencer until his death, when Spencer's nephew, described by one of Garnet's biographers as "overbearing and cruel; the very personification of tyranny," inherited them. With the change of ownership, Henry's mother immediately recognized the life of terror that lay ahead and cunningly and courageously made plans to escape.

Appealing to whatever shreds of humanity that her master possessed, she obtained permission to attend the funeral of a relative who lived ten miles away, a trip requiring an absence of two days. Departing at sunset, the Garnets, along with eight other fugitives, travelled north throughout the night. When daylight came, they found shelter in the woods and swamps and fitfully rested their bodies if not their minds. Henry was not always able to keep up with the adults, who occasionally carried him on their backs. The group eventually reached the Wilmington, Delaware, home of Thomas Garret, a Quaker and a giant in the anti-slavery cause. From there, with Garret's help, they continued on to the appropriately named village of New Hope in the free state of Pennsylvania before going on to New York City, where they took up residence.

For seven years the Garnets made their own way in what must have seemed to them a strange new land of the free. However, neither time nor distance assured their safety. At what should have been the relatively carefree age of fourteen, Henry arrived home one day from his job as a cook and a steward aboard a schooner that sailed between New York and Washington to find his family missing. His father, who was tall and athletic, "carrying in his every movement strength and dignity," had leapt from an upper-storey window and fled. His mother, who, despite her past oppression, was "the very soul of fun, wit, frolic and laughter," was being hidden by neighbours. His only sister, now seventeen, had been captured and jailed as a "fugitive from Justice." All of the family's furniture had been either stolen or destroyed. Henry Garnet became enraged upon learning what had befallen his family and was fixated on seeking revenge. Luckily his friends had cooler heads and persuaded him to go into hiding on Long Island.

Recognizing that vengeance could come in many forms, Henry seized the opportunity to become educated. At the African Free School in New York, he received his educational foundation. Then in 1833 he attended the Canal Street Collegiate School and studied Latin, among other subjects. But prejudice prevented him and his fellow black students from receiving the same instruction as their white counterparts, as they were not allowed in the same classrooms. Two years later he travelled five hundred miles to attend the Canaan Academy in New Hampshire, where the attitude toward black students was even more vicious. After Garnet had been there for an uneasy three months, a mob brought sixty-five teams of oxen and pulled the school off its moorings and set it on fire. They then attacked the house where the black students boarded, firing bullets into the rooms.[30]

On the same day that the academy was destroyed and bullets came flying into Garnet's dormitory room, a young woman named Julia A. Williams arrived in town. Her experience had been only slightly less traumatic than Garnet's. Born in Charleston, South Carolina, on July 1, 1811, she came to Boston while still a child. The joy that must have accompanied her to the free state of Massachusetts was no doubt tempered by her leaving part of her family, including her sister Diana, behind in slavery. Julia's early life in the heart of the South created in her a hunger for religion and for education, and she was baptized into the Baptist Church at the age of eleven.

Several years later, when the opportunity arose, she became a student at Prudence Crandall's school for young ladies in Canterbury, Connecticut – until it was broken up by a mob and Miss Crandall was thrown into jail for teaching girls of colour. More technically, she was jailed for attempting "to establish literary institutions in this State, for the instruction of colored persons belonging to other states and countries, which would lead to the great increase of the colored Population of the State, and thereby to the injury of the people."[31] From this sad experience she went to the equally difficult situation at the Canaan Academy. Although these trying events temporarily prevented her from. furthering her education, a fickle providence now considerately arranged for her to meet her future life partner.[32]

Drawn together by similar experiences and by mutual attraction, Julia Williams and Henry Garnet were married a few years later by Reverend T.S. Wright at the Frankfort Street Church in New York City on August 19, 1841. Julia was living and teaching in Boston at the time, and her new husband was stationed in Troy, where he taught at the "colored school" and had been ordained as a ruling elder at the First Presbyterian Church.[33] By then, Henry had also become an accomplished lecturer and writer. He gave powerful speeches before many groups, including the American Anti-Slavery Society, which elevated his stature as one of the leading black figures of the day. Referring only occasionally to his notes, he could bring large crowds to outrage or to tears. A friend described Garnet as having "a salience, a variety, an intellectual incidity, and above all, a brilliancy and glowing fire in our friend's eloquence which gave him his special and peculiar place."[34] He stood erect in his finely tailored clothing and had an aristocratic air about him. By the time he became an ordained Presbyterian minister in 1843 he had become one the greatest public champions of freedom and equality.

Circumstances kept Garnet focused on the cause. On June 20, 1848, while leaving Buffalo on a trip to Niagara Falls, Canada, he was dragged from his seat on a train for sitting in a car that the conductor said was reserved only for whites. When Garnet resisted, he was choked and severely beaten and for a time feared that he would be thrown beneath the wheels of the moving train. A small man of about five feet two inches, he was no physical match for his assailant. He also walked with a cane after having had his leg amputated at the hip, the result of an injury during his youth. The outrage was widely reported by a sympathetic press, and was even featured in the English newspaper *Monthly Illustrations of Slavery* in Newcastle-upon-Tyne.[35] It would later prove to be serendipitous that this attack on Garnet reached the ears of this newspaper's editors, Henry and Anna H. Richardson.

Two years later, in 1850, around the time that Stella Weems arrived into the safe haven of his household, Reverend Garnet accepted an invitation to give anti-slavery lectures in the British Isles. Garnet's main focus was to discourage the use of produce grown by slave labour:

*Henry and Anna Richardson, editors of the British abolitionist newspaper* Monthly Illustrations of Slavery, *who were instrumental in drumming up support for the Weems family* (from the book *A Historical Sketch of the Society of Friends,* by John William Steel, 1899)

*Gerrit Smith, a millionaire philanthropist and abolitionist who three times ran for president* (Library of Congress image cwpbh 02633)

chiefly cotton, sugar, rice, and coffee. Leaving part of his family behind, Garnet and his five-year-old daughter, Mary, made the transatlantic trip on the Cunard line of steamers. After boarding, he was forced to take an expensive, solitary state room rather than the cheaper second-class cabin, "lest there should be trouble" with the white passengers.[36] While naturally torn at leaving his family, including Stella and his pregnant wife, it probably never occurred to him that they would be at risk in their Geneva home, where they lived surrounded by the many parishioners of his church.

Perhaps Garnet had not counted on the magnitude of the terror that rippled through the free states following the September 1850 passage of the Fugitive Slave Act. Many of the blacks in his Geneva congregation were particularly vulnerable, as two-thirds of them – including all of his family – were technically fugitive slaves. Seventeen of these parishioners were forced to flee to Canada in the act's aftermath.[37] In one of his moving speeches to a large and enthusiastic audience in Gateshead, England, Garnet estimated that those members of his own flock had joined forty thousand other fugitive slaves who had found shelter in Canada.[38] He considered Canada to be the "safety valve" for the American Republic, which would explode in a violent "liberty or death" struggle if blacks could not flee to the British colony.[39]

Before he left Geneva, Garnet had left instructions with his wife to contact Gerrit Smith, a good friend and one of the champions of the anti-slavery cause, in the event of an emergency. Garnet sent money home when he could. In November 1850, he sent forty-nine dollars to New York abolitionist Lewis Tappan to forward to Julia, but even that amount would not be enough to cover his family's expenses.[40] By December the money had still not arrived and they were nearly destitute. By now Julia had delivered a second son, named Henry, another mouth to feed. Samuel Rhoads, a Quaker abolitionist who was a friend of both the Garnets and Anna Richardson, wrote to Lewis Tappan and asked if he could ascertain how Julia was faring. Both Rhoads and Richardson were willing to lend aid if necessary.[41] Julia was forced to follow her husband's advice on St. Valentine's Day, 1851. She wrote to Gerrit Smith that she feared the money her husband had mailed must have been onboard the steam ship *Atlantic*, which had not been heard from since it left the port of Liverpool on December 28 and was presumed lost at sea. She had written to Henry in Europe but had so far received no reply.

To compound her troubles, both of her sons were sick, five-year-old James particularly so, although Julia was optimistic that he was "not dangerously ill."[42] Two weeks later the mother's hopes careened into despair when James died on March 1. The forty-eight dollars that Henry sent to Tappan for his wife one month later could do nothing to lighten her tremendous grief. Ever the friend of the downtrodden, Gerrit Smith paid for Julia and her children to travel to England to be reunited with their husband and father.[43]

◆

Meanwhile, Henry Garnet was living "a new life" in what he described as "a new world." He was astounded that in Britain he was treated with equality and did not receive any of the abuse that was the norm in North America. Britain had a tradition of anti-slavery activity. Slavery itself was completely abolished there in 1778, when Scotland followed the course set earlier in the decade by England and Ireland. In 1807, George III had given his royal assent to a bill abolishing the African slave trade, with the law coming into effect on January 1, 1808. Then on August 1, 1834, an imperial decree signed by George III came into effect that outlawed slavery in all of Britain's colonies – including her possessions in the West Indies and British North America, which would later become known as Canada. Not content to see slavery eliminated within Britain's borders, many sought to continue the crusade and eradicate its stain from the globe. Anti-slavery organizations took root across England, Wales, Scotland, and Ireland.

Henry Garnet was welcomed by many of these groups, starting with the August 14, 1850 meeting of the British and Foreign Anti-Slavery Society, where he joined Chairman Joseph Sturge, Secretary John Scoble, and the other members in expressing their sympathy for William Chaplin, who was in an American prison for aiding in the escape of slaves. The pain was particularly acute for Garnet, who was a personal friend of Chaplin's. They had worked together, including an occasion two years earlier when they had held triumphant meetings in Philadelphia after helping with the escape of some girls whom Garnet was to take to safety in the west.[44]

Garnet would spend the next two and a half years travelling across Ireland, Scotland and England, lecturing with great effect to the assembled audiences on the evils of buying produce that had been grown with slave labour. Whether he spoke in large cities like London, Belfast, Glasgow, and Edinburgh, or smaller places like Greenock, Paisley, Ellensboro, Hamilton, Falkirk, Kirkaldy, and Dundee, he connected with and moved ordinary citizens. He was immensely popular and left a lasting impression with his eloquent delivery mixed with both pathos and humour – telling one audience that it was so dangerous to be an abolitionist in the United States that they might go to bed one night and get "up in the morning with their heads off."[45]

He was also in a position to meet with most British anti-slavery leaders, including the various members of the Sturge family of Birmingham, George Gallie of Glasgow, and John Scoble from London. At times he shared the newspaper columns or the podium with other black leaders from the United States such as Reverend J.W.C. Pennington, William Wells Brown, and Alexander Crummell, and from Canada, such as Samuel Ward from the Canadian Anti-Slavery Society and Josiah Henson from the Dawn Settlement. Garnet's familiarity with all of these people would pay unexpected dividends to Stella Weems's family in the very near future.

But Garnet's separation from his loved ones had been weighing heavily on him for several months. He dearly loved children, and an admiring friend commented that "they all loved him; everywhere they flocked around him; everywhere he was the object of their idolatry; so great was the playful element in his nature, so long did he carry the feelings of childhood into the maturity of age, that children forgot his seniority and thought themselves for the time romping and sporting with a playfellow." Likewise, he was interested in young adults of Stella's age, who "delighted to come to his house and spend long hours in the joyous converse which he would pour out sparklingly, hour after hour." It would be nice to get acquainted with Henry Jr., the newest member of his family, and he especially missed his Julia, who excited the same "gallantry" in him after their marriage as she had before it.[46]

On July 7, 1851, Henry Garnet wrote to Gerrit Smith from London in anticipation of his wife and "little ones," who had not yet arrived but were expected any day. Finally on August 28 they arrived at the port of Liverpool.[47] Stella Weems accompanied her adoptive mother, thereby putting an ocean between herself and the American slave hunters. Garnet's long-suffering wife was honoured on her arrival with the presentation of a ceremonial object, likely patterned after a tool used to separate wheat from straw, called a "free labor flail," in recognition of her own stand against purchasing goods produced through the toil of slaves.[48] A newspaper editor later articulated how worthy Julia was of the accolade: "Her devotion to the anti-slavery cause, and her sacrifices for the fleeing fugitives, may not be recorded by human pen but the recording angel has written them."[49]

The Garnet family lived briefly at 89 Blandford Street in Newcastle-upon-Tyne.[50] The British Isles offered an entirely different atmosphere, and nowhere was this more pronounced than at Newcastle, where Quakers Henry and Anna Richardson led the anti-slavery movement. It was this couple who had originally invited Garnet to lecture to audiences throughout Britain and who had offered him a place in their home. Anna devoted her time to distributing and collecting subscriptions for the American anti-slavery newspapers the *North Star* and its successor the *Frederick Douglass Paper*, which was only fitting as she,

*Frederick Douglass, editor of the anti-slavery newspapers the* North Star *and* Frederick Douglass Newspaper
(Library of Congress image cph 3a18122)

along with her sister-in-law Ellen Richardson, had been responsible for raising the money to purchase and grant the freedom of Frederick Douglass, the newspaper's editor.[51]

The Newcastle Ladies' Negro Emancipation Society held a celebration of welcome for the entire Garnet family. The Independent Chapel was filled to capacity with people of different denominations. Speaker after speaker denounced slavery and the monstrous Fugitive Slave Act, which forced people like Stella Weems and the Garnets to flee their homeland. Resolutions were presented and unanimously endorsed that shame should fall on Christian churches that supported the institution of slavery and "that God had made of one blood of all the nations of the earth." The entire house joined in raucous applause.[52]

Similar sentiments were expressed when the Garnets moved to Scotland in early 1852, for their final months of spreading the anti-slavery and free-produce message across the British Isles. Stella could not help but be amazed at the genuine outpouring of affection there. Perhaps even more importantly, another group known as the Glasgow Female New Association for the Abolition of Slavery selected the New York Vigilance Committee as the organization that would receive the greatest share of the benevolent funds that they had raised.[53] Stella's family would later be among the principal benefactors of this generosity.

As 1852 drew to its close, Stella was preparing to accompany her adoptive family on a move to Jamaica, where Garnet would assume his new appointment as a missionary for the United Presbyterian Church of Scotland. Before the family departed from Glasgow, the Glasgow Female New Association for the Abolition of Slavery held a soirée in tribute to the Garnets.

As Stella and her adoptive family were about to depart for the West Indies, they received a letter from a New York City abolitionist informing them that the Hardings had sold Stella's mother, two sisters, and five brothers to slave traders and that they would be separated! She had never even had the chance to see her baby brother, Sylvester, who had been born after she had fled two and a half years earlier.[54] The news was more than her fragile emotional psyche could handle. Would she ever see her family again? Was the price of her own freedom too dear? And worst of all, could her escape have ignited a series of events that enraged her former owners and led to the retaliation against her dearest ones? Garnet described Stella as someone who was "overwhelmed with grief, and presents in her person an object of intense mental suffering. Her distress is so great I fear she will lose her reason."

Stella's pain was particularly profound, but none of the Garnet family was immune from the shock and the hurt. The stress of hearing the news caused the reverend to faint on a Glasgow street, leading him to receive medical treatment.[55] In a letter he wrote on Sunday evening, October 17, 1852, to his friends Anna and Henry Richardson, he movingly described the shadow that had fallen on his household: "There is a sorrow in my dwelling! The light of joy that cheered my hearth has been put out by one rude blast of a storm of severe affliction . . . Stella is but little less than a maniac; and all of us are smitten as if by death. It is worse than death; in the grave, the weary are at rest, the wicked cease from troubling, and the slave is free from his master . . . O what a world it is! What cruelty, what inhumanity does man show towards his fellows! Stella's grief is heart-rending; and we fear her mind will give way."[56]

JOHN WEEMS WAS FRANTIC to find a way to buy Arabella and their children before it was too late and they were sent away to the South forever. The nightmare of all slaves had come true for him.

At the beginning of April 1852, John had decided to make his way north – he knew not exactly where – to search for his daughter, Stella, and his sister-in-law and brother-in law. He hoped that they could help him quickly raise the money to purchase his family's freedom. He

*Reverend Charles Bennett Ray,
co-founder and editor of* The Colored
American, *a weekly newspaper
published in New York that
championed abolition and the
improvement of free blacks' lives* (New
York Public Library, image 1219249)

stopped first at New York City to seek out a friend, probably someone who had ties to Washington's Underground Railroad network, who might help with fundraising or perhaps even locate Stella and the Bradleys. Not finding his friend there, John proceeded to Boston to look for him, again with no success.

He then returned to New York, which had, as did many other places in the United States and Canada, a "vigilance committee" to help runaway slaves and free blacks. Fortunately in Brooklyn he found Reverend Charles Bennett Ray, a black Congregationalist minister who was well connected in the extensive web of anti-slavery activists as the co-founder and correspondence secretary of the New York State Vigilance Society and former editor of the slavery newspaper *The Colored American*. Ray knew that Stella was with Reverend Garnet in the British Isles and that the minister's speaking engagements there were gathering great attention from a sympathetic public.

When John returned to Washington, he learned the heartbreaking news: the Hardings – attracted by the prospect of sudden wealth or at least a loosening of their financial bindings – had sold his wife and children to the slave traders for the goodly sum of $3,300. Arabella and their sons had been transferred to a slave pen in Washington, D.C., where they would be sold and sent to the South forever. Meanwhile, their remaining daughters had been sold to slave traders and were now held in the nearby town of Unity, Maryland. In an act filled with venom, the Hardings had stipulated that the Weems family not be sold to anyone in the vicinity of Washington.

Fuelled by desperation and love, John used his best powers of negotiation to save his family. A noble man in Washington pledged to loan him $1,600, but only if John could raise the remaining $1,700. This proved impossible to do in a short period of time and the pledge was lost. Such was the peculiar nature of the pledge – it was to be all or nothing, perhaps because if the entire family were purchased, they could all work to repay it.

The slave trader then offered John his wife and two-year-old Sylvester for nine hundred dollars. By appealing for donations in Maryland, John raised four hundred. To collect any more, he knew that he would have to travel out of the Slave States and into northern cities, where there was more opposition to slavery. The laws aimed at ridding Maryland of free blacks meant that he would need a permit to get back into the state. Complying with the details of the law, he got three white men in Montgomery County to sign a paper attesting to his good character, which he presented to the county's Orphans' Court for permission to leave the jurisdiction for thirty days and then re-enter.[1] This was the same Orphans' Court that two years earlier had put a price on John Weems's family and made the final ruling on their division among Adam Robb's heirs. Fortunately the court showed mercy this time and granted John's request.

John raised another two hundred dollars in Boston, Philadelphia, and New York, but he was still short by three hundred. In late September he met with Reverend Ray, who promised to write to Henry Garnet in Scotland to see if the British abolitionists would contribute to the fund.[2] Garnet's popularity there suggested that they would, but it would take weeks for Ray's letter to cross the Atlantic and for the overseas fundraising to begin. Time was running out. It was becoming clear that John's children would be lost to the South and probably his beloved Arabella as well.

*

As the Weems family was suffering from their personal tragedy, a serialized story entitled *Uncle Tom's Cabin, or Life among the Lowly* by Harriet Beecher Stowe appeared in the American anti-slavery newspaper *National Era*. Like nothing else before its publication (eventually it appeared in book form) this story accelerated the abolitionist movement and appealed to widespread popular sentiment.

The sympathetic characters became for many readers the embodiment of southern slaves. The title character is pious and loyal and would rather be sold at the New Orleans market than run away because he feared that the slaves left behind would suffer the consequences. He befriends Evangeline, or Little Eva, a pure-of-heart child who is dying of consumption and who has a wisdom and humanity that transcend colour. Simon Legree is the cruel and drunken master who causes Tom to be beaten to death. George Harris is a skilled slave who runs away to Canada, soon to be joined by his beautiful wife, Eliza, and their son. This family is fair-skinned enough that they are able to pass as white. Sympathetic conductors along the Underground Railroad route care for Eliza and her child, who are being pursued by their Kentucky slave owner and who desperately jump across ice floes on the Ohio River during their daring escape. Kindly Quakers assist them on their flight.

*Uncle Tom's Cabin* was wildly popular across all classes. Three hundred thousand copies were sold in America in the first year alone.

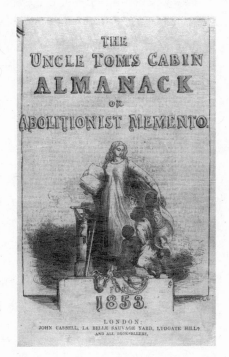

*Seizing upon the unprecedented popularity of* Uncle Tom's Cabin, *organizations rushed to publish tracts containing stories about the barbarity of slavery.* (New York Public Library image 413868)

The book's influence reached into the political arena and helped to inspire a movement to repeal the Fugitive Slave Law. But its most profound and lasting effect was on ordinary citizens. It inspired people to become more active and vocal in the anti-slavery movement and the Underground Railroad. Among them was George Washington Williams. Although only a small child when Stowe's book was written, he deeply felt its impact and would write in his own book, *History of the Negro Race in America 1619–1880*:

But the uncounted millions of anti-slavery tracts, pamphlets, journals, and addresses of the entire period of agitation were little more than a paper wad compared with the solid shot "Uncle Tom's Cabin" was to slavery. Written in vigorous English, in scintillating, perspicuous style; adorned with gorgeous imagery, bristling with living "facts"; going to the lowest depths, mounting to the greatest altitudes, moving with panoramic grandeur, picturing humanity forlorn and outraged; giving forth the shrillest, most despairing cries of the afflicted, and the sub- limest strains of Christian faith; the struggle of innocent, defenseless womanhood, the subdued sorrow of chattel-babyhood, the yearning of fettered manhood, and the piteous sobs of helpless old age, – made Mrs. Harriet Beecher Stowe's "Uncle Tom's Cabin" the magnifying wonder of enlightened Christendom! It pleaded the cause of the slave in twenty different languages; it engrossed the thought of philoso- phers, and touched the heart of youth with a strange pity for the slave. It covered audiences with the sunlight of laughter, wrapt them in sorrow, and veiled them in tears. It illustrated the power of the Gospel of Love, the gentleness of Negro character, and the powers and possi- bilities of the race. It was God's message to a people who had refused to listen to his anti-slavery prophets and priests; and its sad, weird, and heart-touching descriptions and dialogues restored the milk of human kindness to a million hearts that had grown callous in an age of self- seeking and robbery of the poor.

Stowe's fictionalized account of life in slavery was widely and vehemently attacked in the South. Slave owners asserted that the cruelties depicted in the novel were not only overstated but blatantly untrue and that southern society was unjustly characterized. The experiences of the Weems family, and those of thousands of others, make that argument absurd.

In Britain as in North America, the public mind was fresh with Harriet Beecher Stowe's imagery of the beautiful and delicate Rosa, whose mistress accused her of not knowing her place. When Rosa commits the crime of trying on her mistress's dress, she is issued a written order to receive fifteen lashes in the whipping house. *Uncle Tom's Cabin* also drew a mental picture of Emmeline, a young slave raised in the refined atmosphere of New Orleans society who is the lust object of her depraved new owner, Simon Legree. It took little imagination to put the beautiful Catharine Weems in Rosa's or Emmeline's place.[3]

Now recovered from his shock on hearing that the Weems family had been sold, Henry Garnet quickly spread the word around Britain. British newspapers, which had often covered Garnet's speaking engagements, quickly picked up the story and appealed to the emotions of their readers. Stowe had written that the death of one of her own sons less than three years previously had impressed upon her the sorrow that a slave mother must feel when any of her children were torn away from her.[4] Now some newspapers challenged women to demonstrate with practical generosity the feelings that Mrs. Stowe had stirred within them. At least one paper described the Weems family's tragedy within a longer article devoted to a story on Stowe and her family. The newspaper mentioned Reverend Garnet and brought special attention to Stella Weems, who was among them, and to Catharine, who had unknown horrors awaiting her.[5] Catharine's skin was very light, which drew additional public attention to her plight. Curiously, abolitionists often expressed moral outrage when slaves were as nearly as fair-skinned as their owners, as though it was more criminal for them to be enslaved than for someone darker.

Many newspapers were happy to report on the story, as if doing so wiped any remaining stain of slavery from Britain's hands. With righteous indignation, British writers almost gleefully seized the opportunity to mock the grandiose language of the American Declaration of Independence: "We hold these truths to be self-evident: That all men are created equal; that they are endowed by their Creator with certain inalienable rights; that among these are life, liberty and the pursuit of happiness."[6] These words rang hollow to many Britons.

Garnet himself quickly sprang to action to raise money for the Weemses, and addressed an anti-slavery crowd at the Presbyterian Church in Glasgow. Within three weeks a Scottish steamer carried news of the meeting to the United States, and a Philadelphia newspaper, *North American and United States Gazette*, made the story more widely known.[7] The relatively new telegraph network ensured that it would spread along the eastern seaboard, and the *Boston Daily Atlas* and *Vermont Watchman and State Journal* carried the dispatch.[8] Overjoyed at the public outcry over the past three weeks about the Weemses' situation, Garnet heaped praise on his "adopted" empire, "whose Government above all others of the earth give the best illustrations of civil and religious liberty."

As the time was nearing for Garnet and his family to depart for Jamaica he left a parting challenge: "I know of but two ways by which the benefactors of the family of John Weems can form a just estimation of their deed of mercy – by their supposing what would be their feelings if their beloved relations and friends were sold and redeemed from the slave-traders, who are the meanest and the most heartless of all the wretches who prowl on the outskirts of the human family; and also, by realizing the value of the words of our Lord, 'inasmuch as you have done it unto one of the least of these my brethren, ye have done it unto me.'"[9]

British newspapers also reported that one half of the money needed to redeem Arabella Weems and her seven remaining enslaved children

*A typical British abolitionist logo, the seal of the British & Foreign Anti-Slavery Society depicted a male slave in chains.* (Library of Congress image cph 3G05321)

had been raised. Anna and Henry Richardson alone had raised 145 pounds and had been promised another hundred more. The Richardsons championed the cause and made impassioned pleas to other anti-slavery societies to become involved in the fundraising. George Gallie of the Glasgow Emancipation Society in Scotland quickly raised fifty pounds; Reverend Alexander Somerville of Edinburgh raised thirty; and a Mr. Turner added another six. The editors of the *Gateshead Observer* and *Newcastle Guardian* joined with the Richardsons as guarantors that the cause was legitimate and that the money would be spent as intended. They also pledged to be "channels of help."[10] Edinburgh's Edmund Sturge, who came from a remarkable family of anti-slavery activists, joined in as a subscription agent to seek out and collect pledges.[11] Organizations such as the Glasgow Female New Association for the Abolition of Slavery pitched in as well.[12]

Joseph Sturge, Edmund's brother, one of Britain's foremost anti-slavery activists and the founder of the British and Foreign Anti-Slavery Society, also took a keen interest in the Weemses' case and was regularly apprised of developments. The family's situation was no abstraction for him. On an earlier trip to the United States, he had visited a slave pen in

Baltimore. Sturge was not fooled by the cleanliness of the facility nor by the courtesy extended to him by the keeper. He was skeptical of the owner's assurances that the slaves were well fed and that he never separated families. The Englishman saw the bolts on the doors and the bars on the windows, and he felt the lingering presence of those who had passed through the pen on their way to the Lower South. A devout Quaker, Sturge was gentle and thoughtful. His observations and feelings about slavery were reinforced by the many friendships with abolitionists that he cemented on his visit to the United States, most particularly with Lewis Tappan. He carried those friendships and experiences back to England with him, even more resolved to be at the forefront of the fight.[13]

*The interior of a slave pen* (Library of Congress image cwpb 01472)

The pages of the *Gateshead Observer* kept the Weems family's story before their readers. Its editor, James Clephan, stepped forward to announce that he would also accept donations and forward them to the Richardsons. The editor of the *Christian News* did the same.[14] Being realists, the abolitionists had thought that they would be able to raise only enough money to purchase Arabella and the girls, but Clephan listed the names and ages of all of the family: Mrs. Weems, 41; Catharine, 18; William Augustus, 16; Charles Adam, 14; Joseph, 12; John Lewis, 10; Ann Maria, 10, and an infant whose age and name were unknown to him.[15]

And the money flowed in – from Yarmouth, Edinburgh, Airelands, Brighton, Garrycloyne, and Darlington. People gave what they could afford; some several pounds, some a few shillings, others only a few pence. Some donors gave anonymously, the purest form of charity.[16] It began to look as though there would be enough to buy not only John's wife and daughters but his sons as well. Perhaps there would even be enough to whisk the family to the free dominions of Queen Victoria.[17] This British generosity was a wonderful surprise to John Weems, who was dejected after his fundraising attempts in the United States.

But for many abolitionists this idea of purchasing slaves presented an insurmountable moral dilemma. The December 1852 edition of the monthly *Anti-Slavery Advocate* carried a lengthy article on this issue. It referred to the appeal for funds that had been made in the various religious and philanthropic newspapers throughout the country on behalf of the "Weims" family (as the surname was consistently spelled in Britain). Prompted by the discussion swirling around the family, the *Advocate*'s editor reiterated and expanded upon the stance that had appeared in the first edition of the newspaper:

> While we would willingly help in the release of a near relation or
> friend from the clutches of the slaveholder, we consider the claims of
> the body of American slaves upon our sympathy and assistance, as
> much stronger than those of any particular family with whom we have

no acquaintance. All that we, as abolitionists, give to individuals, is so much taken from what we should devote to the mass of sufferers. Buying slaves is not anti-slavery business, for it does nothing to help on the redemption of the race, or the abolition of the system; but leads us away from our proper work – the exhibition of the evils of slavery, and the instruction of the English people as to the best means of viewing the subject in its religious, social, and political aspects.

The writer of an open letter that appeared in the *Daily Mail* on November 17 agreed. After referring specifically to the Weems family, he warned against allowing appeals to human sentiment to interfere with what was right. While recognizing that the Weems family's situation tugged hard at the emotions, he feared that purchasing them would make the number of similar cases multiply. If the British public extended an act of kindness to the Weemses, other slaves would be subject to even more cruelty. The writer even suggested that this family, as well as the fictionalized characters in *Uncle Tom's Cabin*, would raise such sympathy that the slave owners would increase the price of their "property," knowing that abolitionists would pay inflated prices for the satisfaction of restoring them to their loved ones.[18]

Harriet Beecher Stowe later agreed with this argument, even though she herself had contributed toward purchasing some of the Edmonson family. She believed that the ransom of slaves "is of doubtful utility, and it is more than probable that many masters play upon the sympathies of Northern people to enhance the value of their slaves."[19] Likewise the London *Morning Advertiser* advised that, despite the anti-slavery revival that was sweeping the country, "warm-hearted" people should not be misled into believing that by contributing to causes such as the Weems fund they were furthering the goal of abolishing slavery when they were, in fact, retarding it.[20]

London's *Anti-Slavery Advocate* chided a Reverend Edmond Kelley who, having raised the required money to buy his wife and four children was now, six months later, attempting to raise enough to purchase his own freedom – even though he was already on free soil and beyond the grasp of his master! Although he only needed just over 116 pounds for his purposes, what was to prevent him from raising one thousand, the newspaper asked.[21] A contributor to the *Anti-Slavery Reporter* cautioned its readers to beware of fraudulent collectors who wore a minister's collar and surrounded themselves with adorable children and "with a well told tale of distress" to prey on their sympathies. Mrs. Stowe's work had made the public vulnerable to those who were seeking to line their own pockets.[22]

A cloud even hung over the head of Josiah Henson, who had previously belonged to Adam Robb and was now in England. Henson was attacked in the British press by agents of the American Free Baptist Mission for collecting funds for the Dawn Settlement without authorization.[23] Members of the British and Foreign Anti-Slavery Society and representatives of other denominational groups came to his aid and at a public meeting condemned the accusers. Joseph Sturge of the society, who incidentally had been involved in the original fundraising effort for the founding of the Dawn Settlement, contacted Lewis Tappan in New York to inquire about Henson's character.[24] Tappan reported that although there was not much evidence that the large sums of money donated to Dawn had been well spent, Henson himself was well respected.[25] The BFAAS resolved that Henson be permitted to continue his work unmolested and that he be welcomed and supported by all those opposed to slavery. They further ordered that Henson's name be cleared in the pages of several British and American newspapers.[26]

Inevitably, even Harriet Beecher Stowe was caught in the verbal crossfire. The *Anti-Slavery Advocate* dared to express publicly what many others were thinking in private. Mrs. Stowe, who before the publication of *Uncle Tom's Cabin* had never been involved in the abolitionist debate, was suddenly the face and the voice for all things anti-slavery. Despite her self-appraisal as "a little bit of a woman – somewhat more than 40 – about as thin & dry as a pinch of snuff – never very much to look at in

77

*Harriet Beecher Stowe, author of* Uncle Tom's Cabin, *became the face of the anti-slavery movement.* (New York Public Library image 484074)

my best days – & looking like a used up article now," her reputation had reached gigantic proportions.[27] As a result, others who had dedicated a great part of their lives to the cause were pushed into the shadows. Almost as an aside, one writer suggested that people like Anna and Henry Richardson and Henry Garnet, who championed the elimination of slavery by boycotting goods that were grown from slave labour, were unrealistic dreamers. His primary argument, however, was that those who were tripping over each other to throw money into Stowe's hands to end slavery were misguided and that they should be giving to proven organizations with a track record of using funds wisely.[28]

Across the Atlantic, abolitionists also wrestled with the issue. The editor of the *New York Tribune* admitted to having contributed to the purchase of forty or fifty slaves, some within the past year. And, although he might donate again in "cases of special urgency, like that of the Edmundson girls" he said that he would attempt to avoid it. He likened the idea to a pirate ship coming to port and people buying the stolen goods.[29] Mrs. Abbey Kelley Foster, a delegate at the Massachusetts Anti-Slavery Society annual meeting in Boston, announced that if the man (presumably John Weems) whom William Lloyd Garrison had spoken about earlier in the day wanted money, he should not get it from abolitionist societies, which were working on a larger scale to end slavery. Rather, he should come to the city of Worcester, where he could raise one hundred dollars from people who were not ordinarily committed to the cause.[30]

A fifteen-year member of an anti-slavery society in Philadelphia wrote to the *Nonconformist* newspaper in Britain to protest the efforts being made there. Signing the letter "an American Abolitionist," he wrote of the deluge of requests his organization had received for similar assistance in purchasing a loved one. He mentioned a particularly touching appeal for money to buy a woman who was held in a Baltimore slave pen. Upon reflection, the society had wondered whether all of the inmates of the pen might be considered worthy of special sympathy if their circumstances were known. At that point they collectively resolved "that we will discourage such contributions, because those who give aid in this way erroneously imagine they are promoting the cause of human freedom, when they may, in fact, be only transferring the bonds to others, equally entitled to their liberty."[31]

The *New York Daily Times* reprinted an article that had originally appeared in the *London Daily News*. The writer appeared sympathetic to the "peculiarly hard" case of the Weems family, following the "breach of promise" by the slave owner that took place even while John Weems was raising the money to purchase his family. The author also mentioned the heartfelt appeal made by Stella, and alluded to the terrors possibly awaiting the attractive Catharine. Nevertheless he argued that "the indulgence of our feelings is, no doubt, easily obtained; but there is a disagreeable question attached to the case – a question whether the act is right."[32]

In the United Kingdom the debate raged on, not only in the columns of the press but also in meetings of dedicated English philanthropic groups. In an address made to the anti-slavery women of Great Britain at London's Stafford House, A. W. Weston candidly warned that devoting time and money toward purchasing slaves was "a profitless and a hopeless task."[33] At a special meeting called in January 1853 to respond to Anna Richardson's appeal on behalf of the Weems family, the Bristol & Clifton Ladies Anti-Slavery Society expressed their resistance to the idea of fundraising for the Weemses and openly discouraged others from becoming involved:

> Resolved unanimously that altho' we deeply deplore the sufferings of
> our brethren in American bondage, & always rejoice when we hear
> of the escape of fugitives, & altho' we fully appreciate the kindly
> feeling which calls forth the efforts now being made to purchase a
> family out of Slavery, yet we cannot consistently with our sense of
> what is right, collect money for this purpose – believing that by so
> doing we sanction the practice of trading in human beings, enhance
> the value of slave property, induce dealers to procure a larger supply
> of slaves to meet the increased demand & tho' releasing a few individ-
> uals retard the emancipation of three million of their less fortunate
> fellow-sufferers.
>
> That we consider the efforts made in this land to purchase the man-
> umission of Slaves as calculated to divert the attention of the British
> public from the great duty of arousing the American nation to a sense
> of its guilt, & of guarding the religious bodies of this country from
> sustaining Slavery by alliances with those in America which uphold
> the system. It was determined to send this resolution for insertion
> in the forthcoming "Advocate," the "Morning Advertiser," "Bristol

Mercury" and any other newspapers to which we have access, Also to Mrs. Richardson with a note from the Secretary to the Edinburgh, Glasgow, Dublin, Clapton A. S. [Anti-Slavery] Societies.[34]

No less a publication than the Scottish Quaker journal the *British Friend* applauded the stance that the Bristol & Clifton Ladies Anti-Slavery Society took on the issue of opposing fundraising to redeem the Weems family. They saw no contradiction in praising fundraising efforts for Harriet Beecher Stowe in an editorial opinion on the very same page.[35]

Despite this opposition, donations and pledges for the Weems family continued to arrive from Glasgow, Edinburgh, and other cities. Susan Edmonstone Ferrier of Scotland was so inspired by Stowe's book that she decided to help at an emancipation bazaar with the hope of raising enough money to purchase at least one slave. In an unfortunate choice of words and a misguided attempt at humour, she wrote to a friend that "I'm going to work like a nigger for it!"[36]

The money was placed in what was christened the "Weims Ransom Fund," and the Richardsons as well as Edmund Sturge and George Gallie took charge of its collection.[37] Anna and Henry Richardson took a particularly active role, including publishing an account of the Weems family's tragic plight in their monthly abolitionist newspaper *The Slave*, which had a regular printing of 3,500 copies. The dedicated couple had no interest in making a profit from their paper, charging one farthing per copy, which was exactly their cost.[38] They wanted only to use all of their means to wipe slavery from the face of the globe. While debate simmered that it was far better for abolitionists to devote their energies to fighting the institution of slavery, there were some situations, such as that of the Weems family, that tugged at the heartstrings enough to make an exception. The Richardsons knew only too well the benefits of freeing individual slaves. In addition to purchasing the liberty of the most important black leader of the day, Frederick Bailey, who became known in freedom as Frederick Douglass, they would soon spearhead the effort to do the same for William Wells Brown, another prominent figure.[39] No one could deny that those singular acts of kindness had left a lasting mark on the anti-slavery movement.

To Anna Richardson it was just as important to pay attention to the "ordinary" slave as it was to purchase the freedom of these prominent men. While recognizing that there was deep-seated opposition to paying ransoms to slave owners, she felt that it was "at least as Christian an act to give money to set people free from bondage, as it is to give it to the same slaveholders for the purchase of their slave-grown produce. This one act makes the victim of his oppression unspeakably happy; the other adds to the weight of his chains."[40] In addition, the Richardsons reminded their readers that Stella Weems and her adoptive parents had met with many people across England, Ireland, and Scotland. "They have sat at our tables, and mingled in the pleasures of many a British hearth; they have become almost naturalized amongst us." Simply witnessing Stella's uncontrollable grief made it impossible to stand by and do nothing to console her.[41]

One of the more famous slaves stepped up to voice his support for the Weemses. William Craft and his wife, Ellen, had captured the imagination of anti-slavery proponents on both sides of the Atlantic. Their ingenious mode of escape from Georgia involved light-skinned Ellen dressing as a man and pretending to be the master of the darker-hued William. To hide the fact that she had no beard, they placed a cloth around her chin as if to soothe an aching tooth. To prevent her from having to register her name at any hotels along the way, they placed her right arm in a sling. To make her look totally dependent on her servant, she pretended to be lame and carried a cane in her left hand. Their flight to the free states was successful, but the passage of the Fugitive Slave Law forced them to move to Britain, where they were treated as celebrities. William's voice carried a certain weight when he declared in a letter to the Richardsons that he was normally opposed to paying the owners

*Ellen Craft escaped from slavery in Georgia disguised
as a man, becoming one of the most famous runaways
in history.* (New York Public Library image 413063)

for slaves once they had escaped and reached freedom, but the Weems family did not fit into that category. Were he in their place, he said, he would do anything within his power to secure his family's liberation.[42]

A Washington lawyer named Jacob Bigelow who had stepped up to take William Chaplin's place in the Underground Railroad also vowed to do what he could to help the Weems family. Bigelow admitted that he once was opposed to purchasing slaves even when the object was to give them their freedom. But now he was "very summarily cured of my theory, when I came to practise upon it." He had a chance encounter with Arabella Weems and her sons as they were herded like cattle in a drove of slaves under a broiling sun from Maryland to the slave pens of Washington's National Man-market. Bigelow was on a mission on behalf of Harriet Beecher Stowe to purchase the mother and two sisters of the celebrated Edmonson girls, Mary and Emily, who became the most famous members of the ill-fated mass escape aboard the *Pearl*. The vision of Arabella Weems, her children and the others with them had left an indelible mark on his being, as this excerpt from a newspaper article he penned shows:

> Let any whole-hearted Englishman, whatever his theory might be, have seen this human drove, just parted from all their friends; let him have observed, for a moment, their sad countenances, as they were urged onward on foot in a broiling sum; let him have followed them to their loathsome 'slave pen,' and thence on their long journey to the cotton-fields of some Alabama Legree, and my word for it, that man's heart and purse are open for their deliverance right quickly.[43]

Bigelow had lived an interesting life thus far. Born in Waltham, Massachusetts, on August 26, 1790, he had moved to Boston, a hotbed of abolitionist fervour, while still a young man. From there he moved north to Montreal for several years to work in the mercantile business. He further expanded his perspective by travelling to Europe on two different occasions. Married to Eliza Southgate when he was thirty, he had two sons while living in Lower Canada, as Quebec was then known. The Bigelows experienced the agony of losing a child when their eldest son, Joseph, died just short of his ninth birthday. The remainder of the family soon returned to the United States, moving to Michigan City in Indiana. Again death struck their family, this time taking Eliza. Robbed of his loved ones, Bigelow devoted more and more of his time to easing the suffering of others, whenever he could allow time away from his law practice. By Bigelow's own admission, "I have for years, cheerfully regarded one half of my time as appropriated to aid the oppressed in some form or to oppose the oppressor."[44]

Events across the ocean temporarily deflated even Bigelow's optimism. The slave trader who had promised to wait to sell Arabella and her sons while the ransom fund was being raised eventually gave in to the demand of Adam Robb's heirs for a sale. The timing coincided with the return of the panicking John Weems to Maryland before his thirty-day permit expired. He arrived in Washington just in time to say goodbye to his family, who were about to be sent, along with a group of others, from the slave pen to the southern market. John begged the slave trader to leave his wife and youngest child so he could have a little more time to finish raising the rest of the money. He was refused. A heartbreaking scene ensued, such as can only be imagined and never adequately described, although the words of one observer of a similar scene perhaps come close:

> Wives were there to take leave of their husbands, and husbands of
> their wives, children of their parents, and parents of their children.
> Friends parting with friends, and the tenderest ties of humanity
> severed at a single word of the inhuman Slave Broker before them.
> A husband, in the meridian of life, begged to see the partner of his
> bosom. He protested that she was free – that she had free papers, and
> was torn away from him and shut up in the jail. He clambered up to
> one of the windows of the car to see his wife, and, as she was reaching
> forward her hand to him, the black-hearted Slave Dealer ordered
> him down. He did not obey! The husband and wife, with tears streaming down their cheeks, besought him to let them speak to each other.
> But no; he was knocked down from the car, and ordered away! The
> bystanders could hardly refrain laying violent hands upon the brute.[45]

Amid their tears, John asked Arabella to try to get word of her whereabouts to him when she was sold. He returned to an empty house: once there were nine; now there were none.

The melancholy news found its way to the ears of fundraisers and into the columns of newspapers across the ocean. Among them was the *Gateshead Observer*, which corrected the ages that appeared in an earlier article and detailed the story: Mrs. Weems, 40; William, 17; Adam, 12; Joseph, 8; John Lewis, 6; and infant Sylvester, aged 2, had been sold at auction "and carried off – it was supposed to Alabama." There was little hope that their destination could be discovered.[46]

# CHAPTER 5

IN BRITAIN, DECEMBER 17, 1852 was departure day for Stella and the Garnets, including the latest addition to the family, an infant son born on British soil whom Henry called "his little black John Bull."[1] All the Garnets could do for Stella's family was wonder about them and pray. The early part of their voyage did nothing to lift the depression. After setting off aboard a steamer from Southampton, the family sheltered themselves from the strong winds in their second-class cabin. The weather soon became so severe that a huge wave destroyed part of the ship, carrying away the figurehead and the breakwater. Terrified, each of the one hundred passengers on board thought they would sink to the bottom of the Atlantic at any time. With the Weems case fresh on his mind, Garnet took solace in the thought that even if they never reached their destination, at least they would all be together. The captain and crew employed their considerable nautical skills before deciding to limp into the Spanish port of Madeira. They stayed there until repairs could be made, and then continued their frightening and lengthy course for the Caribbean.[2]

Tragedy again struck the beleaguered family when the ship arrived in Jamaica. The Garnets' baby, whose birth they had celebrated so recently, died. The grief-stricken father held firm to his faith as he painted a peaceful and comforting picture in a letter written to his friends back in England: "Of course you have heard that little R. sleeps in Jesus.

His remains, beautiful in death, lie in Kingston, where we laid them on the day of our arrival. He died instantaneously of a convulsion occasioned by teething, at the very moment the ship touched the shore of Jamaica. He died while playing in his mother's arms, with a little white dress on. We lent him to the Lord, and He took him altogether to Himself. Blessed be His holy name."[3]

Despite their seemingly relentless trials, the move to the tropical paradise of Stirling, in Jamaica's Westmoreland Parish, offered some consolation. Garnet had the distinction of being the first black missionary ordained and employed by Scotland's United Presbyterian Church.[4] In contrast to the financial uncertainty of some of his earlier positions, he was guaranteed an annual salary of 150 pounds. In a gracious gesture, the presbytery had agreed to pay Stella's passage to accompany her adoptive family. In addition, one of its ministers was actively raising money to send to John Weems in America, to help him purchase his wife and children. By February 15, 1853, that minister had raised 150 pounds to bolster the fund, which was approaching a total of one thousand pounds.[5]

The Reverend Garnet felt greatly encouraged that "after a long life of wandering up and down, we are at last *at home*." His family was pleasantly surprised at their new English-style cottage, set on three acres of land surrounded by a cactus hedge and stately trees. The flowers were in bloom year-round, hills surrounded them on three sides, and the sea was in the distance. Both the church and the schoolhouse were large and comfortable. The people were attentive and welcomed them with kindness. All of his remaining family, including Stella, were healthy and well. He optimistically asked in one of his letters to England if the Weems family were on their way to being liberated, adding that Jamaica would make an ideal home for all of them.[6]

But the months passed slowly, with little news to comfort John Weems, other than the fact that his daughters, Catharine and Ann Maria, were still being held in nearby Unity, from where they might be sold at any time. The girls were held by Charles M. Price, who listed his occupation as an innkeeper on official documents but was building a reputation as a notorious slave trader. Although he often worked independently, Price had also formed a partnership with a John C. Cook who had moved to D.C. from Charles County, Maryland, in 1843 after his trading business there became insolvent.[7] Both were no doubt involved at some level in the widespread network of agents of George Kephart, the largest trader in the area and Price's grandfather-in-law.

The two fledgling dealers were beginning to expand their business into the lucrative southern market and by November 12, 1852, the firm of Cook & Price was dealing in slaves in the growing town of Eufaula, Alabama.[8] To supply demand in the South, they transported their wares overland and by steamship along the eastern seaboard. Mandatory slave manifests intended to ensure that no ships defied the U.S. law prohibiting the transatlantic slave trade (but ironically allowing domestic traffic to thrive) reveal that Price shipped thirteen slaves – ranging in age from one to twenty years, but predominantly teenagers – from the port of Charleston, South Carolina, to Savannah, Georgia, aboard the steamer *Calhoun* in 1853. John Cook sent sixteen slaves ranging from one to forty years along that same route on the *Metamora*.[9] Before being allowed to proceed to the next port, both Price and Cook dutifully listed the name, sex, age, height, and "class" or colour of each individual and signed the manifests as follows: "Owner of the within specified Slaves, do solemnly swear, to the best of our knowledge and belief that the Slaves, herein described, were not imported into the United States, from and after the first day of January, one thousand eight hundred and eight, and that under the law of this State, they are held to service and labor."

Charles Price was demanding the inflated price of $1,600 for Catharine Weems, a value based not on her ability to work in the household or in the fields, but on her beauty. The budding slave trader was acquiring a knack for judging the intent and the purse of would-be buyers. He knew that soft hearts and a large ransom fund would give him a tidy profit on his investment in a short time. A precedent had already been set in another case that Jacob Bigelow, William Chaplin, and Harriet Beecher Stowe's brother, Henry Ward Beecher, had been involved in. The slave driver who three years previously had purchased Mary and Emily Edmonson for $1,500 had demanded and received $2,250 because the girls' "comeliness, intelligence and piety" would hold a special attraction for any hot-blooded owner.[10]

By now the ransom fund was large enough for John to buy one of his daughters, and he was forced to make the agonizing choice of whom to free. The very thought of what lay in store for Catharine would send convulsions through the mind of any parent, and made the excruciating decision a little easier. He hoped that Ann Maria had a little more time before she would be looked upon as a mere object to satisfy her master's sexual pleasure.

On a Monday morning in early March 1853, Catharine Weems was a slave. By noon of that same day, she was suddenly free. Catharine's manumission was duly recorded at Washington's city hall so there could be no ambiguity about her status.

Later that day, Catharine accompanied her father for a joyful reunion at the home of her aunt, who lived in another part of the city. From there she went to live temporarily in the home of a family named Boynton, who belonged to the same church as Jacob Bigelow. Sylvanus Cobb Boynton, a smart, fat and comical man, was an up-and-coming lawyer and had attended Oberlin College in Ohio, which had a strong anti-slavery tradition.[11] He and Eliza had been married for only two years, but the couple opened their home to this young person in need. Catharine's supporters hoped that she could stay until she got "used to herself as a free woman."[12]

The transition from slave to free person was not an easy one. Liberty was a foreign concept to those who had never experienced it. As Benjamin Slight, missionary to former slaves in Amherstburg, Canada West, explained, "their former bondage has shackled their minds."[13] When fifteen slaves from Louisiana were told that they would be freed, their equally perplexed owner wrote: "The good news seemed to have little effect upon them. They had come to consider that slavery was their normal condition. They did not know what freedom meant."[14] Harriet Tubman, upon first crossing the line into freedom, had to look at her hands to see if she was the same person. She reflected that "I grew up like a neglected weed, ignorant of liberty, having no experience of it . . . Now I've been free, I know what a dreadful condition slavery is."[15] Similarly, Mrs. Joseph Wilkinson movingly and simply said: "I considered my clothes and the little things I had when in slavery my own but I didn't see it as I do now. I see now that every thing I considered mine didn't belong to me, but could be taken away from me at any time. I didn't set the same store by my little things that I do now, for I didn't see things then as I do now."[16]

Catharine and her father visited Jacob Bigelow's office, where they expressed prayerful gratitude to those who had contributed money to pay her ransom. The experience was so moving that Bigelow felt no one who had witnessed such a scene could ever again question the propriety of buying slaves for the sole purpose of freeing them. He passed along the heartfelt appreciation of himself and the Weems family in a letter intended for the British humanitarians who had helped them: "With all my heart I thank you and the dear friends who have so nobly responded to your call for the redemption of this family from slavery. The Lord is very rich. In his own way, which is the right way, may you and they be rewarded."[17]

A noted abolitionist at the time had likened attacking slavery by freeing a single slave to "an attempt to bail out the ocean with a teaspoon."[18] But sometimes a teaspoon was all that it took.

*

Any joy that came to the Weems family and their supporters arrived in small doses. British newspapers reported that Arabella and the boys had been sent south in a coffle, possibly by the dealers Cook & Price.

*A coffle of slaves in chains passing the Capitol building in Washington, D.C.*
· (Library of Congress image cph 3a06254)

Transporting them by ship would have been much simpler and quicker, but it was more economical to send them on foot. It would have taken fifty days to make the punishing walk from Washington to New Orleans. The total cost for slave drivers, wagons that carried supplies and food, and additional expenses along the way was $44.40 per slave in a coffle, whereas the direct cost would have been $46.40 if they were sent by sea. Costs such as insurance, fees to notaries to register purchases, losses by escape or death, and money transfers between districts could add $31.85 per slave.[19]

In 1836, while travelling on a topographical surveying mission, George William Featherstonhaugh, the first U.S. government geologist, witnessed a slave coffle on its way south. He later included the scene in the published account of his travels, *Excursion Through the Slave States from Washington on the Potomac to the Frontier of Mexico*.[20] Although this trek took place several years before Arabella and her sons made that same trip, it is easy to imagine them experiencing the same horror:

> Just as we reached New River, in the early grey of the morning, we came up with a singular spectacle, the most striking one of the kind I have ever witnessed. It was a camp of negro slave-drivers, just packing up to start; they had about three hundred slaves with them, who had bivouacked the preceding night in chains in the woods . . . It resembled one of the coffles spoken of by Mungo Park, except that they had a caravan of nine wagons and single-horse carriages, for the purpose of conducting the white people, and any of the blacks that should fall lame, to which they were now putting the horses to pursue their march. The female slaves were, some of them, sitting on logs of wood, whilst others were standing, and a great many little black children were warming themselves at the fire of the bivouac. In front of them all, and prepared for the march, stood, in double files, about two hundred men slaves, manacled and chained to each other. I have never seen so revolting a sight before! Black men in fetters, torn from the lands where they were born, from the ties they had formed, and from the comparatively easy condition which agricultural labour affords, and driven by white men, with liberty and equality in their mouths, to a distant and unhealthy country, to perish in the sugar-mills of Louisiana, where the duration of life for a sugar-mill does not exceed seven years! To make this spectacle still more disgusting and hideous, some of the principal white slave-drivers, who were tolerably well dressed, and had broad-brimmed white hats on, with black crape round them, were standing near, laughing and smoking cigars.

The January 29, 1853 edition of Glasgow's *Christian News* reported that although nothing had been heard from Arabella and the boys, it was not yet time to be discouraged. A determined Jacob Bigelow encouraged the readers, writing that "somehow or other, their benevolent purposes will be accomplished. It is plain that every nerve will be strained to gain the desired end." He suggested that perhaps John Weems would travel south to try to seek out his family. John's supporters had gone so far as to contact "one of the most noble-hearted men in the House of Representatives," to ask for his assistance in the search for them. John's allies hoped that the Weemses' case would come up for debate before the U.S. Congress and that the entire country would hear of this outrage against humanity.

Word reached Anna Richardson in Newcastle. She was heart-broken at the news that Arabella and all of her sons had been lost to the South. She and her husband, Henry, had intimately felt the grief of Stella, who had been a guest in their home. "Oh the enormity of this traffic in the flesh and blood of our fellow creatures," she wrote in a letter to Charles Ray. Even though she was on the other side of the ocean, she vowed on behalf of many others that "if God grant us grace and strength to continue the conflict, some of us do not mean to rest till the direful iniquity is searched out, in the present instance, to its very core."[21] Anna went on to express her well-considered thoughts:

> Thou wilt have observed the increasing earnestness of the British
> public to carry their point, and their fixed determination to rescue the
> captives. As the present information is not very definite, we defer
> printing anything about it till more comes in, and we are not even
> saying much about it to our friends. As soon as ever it is known how
> the case stands, be very sure, my friend, that British blood will be up,
> and that there will be one loud continuous shout through the land, that
> agitations and remonstrances must be set on foot, and that we will not
> rest till the Weimses are free. My husband and I had not ventured to
> expect in an early instance that so much interest could be felt in this
> case, as it may be considered comparatively a common one, without

any special atrocious features, but perhaps the masses in this country did not know till *Uncle Tom's Cabin* was in every one's hand, what some of us knew – that these horrible things were of daily occurrence and comparatively a matter of as commonplace frequency as the holding of our own sheep and cattle markets. The British public knows it now and more than this is identifying itself with the present sufferers. The newspapers have voluntarily taken up the theme and it would have been impossible for £1,000 to have been thrown down with greater alacrity. It has not been given in large sums, not with a tone of taunt or defiance, but has come in, in little sums, in hundreds of cases from people of very small means and with a groan of pity – and with a determination for Christ's sake to do the little that the giver could. Filled with this determination, there has been strength of purpose in the giving that will not relax till the object in view is gained. It has been given religiously, tearfully, prayerfully, and though all of us abhor giving money to bad men for the freedom of the bodies and souls of our fellow-creatures, this feeling has been overpowered by the stronger necessity of doing as we would be done by, in similar circumstances.[22]

Anna Richardson echoed the thought previously expressed by Jacob Bigelow: whether it would be safe for John Weems to travel south to seek out his family, or whether some other trustworthy person should be sent. However the ends were to be achieved, she and her husband agreed that whatever was reasonable and manageable should be done. They desperately wanted to be kept up with any developments in the case and hoped that the family would eventually be reunited with Stella in Jamaica.

John finally discovered the whereabouts of Arabella and their two youngest boys. They were in Montgomery, the capital of Alabama, which had displaced Mobile as the largest slave-trading centre in the state. Two of the biggest traders in Maryland and the District of Columbia had recognized its importance and were among those dealing there: Bernard M. Campbell of Baltimore, who coincidentally had sent a possible relative of the Weems family, Martha Weems, to the slave port of New Orleans around the time that Arabella and the boys had gone south; and George Kephart, who had been selling slaves into that market for several years.[23]

Most citizens of Montgomery, like their southern neighbours, accepted slavery as part of life. No doubt expressing the prevailing sentiments of their readers, newspaper editors had little patience with the contrary opinions of outsiders. Showing that even in the mid-nineteenth century, the world was becoming a relatively small place, they observed the British anti-slavery movement with disdain. In a response to an appeal made by a group of British women to their American counterparts to speak out against slavery, the 1852 Christmas Day edition of the city paper *Advertiser and State Gazette* editorialized on the front page that "the efforts of Mrs. Stowe, and her sympathizers in England, to injure the moral standing – to say nothing of the property – of the women of the South, the best, purest, and most intelligent portion of God's own fair creatures, should be repelled and counteracted." A later edition applauded the response from Julia Tyler, the wife of former president John Tyler, which in essence told the British women to mind their own affairs and worry about conditions in their own country.[24] James Hambleton Christian, one of the Tylers' slaves, had no use for the president who, he claimed, treated his plantation slaves very cruelly, but Christian was fond of the first lady, who protected them and treated them well. His experiences as a domestic servant in the White House afforded Christian many uncommon luxuries and opportunities, and Julia Tyler failed to grasp that the lives of other slaves were radically different, he said.[25]

An article in the January 13, 1853 edition of the *Advertiser* lamented that "the effect of this pernicious book [*Uncle Tom's Cabin*] in England has been to stir up among the pseudo-philanthropists of the Kingdom a prodigious quantity of *sympathy* for the sleek, well-fed and clothed negro slaves of this country." The writer was quite certain that "the present form of Government of England will be blotted from existence much sooner than the system of slavery in this country will be abandoned." Many of her critics repeatedly attached Harriet Beecher Stowe for having written what they considered to be a book full of lies and misrepresentations.

With the Montgomery newspaper clearly following events in the British press, the possibility arose that other readers below the Mason–Dixon Line would notice the coverage of the Weemses' plight. Many only scratched their heads at all the fuss: the separation of families was certainly not news in the South.

◆

Before being forcibly removed from the Washington slave pen, Arabella had promised her husband that she would somehow get word to him – a promise that John was uncertain she would be able to keep. Perhaps she did not truly believe it herself. No doubt thousands before her had made similar pledges. Faced with such a tragic fate, few slaves were able to fathom that life could be so cruel as to make the separation permanent – but it often was.

Arabella was perhaps not a typical slave. Time and again she overcame the most daunting of obstacles. Somehow she found a way to send John an envelope containing a small piece of a velvet vest that had belonged to him, along with a swatch of cloth from a pink muslin frock that had belonged to Catharine. Despite her terror at the prospect of travelling in a slave coffle to the Deep South, she had had the presence of mind to carry those pieces of clothing with her. Maybe it was an attempt to hold onto memories. Maybe it was a calculated act. It was common practice among slaves to send something of intimate sentimental value such that only the sender and the recipient could know that it truly came from a separated loved one.[26] It was always a challenge to find someone in the new surroundings who could be entrusted to send the precious package to the north. Many southern postmasters would not knowingly handle such a parcel. John must have been moved beyond tears as he held the tattered mementoes between his fingers.

Once they had discovered the location of Arabella and her sons, those involved with the ransom fund assumed that it would be relatively easy to purchase the youngest boys, because these two were too young to be of immediate value to their owner. In fact, they would only be a distraction to the mother, whose work might be neglected as she tended to her children. Arabella, John Jr., and Sylvester had actually been the beneficiaries of a recent law passed by the governor of Alabama, which cited "relations which moral duty requires us to respect."[27] The law stated that no child under the age of ten could be sold without including the mother. However, considerations of the heart were not allowed to interfere with the business of slavery, so there was a clause that this restriction could be waived if it injured the purchaser's interests. If so, a child could be sold separately, unless he or she was under the age of five. A further caveat stipulated that any slave offered for sale as a result of a legal decree or settling of a financial obligation "must be offered, and, if practicable, sold in families [i.e., the mother and her young offspring]; unless some party in interest made affidavit that selling them together would be to his material disadvantage."[28]

Charles Ray and Jacob Bigelow were resolved that no legal loophole would be allowed in this case and that Arabella and both boys would be included in the purchase. However, an unforeseen wrench was thrown into the works. A rumour that the slaveholders of Alabama had heard of the British subscription appeared in the very same article that trumpeted the release of Catharine Weems.[29] The rumour was indeed fact. The southern press had got wind of the international fundraising effort and put the story before their readers. Word quickly reached the traders and the planters. Just as critics of the practice of ransoming slaves had previously suggested, the news dramatically raised their price. The owner demanded $2,100 – far more than the $1,600 that the Washington slave traders had demanded of John just a few months before. Bigelow and Ray stood firm, refusing to knuckle under to the exorbitant request. The abolitionists began to realize the harsh reality of their situation. In their zeal to raise the money for the family's redemption, and in the intense interest that had ensued, they had been somewhat reckless in keeping the public too well informed. Britain was a long way from Alabama, but news travelled in both directions. When the abolitionists realized what was happening, private correspondence became just that. Rather than finding its way into the columns of the British anti-slavery press, the recipients of news about the Weems family kept silent. In a letter from Scotland, Reverend Somerville reluctantly informed the Garnets that it had been some months since he had heard anything about the Weems family.[30] Anna and Henry Richardson's monthly newspaper *The Slave*, which had been perhaps the most vocal, backed away from revealing further substantial details. It focused instead on unrelated stories, such as a tribute to the Church of England, which planned to form a branch of the "Colonial Church and School Society" to establish schools for fugitive slaves in Canada.[31] Arabella and her children, who were to be the beneficiaries of this international goodwill, had become the victims of its public excess, however inadvertently.

But Jacob Bigelow would not allow such an impediment to halt progress in the case he had taken so much to heart. He arranged with the same slave trader who had originally carried away Arabella and her two youngest sons to purchase them and have them returned to Washington. With apparent disgust, Bigelow informed his British friends that "many shameful and mean pretences were set up" to inflate the price and to interfere with the transaction. When threatened with legal prosecution, the slave owner finally relented and honoured the previous agreement. The ransom price of $1,675 was withdrawn on July 8, 1853 by William E. Whiting, the American banker of the Weems ransom fund, and paid by Charles B. Ray, who served as Bigelow's agent upon delivery of the "entire package" to

Washington. Upon their arrival the free papers were "duly made and their freedom secured."[32] Unfortunately, Bigelow was out of town in Massachusetts when Arabella, Sylvester, and John Jr. were returned to the District of Columbia, so he missed the opportunity to witness the event and to receive the gratitude that he so much deserved.

By October 9, 1853, the news had reached England. In a letter to Charles Ray, Anna Richardson rejoiced "for Airay Weims and her two boys to be restored to their home, and sincerely thank the various parties concerned for the kind care they have taken in the matter."[33] John, Arabella, and the two boys took up residence in the countryside just outside of Washington, in the new home that John had secured in their absence. They were fortunate to find jobs that paid relatively well, and their relief and happiness were immeasurable.[34]

However, shortly after their reunion, a tragedy of Old Testament proportions again visited the family. Sylvester, the family's youngest child, died just after he had been freed. Now, only John Jr. remained in his parents' household. Stella, in faraway Jamaica, never got to meet her youngest brother. At least Catharine was living nearby and could share in her family's sorrow. Sarah Tappan, a future friend, later surmised that "hard as it must have been to lay this little one in the grave, the bereaved parents had far less cause to weep for him, than for his brothers in bondage; for they could feel that he was gone."[35] Ann Maria, Augustus, Joseph, and Adam were still tightly held in the grasp of slavery. Only John and Arabella knew the degree of anguish they felt at this new loss; their sufferings were so many and so close together as to make it impossible to distinguish where one began and the other one ended.

It was decided that some of the money that had been raised would be used to send John Weems south in search of his sons. The uncertainty as to their final destination made it difficult to know where to begin. The slave-trading network was wide ranging across the South, and there were extensive dealings among traders. When the traders herded the slave coffles overland, shipped them by water, or boxed them by rail,

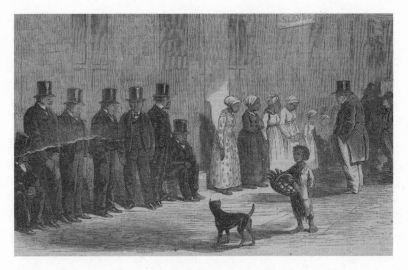

*A sketch of slaves waiting outside a New Orleans slave pen before the auction. Judging from their clothing, these slaves might have been house slaves or body servants, rather than field hands.* (New York Public Library image 812594)

there was always a chance that they might sell the slaves along the way. John Weems, under the guidance of his friends, made the educated guess to search first in New Orleans.

John found no comfort as he wandered the New Orleans streets in the summer of 1853. Thousands of European immigrants were drawn to the bustling city to work at widening canals, digging ditches, installing water and gas mains, and building roads. Sanitary conditions were abhorrent and the levees and back streets were foul. Yellow fever arrived in May aboard a ship carrying Irish immigrants and quickly spread, killing hundreds and causing thousands more to flee in panic, blocking every route. According to one observer, the floors of the charity hospital were filled with sick paupers, who died at a rate of one every half-hour. By August 22, a victim was dying every five minutes.

John's quest would have led him to the various slave marts and auction houses. A visitor to the city described his impressions of these:

I saw nothing especially repulsive in these places excepting the whole thing; and I can not help feeling a sort of astonishment that such a thing and such scenes are possible in a community calling itself Christian. It seems to me sometimes as if it could not be reality – as if it were a dream.

The great slave-market is held in several houses situated in a particular part of the city. One is soon aware of their neighborhood from the groups of colored men and women, of all shades between black and light yellow, which stand or sit unemployed at the doors. Accompanied by my kind doctor, I visited some of these houses. We saw at one of them the slave-keeper or owner – a kind, good-tempered man, who boasted of the good appearance of his people. The slaves were summoned into a large hall, and arranged in two rows. They were well fed and clothed, but I have heard it said by the people here that they have a very different appearance when they are brought hither, chained together two and two, "in long rows, after many days" [of] fatiguing marches.[36]

Dispirited after two months of unsuccessful searching for his three sons, John Weems returned to New York City on September 14, 1853 on the steamship *Metropolitan*.[37]

CHAPTER 6

IN THE 1850S, THE ISSUE OF SLAVERY was constantly on the minds
and the lips of the Weemses' neighbours in Washington and nearby
Maryland. Politicians ranted about it, on one side or the other. Blacks
bemoaned it. Abolitionists published tracts about it. Newspapers on both
sides of the Atlantic carried endless articles about it. The faithful prayed
about it. But the time for an answer had not yet arrived. Business continued as usual.

The Hardings, now minus the Weems family, still owned and paid
"property taxes" on twenty-six slaves who remained on their farms in
Montgomery County. Both of the four-year-olds, Alexander and Fanny,
were assessed along with the older children and the adults.[1] Charles A.
Harding continued to add to his stable of slaves with little regard for
age. On July 23, 1853, he acquired twenty-one-year-old Horace; Mary,
nine; Axie, five; Isaac, four; and a one-half interest in a negro man
named George, about twenty-four years old. Each was termed a "slave
for life," a reflection of the fact that the practice of granting freedom
after slaves reached a certain age was disappearing and that anti-black
laws were strengthening. These slaves were included in Harding's
purchase of a farm of nearly two hundred acres as well as "one horse,
carryall [sic] and harness, five shoats, one sow and seven pigs, four head
of sheep, two calves" and various crops – corn, wheat, rye, oats, grass,

and potatoes. The deed dictated that Charles Harding would have use of the slaves only for a fixed period of time, as he was to hold them in trust for the children of the sellers, Isaac and Eliza Soper, and divide them between these two when the youngest reached twenty-one.[2]

The new Democratic mayor of Washington, John Walker Maury, was determined to enforce any laws and ordinances that would torment the black population. Shortly after Catharine, Arabella, and John Jr. began to settle into their new world, the mayor took steps to remind everyone that equal rights did not apply in his city. He reached back to a municipal ordinance that had been put into effect in 1827 – over a quarter of a century earlier. It decreed that "no free black or mulatto person shall be allowed to go at large through the city of Washington, at a later hour than ten o'clock at night, without a pass from a justice of the peace or a respectable citizen." The first to feel its sting was "a most respectable and orderly citizen" who was arrested for violating the ordinance – a sign of things to come.[3]

By the early 1850s, Alexandria had displaced Washington as the major market for slaves bound for the Deep South. The city had become part of the state of Virginia in 1846 and was under no obligation to follow any of the conditions of the Compromise of 1850 that supposedly abolished the slave trade in the District of Columbia. The Compromise was composed of five laws, including the amended Fugitive Slave Act, and was intended to avert a crisis between the free states and the Slave States by placating the South, which felt that its way of life and right to own human property was being threatened by northern liberals. For many years there had been petitions and heated debates over the trafficking of slaves in Washington, the focal point of "the land of the free." Unlike in individual states, Congress had clear jurisdiction over the capital, and had the power to legislate an end to the trade there. However, despite the fact that slave traders could make a simple trip across the Potomac to Alexandria to conclude their business, the sale of slaves was still not an uncommon sight in Washington, and the slave pens continued to hold their prisoners. Even as Congressman Joshua Giddings protested on the floor of the House of Representatives that the laws only supported "the slave-breeding interest" of the District and the Slave States, sales were openly occurring on Pennsylvania Avenue within sight of the Capitol. An eighteen-year-old man was auctioned off for eight hundred dollars and a ten-year-old girl was sold for three hundred dollars. A seventeen-year-old girl had already been sold to the traders and was being held in the slave pen with the very real threat of being removed from the District. Like John Weems, this young woman's grief-stricken father was frantically attempting to raise the one thousand dollars demanded to purchase her before she slipped beyond his grasp.[4]

The local newspapers continued to carry "Negroes for Sale" and "Negroes Wanted" advertisements. Some slave owners looked down their noses at these merchants of misery and were reluctant to trade with them, preferring to deal directly with potential buyers. One owner drafted a document that demonstrated his disgust for slave traders. The master apparently saw no contradiction in his entering into the same kind of transaction, albeit on a much smaller scale:

The bearer, Mary Jane, and her two daughters, are for sale. They are sold for no earthly fault whatever. She is one of the most ladylike and trustworthy servants I ever knew. She is a first rate parlour servant; can arrange and set out a dinner or party supper with as much taste as the most of white ladies. She is a pretty good mantua maker; can cut out and make vests and pantaloons and roundabouts and joseys for little boys in a first rate manner. Her daughters' ages are eleven and thirteen years, brought up exclusively as house servants. The eldest can sew neatly, both can knit stockings; and all are accustomed to all kinds of house work. They would not be sold to speculators or traders for any price whatever.

The asking price was $1,800 for the three of them. However, the seller would consider taking a thousand dollars for the daughters and allowing the mother to be taken on a one-month trial basis.[5]

An article in Washington's *Evening Star* reported that there was great excitement throughout the city resulting from a meeting to raise money to purchase a young woman's freedom. All of the blacks who were assembled there were arrested and escorted to the jail cells of the watch-house. Many of them were free, but some were slaves. According to the local newspaper:

> The law was read to them which prohibits free or slave blacks and mulattoes from assembling unlawfully or meeting in secret: the smallest fine for which offence is five dollars. The municipal statute likewise subjects police-officers to a fine of fifty dollars, in the event of their failing to enter and break up such associations.
>
> Being asked whether they had any thing to say, one of the blacks requested the examination of certain books which he placed on the desk, which consisted of the Holy Bible, Seneca's *Morals* and *Life in Earnest*. Among the private papers was one in the form of subscription for the purchase of a slave woman.[6]

Listed among the contributors were three prominent citizens, all congressmen – Gerrit Smith, $30; W. H. Seward $5; and J. R. Giddings, $1. All twenty-four of the blacks were taken to a room on the lower floor and searched, but nothing incriminating was found. They all swore that they were meeting for benevolent purposes. However, the authorities needed no further proof that a crime had been committed – simply meeting together was a crime in itself. Four men were sentenced to the workhouse, one was whipped, and twenty were fined $5.58 each. The total of the fines amounted to over three times as much money as they had raised for the woman they wished to free.

*

Between 1853 and 1855, time slowly ticked away for the Weems family. The ransom fund had grown large and the Richardsons had sent most of it to New York under the care of Reverend Charles B. Ray, who in turn had given most of it to William E. Whiting, his banker.[7] But Ann Maria, Augustus, Joseph, and Adam were not being freed. Either the fevered passion to free the family had begun to cool with the passage of time, or their supporters had trouble locating the boys, or perhaps their owners refused to sell them.

In Newcastle, England, the Richardsons were becoming uncomfortable with the delays and were uncertain about the status of the money. In 1854, they made an attempt to explain in their paper that the remainder of the family had not yet been freed from bondage by the American abolitionists because "great difficulties have been thrown in their way by the cupidity of the owners of this human property." They noted that over half of the ransom money that had been raised was sitting unused at the Union Bank in Newcastle, and in the hands of the treasurer of the American and Foreign Anti-Slavery Society.[8] They were gradually becoming less confident about the status of the funds in the United States. In a letter dated, in the Quaker style, "sixth month, 27th day" of 1855, they contacted their longtime friend Lewis Tappan in New York City and requested that he take the money that had been entrusted to Charles Ray and deposit it in a bank.

Tappan immediately contacted Ray, requesting a meeting in the privacy of the Tappan home, away from any prying ears in his office. Reverend Ray, despite his dedication to the anti-slavery movement, was careless with financial record keeping – in fact, he kept no written records and relied totally on his memory for details. His recollections of the Weems fund differed somewhat from those of the British abolitionists who had championed the fundraising. After having spent a thousand dollars for the purchase of Catharine and $1,675 for Arabella and the two youngest children, about $2,200 should have remained. Ray had decided to invest much of the remaining money in improvements

*Lewis Tappan, a wealthy New York-based abolitionist who helped establish America's first anti-slavery society* (New York Public Library image 1222696)

to his house and mortgage payments on his land, despite the fact that the funds might be needed quickly and at any time. He had withdrawn the money in quarterly instalments beginning on March 30, 1853 – first $212, then $150, then another $150, and finally a thousand dollars on March 1, 1854. He did not feel that he had acted incorrectly or that he had to take direction from those who had contributed the money. He felt that he had devoted a great deal of time to the Weems case and should be compensated.[9] Also, he had constantly been beseeched for assistance by fugitive slaves who had found their way to his office at 48 Beekman Street in New York. Donations to the Vigilance Committee, which for the most part came from Scotland and New York City, had fallen off dramatically. Yet the numbers seeking help had greatly increased. Rather than turn anyone away, some members, particularly Tappan, had reached into their own pockets.[10] After a discussion lasting nearly three hours in which Tappan argued that Ray had to turn the money over, Ray still felt that he was under no obligation to do so. However, he did promise to speak to his attorney and "do what was right."[11]

Tappan then wrote to the Richardsons and Jacob Bigelow, thoroughly questioning them about their recollections of the financial details and requesting any written documentation. He also wanted to know if any opportunities to redeem the Weems boys had been lost. Although Tappan felt that Ray was totally incapable of handling business matters, he believed that the reverend was not dishonest and that he had earned the respect of both blacks and whites. In Ray's defence, Tappan wrote to the Richardsons to inform them that the reverend had supposed that some of the money would not be needed for a long time and that there was a possibility that it might never be used if they were not successful in redeeming the whole family. In the interim he thought it prudent to use it as security for his property. Tappan expressed his sorrow that "such a temptation was thrown in his way."[12] He also updated Joseph Sturge of the British and Foreign Anti-Slavery Society, who continued to have a keen interest in the case.[13]

On July 21, 1855, three days after their initial meeting, Tappan received a letter from Ray proposing to turn over one thousand dollars.[14] Within the next week, apparently acting on the advice of his attorney, Ray brought a cheque for this amount signed by New York's commissioner of deeds, William H. Maxwell, Esquire, along with an order from William E. Whiting for the balance due on the account.[15] Nearly a month later, on August 16, he promised to give security for the remainder.[16] By Tappan's calculation Ray owed a total of $1,800 for his various withdrawals. A stickler for fiscal detail and for moral virtue, Tappan calculated the daily interest on each of these transactions, adding another $216.33, to bring the total to $2,016.33.[17] Satisfied that all was resolved, Tappan wrote to Sturge that "Mr. Ray has behaved well in putting into my hands money & security & has, I believe, been educated throughout by good motives."[18]

While awaiting the remainder of the funds, Tappan received an anonymously sent package from England, containing a copy of the British anti-slavery newspaper *The Slave*. Curiously, it was edition number 25, which was nearly two and a half years old, dated January 1853. It contained a story about the Weems family. The package was no doubt sent by Henry and Anna Richardson, who edited the newspaper and wished to reignite the fires to free the family using any spark at their disposal.[19]

By now Lewis Tappan and Henry Richardson were regularly exchanging letters – at least as regularly as they could, given that it took two weeks for transatlantic mail to arrive. Jacob Bigelow and Tappan were also in constant contact, with a continuous exchange of letters between Washington and New York. Bigelow, who had never lost sight of their ultimate goal, was hot on the trail of an opportunity to free another slave. Ever the optimist, Bigelow was confident that they would not have to pay much to secure the freedom of the children still held in bondage.[20] Like a stone skipped across the ocean, the ripples from the Richardsons were beginning to have an effect.

Eventually the Weems ransom fund was transferred to Tappan, as the British fundraisers had requested. William Whiting and Anthony Lane would act as trustees. In a gesture that suggested no hard feelings existed, Charles Ray was also included in that capacity.[21] These four men had worked together in the past, and all were executive members of the American Missionary Association, which among many other things supported foreign missionaries, including two ordained missionaries to Canada, their wives, and two female assistants.[22] Tappan was the driving force behind this organization and several others that he was involved in. A capable businessman who had made a fortune before he was twenty-five, he had suffered serious setbacks but had learned from each experience and was prospering again in his later years. He admitted to "being wise too late or rather not wise soon enough."[23] Whatever the timeline, he was now wise, capable, and determined.

Displaying his business acumen, he suggested to Henry Richardson that whatever money was not immediately needed to purchase the Weems children be loaned out at six percent interest. The excess could be used for other "interesting cases of fugitives."[24] Temporarily smitten with some of Bigelow's optimism, Tappan felt "it is probable that no more than $1000 of this fund will ever be required for the precise purpose for which it was raised."[25] After what must have been an excruciating lull, the effort to liberate all of the Weems family was re-energized.[26]

CHAPTER 7

BY THE EARLY SUMMER OF 1854, John and Arabella had slowly gathered fragments of their family back together again. The following year, Arabella gave birth to Mary, their tenth child. For the first time in John and Arabella's lives, there would be no penalty for the child taking the mother's status: Mary would be free for life. Catharine and John Jr. were again – only this time legally – under their parents' protective wing, albeit at somewhat of a distance for Catharine, who was still living with the Boyntons. Baby Sylvester had joined his older brother, Richard, with the angels. Stella was free and living in the Caribbean with Reverend Garnet and his family. Augustus, Joseph, and Adam were eight hundred miles away in Alabama. Ann Maria was still owned by Charles Price in Rockville, Maryland, a short carriage ride away, but considering the exorbitant amount of money that they had been forced to pay for Catharine, she might as well have been on the other side of the country.

Price, then in his mid-thirties, was a heavy drinker and possessed a raging temper. He bought and sold many slaves over the course of a year. He capitalized on acquiring blacks who had been committed to the runaway slave jail in the District of Columbia, as did other slave traders in the area such as John C. Cook, George Kephart, John Davis, Benjamin O. Sheckells, and Price's brother-in-law, Solomon Stover.[1] Angry owners and officers of the Auxiliary Guard were only too willing to turn these troublesome pieces of property over for transport and sale in the Lower South.

Charles Price also acquired slaves by other means. Warren Duvall, a neighbour, owed Price one hundred dollars in January 1854. The two men drew up legal papers for the loan and Duvall put his teenaged slave, Mary Jane, up as collateral, on January 3. On April 15, Duvall signed over to Price for fifty dollars the legal title to the "Mulatto girl named Mary Jane who is now between fifteen and sixteen years old and who is a slave until she arrives to thirty years of age."[2] The stipulation that the girl was to be freed upon reaching the age of thirty was meaningless. Slaves had no rights that they could depend on, and no legal standing to fight their case. This was particularly true when they were owned by a slave dealer who was likely to sell them to southern markets, where no such laws existed.

In the 1853 tax assessment records for their residence near Unity, Charles was listed as owning three slaves – Ann (presumably Ann Maria Weems) and Martin, both age eleven, and Benjamin, age four. Seven of the eight slaves belonging to his father, William Price, were between the ages of two and sixteen.[3] One wonders how useful these children would have been in working in the Prices' tavern and on their farm.[4] In all likelihood, the Prices kept enslaved children on speculation for huge profits later, and at this age they could still be moulded to acquiesce to their owner's bidding. Price specialized in slaves that were young and "likely," as did his father. The term "likely" meant that the slaves – particularly the females – were physically attractive and were therefore suitable for breeding and producing more slaves. It was implied that the girls would also be pleasing enough to satisfy the lusts of their owner.

Price's wife, Caroline Stover-Price, had an evil disposition and took great pleasure in torturing one of her little slave boys, because he was the biological son of her husband. After being married for thirteen years, the couple were still childless.[5] Like many southern wives, Caroline suffered her husband's infidelity. It was common for masters to have both white and mulatto children. Some wives publicly turned a blind eye, while others fought back and demanded that these constant reminders – both the objects of the lust and their children – be sold away. Yet another example of the evils of slavery to both the enslaved and the enslaver, these sexual liaisons were the source of profound pain – to the female who had to submit to unwanted advances, to the slave owner's wife who was hurt and humiliated, and to the black husband who had to stand by in agony, powerless to protect the woman he loved. When a child was born from these physical encounters, more pain ensued for almost everyone involved, with the only possible exception being the master, who was one slave wealthier.

During this time Charles Price moved away from Unity and established his own tavern in the town of Rockville. It was a homecoming of sorts for Ann Maria, as her new master's tavern was on the corner of Jefferson and Washington streets, just across the road from where her old master, Adam Robb, once had his inn. June 1854 marked three years since Ann Maria's nightmare had begun. With her older sister, Catharine, now gone from the Price plantation, she no longer had the comfort of her company.

Jacob Bigelow, who had played such an important part in the purchase of her sister, her mother, and two of her brothers, still could not rest. After purchasing Catharine from Charles Price, he had offered seven hundred dollars for the younger girl. Price had refused and demanded one thousand dollars, the same sum he had received for the elder girl. It was an outrageous price for one so young.[6] There was still $2,200 remaining in the Weems ransom fund two years after it was raised, and Lewis Tappan thought perhaps they should use it to buy Ann Maria.[7] Bigelow refused to consider this extortion. They would have to come up with another way. Bigelow later claimed to have warned Price that "he had better keep his eye on her or he might call her some morning and she would not answer."[8]

Heeding Jacob Bigelow's threat, the Prices forced Ann Maria to sleep on the floor in their bedroom, knowing that she might attempt escape. However, the distance of about twelve miles to either her family's or Bigelow's home in Washington would make undetected flight difficult, especially given the number of advertisements offered for runaways. Hunters were ransacking houses looking for fugitives and no place could be considered safe. Rewards of one or two hundred dollars were offered to blacks to betray the hiding places of runaways. The informants were then often deceived and denied the promised reward.[9]

The Prices also took the added precaution of ensuring that the legal title to Ann Maria was clear and that it was registered at the Montgomery County Courthouse. According to the bill of sale signed, sealed, and dated July 27, 1854, Charles A. Harding was the son of Catharine Harding, who had received the Weems family as part of her inheritance from her late father, Adam Robb. He had previously "contracted" his "negro Girl, Ann Mariah, aged about thirteen years, a slave for life," to Charles M. Price. Harding then sold the girl for the sum of one dollar to Caroline E. Price "in her own name, and as her own property." This legal manoeuvre was instigated by Charles Price.[10] The Prices were only too aware of the transatlantic interest in the Weems family and wanted no impediment to their being the benefactors of the financial windfall that would accompany the bleeding-heart sympathies of the British.

But Bigelow had developed another plan. Ann Maria had two cousins in the area, a twenty-two-year-old male and a female about seventeen, both also slaves. The conductor had full confidence in the young man, whom he described as "bright and clear-headed as anybody." Bigelow felt that Ann Maria's rescue could not be made without their participation and that because of the risk that they would take by helping with the escape, and the consequences they would face, they would have to be freed as well.[11] Just as it took an entire web of anti-slavery sympathizers to come together to raise the money to purchase part of the family, it would take the same to successfully rescue a slave and carry her north to freedom. The rescue would have to be done in secret by only the most trusted individuals. Sadly, even if the rescue were successful, Ann Maria could not return to her father's home in Washington and live openly with her mother and her brother, John Jr. Nor could she live in the Boynton family with her elder sister, Catharine. They were all legally free and had the papers to prove it. But as her sister Stella, her uncle William, and her aunt Annie knew, runaways could never be free in any part of the United States – south or north. Canada and the home of the Bradleys afforded Ann Maria's only option.

Again, the Weems family and Jacob Bigelow would have to rely on some of the people and organizations that had helped them in the past – Charles Ray from the New York Vigilance Committee, Lewis Tappan from several anti-slavery organizations including the American and Foreign Anti-Slavery Society, as well as the American Missionary Association, and William Still and the Philadelphia Vigilance Committee. Bigelow began writing a series of letters to these supporters, shrouded in vague terminology, coded names, and deliberately misleading language.

*William Still, a prominent abolitionist based in Philadelphia, Pennsylvania*
(New York Public Library image 485715)

In some of his written communications with other agents he used the code name William Penn. His nephew recalled his uncle's instructions to some of the fugitives that he assisted:

He was to fill his pockets with crackers or other provisions enough to last him two or three days. At a definite hour in the evening of a particular day he was to go to a certain street corner where he would see a man with a white hat and a silk handkerchief in his hand and was to ask him if he was the Sexton of __ Church. If he said he was, the fugitive was to do whatever he bid him to do. If there were several the man in the white hat would station one upon one street corner and another at a different corner, and so on with the instruction that when he passed by them they were to follow on some distance behind him, thus he would pick up two or three when he came to forks in the road. They would get a glimpse of his white hat, when that was not to be seen they were to press on with diligence. If he met any one he would whistle and call his dog and they were to jump over the fence or hide in the bushes, until the traveler had passed but they had to take their chances of pursuit from the rear. Before daybreak he would send them in the bushes or elsewhere, and leave them in hiding through the day, and at night would appear again. His face they never saw and in two or three days they were delivered to friends in Philadelphia. For this perilous service I think the conductor rec[eived] $40. pr. Head from each fugitive or his friend.[12]

On June 22, 1854, Bigelow wrote to Still: "A person who signs himself Wm. Penn lately wrote to Mr. Wright, saying he would pay $300 to have this service performed. It is for the conveyance of *only one* SMALL package; but it has been discovered since, that the removal cannot be so safely effected without taking *two larger* packages with it. I understand that the *three* are to be brought to this city and stored in safety, as soon as the forwarding merchant in Philadelphia shall say he is ready to send on. The storage, etc. here, will cost a trifle, but the $300 will be promptly paid for the whole service."[13]

Another year went by filled with a series of failed attempts to rescue Ann Maria. The three hundred dollars was secured to pay for transportation to get her into Philadelphia and to pay for the costs of caring for her while she remained in hiding until the resulting furor over her escape subsided.

Thoughts of stowing her on board a train car were quickly dismissed, as the depot would be closely watched by slave hunters. A horse-drawn carriage would be safer, but only marginally so. William Still contacted two or three ship captains who occasionally agreed to stow runaways bound for Philadelphia – for a price. One had previously aided in similar causes and was known in Underground Railroad circles as the "Powder Boy." He, along with his brother, who was also captain of a ship, ventured to Bigelow's apartment to discuss Ann Maria's impending escape, but felt that it was not financially worth their while to accept the risk for a single fugitive slave. Or, as Bigelow would write in the cryptic language of the Underground Railroad, "I had a little light freight for them; but not finding enough other freight to ballast their craft, they went down the river looking for wheat, and promising to return soon."[14] Altruism did not come free.

Ann Maria herself had not yet escaped from the Prices at the time the Powder Boy's ship was docked in the port of Washington. After its departure, the ship's business took the captain to Richmond and Petersburg, Virginia, among other places. On Sunday, September 9, 1855, during the time that the Powder Boy was sailing to those southerly ports, yet another attempt at rescuing Ann Maria met with failure, a disappointment that would by now seem routine were it not so heart-wrenching. The girl must have believed that even God had turned His back on her and her family, even though only a week before her grandmother, Cecilia, had received the sacrament of confirmation in St. Mary's church.[15] A stir among both races in Rockville accompanied the archbishop's visit for the ceremony, but his position on slavery was only a source of confusion for the blacks. On the one hand, he had written that "all men are by law of nature equal, no one is by nature a master of another"; on the other he espoused the view that "nevertheless, since this is the state of things, nothing should be tried against the laws" and "that slaves, informed by Christian custom, should offer obedience to their masters."[16]

Realizing that timing was crucial for all aspects of the plan's coordination, the principals knew that nothing could be left to chance. A plot was hatched whereby a professor at the medical college in Philadelphia known as Dr. H would come to Washington as soon as classes recessed, and continue with the next step after Ann Maria was rescued from Charles Price's home. To cover necessary expenses, Bigelow requested that William Whiting and Lewis Tappan approve the release of two hundred dollars from the ransom fund.[17]

In September and October 1855 an advertisement appeared in both the *Montgomery Sentinel* and *Baltimore Sun* announcing Ann Maria's escape. Arabella had played a significant part in the escape of her youngest enslaved daughter, but of necessity her role was shrouded in mystery.[18]

The newspapers of the time often carried advertisements for lost or stolen articles. On October 8, 1855, an advertisement in Washington's *Evening Post* offered a five-dollar reward for a small bay mare that had strayed from the premises of Joseph Abbott. It could be identified by a scar over its left eye and one on its breast, and by its long tail and mane. A week earlier, Edward H. Edblin had offered the slightly higher price of twenty dollars for fifteen-year-old John Oliver, alias "Brown." When he fled, pretending to be a free person, he wore an old straw hat, a black coat and light-coloured pants. Like the mare, he also had a scar on his forehead.[19] Tilghman Hilleary offered one hundred dollars for his sixteen-year-old runaway "servant" Margery Arnold, described in the *Baltimore Sun* of September 24 as having "a small horizontal scar on her forehead, complexion brown, and a very full suit of hair." She was suspected of fleeing to Washington to join some of her family. Eleven of her family members, including both parents, sisters, brother, aunt, and uncle were named in the advertisement, along with their location. Tragically, these eleven individuals belonged to ten different owners.

In the same paper, an advertisement referred to twenty-one-year-old "indentured apprentice" William A. Hall, who had fled from George O. Blubaugh. Hall; William was slender and had a dark complexion, and was last seen wearing a "brown frock coat, dark pants, and white slouch hat." Anyone who harboured or employed the young man would do so "at the peril of the law," the ad warned. To further demonstrate that the wronged master meant business, the heading sarcastically shouted from the page in bold capital letters: "ONE CENT REWARD"![20]

Other notices showed more serious intent. The large number of ads suggested that the Underground Railroad was particularly active and explained why vigilance to prevent or capture runaways was intense, which explains why it was so challenging to free Ann Maria. Also telling is the habitual mention of where the relatives of the fugitives lived. On September 26, William J. Berry offered two hundred dollars for "my negro man," twenty-seven-year-old Davis Green, who had relatives in Washington. In the same edition, Edmund Plowden offered one hundred dollars each for forty-year-old Hanson and twenty- or twenty-one-year-old Joseph. Hanson was further identified as being "of copper color, about 40 years of age, 5 feet 4 or 5 inches high, well made but spare of flesh; when spoken to generally turns his head away and does not look the speaker in the face." But he was "very smart" and could read, and it was suspected that he could write as well. The ad above this one requested that Thomas and Caroline Lewis and their child be returned to Robert M. Denison. He would pay two hundred dollars for each if they were captured outside of the state or one hundred dollars each if taken within Maryland.

But none of these rewards could begin to compare with that offered by an outraged Charles M. Price:

**$500 REWARD.**

R AN away on Sunday night, the 23d instant, before 12 o'clock, from the subscriber, residing in Rockville, Montgomery county, Md., my NEGRO GIRL "Ann Maria Weems," about 15 years of age: a bright mullatto; some small freckles on her face; slender person, thick-suit of hair, inclined to be sandy. Her parents are free, and reside in Washington, D. C. It is evident she was taken away by some one in a carriage, probably by a white man, by whom she may be carried beyond the limits of the State of Maryland.

I will give the above reward for her apprehension and detention so that I get her again.

CHAS. M. PRICE.

*An outraged Charles Price offered a five-hundred-dollar reward for the return of Ann Maria Weems. (Montgomery County Sentinel, January 5, 1856, courtesy of Maryland State Archives' "Beneath the Underground")*

Jacob Bigelow was probably the white man in the carriage described in the advertisement. He would not have dared to take Ann Maria to her parents' home. Neither was the Boyntons' house an option, nor were her aunt's rooms in Washington, where Catharine had gone on the first day of her freedom. Many of the slaves who belonged to the daughters of Adam Robb were hired out to District of Columbia households, but it would have been far too dangerous to risk trying to shelter Ann Maria with them. Although Bigelow was under suspicion, he had little choice but to keep his young ward in his own home.

Two weeks slowly passed as Ann Maria Weems and Jacob Bigelow waited for Dr. H. to arrive. It is undocumented whether the two unidentified cousins who were to help in the escape were successful in getting away. Perhaps they were among those whose names appeared in the runaway slave ads. At any rate, the stir caused by Ann Maria's escape gave many slaves in the vicinity just cause to worry, as did the huge reward Price offered. The challenge of maintaining absolute secrecy in Bigelow's

*Visible on the right is the corner of Jacob Bigelow's apartment overlooking the post office on E Street and Seventh Street NW in Washington. Ann Maria Weems hid there for two months while waiting for a member of the Underground Railroad to bring her to the free state of Pennsylvania.* (Library of Congress image cph 3A53371)

apartment, located above his office at the corner of E and Seventh streets, was compounded by the presence in another part of the same building of druggist John Callan and his wife, along with their eight children.[21] Feeling helpless, the lawyer sent a letter to William Still beseeching him for help: "And as I am powerless without your aid, I pray you don't lose a moment in giving me relief. The idea of waiting yet for weeks seems dreadful; do reduce it to days if possible, and give me notice of the earliest possible time."[22] A panicking Bigelow sent many other letters to Lewis Tappan, including two in one day on two different occasions. When he got no results he tried signing his code name, William Penn. But Tappan was powerless to speed up the process. Offering cool comfort, his only reply was, "I hoped the matter would be accomplished."[23]

Another five weeks passed before an emissary from the Underground Railroad appeared. But whatever momentary promise was suggested quickly vanished. The agent, known as Dr. T., had nothing of substance to offer, only the sympathy of a fellow anti-slavery crusader. Likewise, Still's letters were only filled with conjecture that the "Powder Boy" would perhaps arrive soon. In New York, Lewis Tappan continued to anxiously await the human "parcel." Another week passed. And another began.

Harbouring Ann Maria caused a great deal of hardship for Jacob Bigelow, who was unable to fulfill some of his personal and professional obligations. He dared to leave his apartment only for very brief periods. But he and his fugitive house guest soon put the time to good use. They had initially christened the runaway with the new name "Ellen Capron" but they soon changed it to a more masculine-sounding "Joe Wright," and decided she would complete the escape dressed in boy's clothing. It would be necessary to drastically change her appearance from the description that appeared in her runaway slave ad as "about 15 yrs of age, a bright molato, some small freckles on her face; slender person, thick suit of hair; inclined to be sandy."[24] She was to spend her time in the apartment becoming accustomed to male garments and perfecting a masculine manner.

*Ann Maria Weems escaped disguised as a man, as Ellen Craft had before her.* (New York Public Library image 1167940)

Abolitionists knew that this ruse of changing gender had succeeded before. Ellen Craft, who had dressed as a man during her flight with her husband, William, was one slave who had employed this tactic. Under the headline "Bloomerism and Slavery," the Canadian black newspaper *Voice of the Fugitive* had trumpeted the story of another slave woman, originally from Mississippi, who had accompanied her master's family to the free state of Illinois. The article stated that "she concluded on that occasion to leave them to nurse their own children, black their own boots, and comb their own hair, or pay for having it done." To that effect, she dressed in her master's clothing and fled while he slept. When he awoke the following morning and couldn't find his pants, he bellowed to his slave to bring his clothes. He received no reply. Incensed, he declared that he would not leave Illinois until she was captured. Upon reaching Canada via friends in the Underground Railroad, the now former slave gleefully said she "wishes to inform him that he need not wait longer in Illinois for her company; that she is now in the enjoyment of British liberty, and whenever she gets ready to return to American slavery, she will let him know."[25]

By mid November, Ellwood Harvey, who was Dr. H., had arrived in Washington to help Ann Maria as promised, much to the relief of all concerned. The doctor was not only a professor but also the dean of faculty at the Female Medical College of Pennsylvania. One of his

*Ellwood Harvey, or Dr. H, whose motivation to help Ann Maria escape was in part a reward that would allow him to buy a teaching mannequin for his medical school* (courtesy Steve Harvey)

*A sketch of a slave auction in Richmond, Virginia* (Library of Congress cph 3a17645)

immediate incentives for helping was the need to raise money to purchase a mannequin as a teaching tool for the cash-strapped college. The
college had been opened only since October 1850. Founded by a Quaker
who had the revolutionary idea that women should be afforded the same
opportunity as men, the college would boast an initial graduating class
of eight women. In those early days, the college consisted of a few small
rooms that could be reached from the street only by a dark and narrow
passageway. Harvey had been promised a goodly sum of three hundred
dollars for his humanitarian effort, but this was not his only motivation
for helping Ann Maria escape.[26]

On Christmas Day 1846, almost nine years earlier, he had witnessed
a scene that made a deep impression on his soul. While attending what
he thought was a land sale near Petersburg, Virginia, he unexpectedly
discovered that it was also a public slave auction. The slaves had been
told that they would not be sold that day. After the land had been sold,
all were astounded to hear the auctioneer cry, "Bring up the niggers."
Dr. Harvey stared in helpless amazement as the slaves gradually
grasped what was about to happen. He watched as mothers gathered
up their babies and ran to hide in the slave huts. The older children,

in a futile attempt to hide themselves, ran behind trees and buildings. The men stood frozen and unable to speak as they realized the horror about to befall them.

As the sale in human flesh began, Harvey was saddened to see old men relinquish whatever little bit of pride they possessed and exaggerate their infirmities and worthlessness so that they would not be sent to the southern cotton fields. Those who were most successful at this ruse soon learned that they were worth only between thirteen and twenty-five dollars. A fifteen-year-old boy, with whiter skin than many of his tormentors in the crowd, struggled to demonstrate his approaching manhood as he trembled and wiped away tears rather than give spectators the satisfaction of seeing him cry. His ordeal was heightened as the crowd made "vulgar jests" about his colour, even as his mother came rushing to the doorway of a nearby hut to scream her agony at losing her child. Next up was a young woman who placed her baby into the arms of an old woman and walked mechanically toward the auction block before collapsing. Dr. Harvey and his companions could stomach no more and returned to their carriage and departed.[27]

Compelled to let the world know about the scenes that had so sickened him, Dr. Harvey sent an account of the auction to the *Pennsylvania Freeman* newspaper. Gerrit Smith was so moved by the account that he decided to "scatter it over our Country in a hand bill form."[28] Smith also "scattered" it as far as Britain, where it was published as the forty-eighth tract in the *Leeds Anti-slavery Series*. Several years later, Harriet Beecher Stowe was so touched that she published it in *A Key to Uncle Tom's Cabin*. This, along with hundreds of other first-hand accounts, was intended to silence any critics – and their numbers were legion – who declared that she had dramatically overstated the evils of slavery. In its own way, Harvey's moving description provided an incontrovertible argument to the contrary, and the experience propelled him to accept the challenge of accompanying Ann Maria to safety.

As soon as the semester ended at the medical school, Harvey rented a black horse and carriage in Baltimore and drove from there to Washington. Within three minutes of arriving at Jacob Bigelow's door, the doctor's calm and thoughtful manner reassured the lawyer that he was "perfectly competent to execute his undertaking." As Ann Maria and the doctor prepared to leave, Bigelow's worry subsided, and he could finally turn his attention to other matters – that of another "half dozen or so of packages here pressing for transportation; twice or thrice that number also pressing, but less so than the others." His self-sacrifice and bravery in continuing to help other "packages" to freedom was apparently not in the least diminished.[29] However, before totally turning his focus elsewhere, Bigelow wrote a hasty letter to Charles Ray informing him that

I have a friend passing through this city on his way to New York, and I mean to avail myself of his kindness to send to your lady the little parcel she has been so long expecting. You can name it to her, and I now suggest that as soon as you find it convenient, you send me back by express the wrapper and covering in which the valuables are packed, for I have another similar parcel to send, and shall find these things exactly convenient for the purpose. My friend intends to leave here on Monday morning, with his own conveyance, taking it leisurely, and may not reach New York before about Thursday, but of this I shall speak more exactly before I close. I need not suggest to you how anxious I shall be to get the earliest news of the arrival of the package without breakage or injury.[30]

In a second letter to Ray, Bigelow relayed an appeal from Arabella, whose experiences had taught her only too well the importance of having some tangible reminder of a loved one to cling to: "I am requested for the gratification of Joe's mother that you will be pleased on his arrival, and *before he changes his sex*, to have his daguerreotype taken for her use."[31]

The abolitionists decided that "Joe" was to act as a coachman for Dr. Harvey. They would boldly meet at midday in the crowded street in front of the White House, rather than risk meeting again at Bigelow's home. As the two men shook hands and wished each other well, the "young man" jumped aboard the carriage and took the horse's reins in hand. It would be two nights' journey through Maryland before they reached the free state of Pennsylvania. They met with their first obstacle at the turnpike gates on the toll road leading out of the city, where the guards hesitated to let the "servant" pass, suspicious that he might be a runaway slave. It was ironic that Ann Maria should have problems at this point; many years earlier, in 1817, Adam Robb had been appointed a commissioner to sell shares of stock to finance the construction of the turnpike.[32] It was also the place where William Chaplin had been captured as he had attempted to whisk two slaves to freedom six years earlier. Ann Maria and Dr. Harvey were more fortunate, and after answering questions to the satisfaction of the guards they were finally allowed to proceed.

Further displaying his cool, the doctor decided to spend one of the

Philadelphia Inquirer *photographs show a 1938 reenactment of Ann Maria Weems's escape dressed as a buggy driver.* (courtesy Steve Harvey)

nights in the home of an old friend who was himself a slave owner. This family was aware of Dr. Harvey's opposition to slavery in his younger days. It was therefore necessary for the doctor to act as though he had exchanged his youthful idealism for a mature acceptance of societal realities. Putting on the air of a firm master, he directed his "slave" to behave properly. Later, pretending to be slightly ill, the doctor informed his hosts that his slave would need to sleep in the same room as he, to answer to his needs. After a night's sleep, the two rose early and thanked their friends, who were honoured to have had such a distinguished visitor. They never suspected the subterfuge.

Their next obstacle appeared when they tried to board a ferry on the banks of the Susquehanna River. A gang of men at the boat were not fooled by Harvey's protests that his young charge was not a runaway. Only a display of physical bravado saved Ann Maria. Harvey, a man of robust build, removed his coat and challenged their tormentors with a torrent of obscenities. Suitably intimidated, they reconsidered their objections. The doctor and his "boy" were allowed to continue on their journey.[33]

By mid-afternoon of the next day – appropriately during the week of Thanksgiving – they arrived at the home of William Still. Still had temporarily stepped out, so the doctor hurriedly told Mrs. Still that he was leaving "the young lad" there for a while, then quickly departed. When Mr. Still returned, he asked the young person if he was the one the doctor had brought from Washington. "Joe" denied it and replied that he was from York. Puzzled, Still asked why the doctor had brought Joe to his home, when Still had been expecting a young girl dressed in boy's clothing. "Joe" got up and walked out of the house. A perplexed Still followed. The well-trained fugitive explained that there were other people inside – Mrs. Still, a hired servant girl, and another runaway woman – and the doctor had told her not to reveal her true identity to anyone other than himself. Still was relieved and amazed to learn the truth, that it was actually a female standing before him.

As was his custom with all of the fugitive slaves who sought the assistance of the Vigilance Committee, William Still carefully recorded an
account of Ann Maria's visit. His notes are probably the most important
surviving records of the Underground Railroad. They are rich with
detail, saving for posterity the names of the owners and the conditions
individuals experienced in slavery and in escape. A particularly meaningful and thoughtful touch was his inclusion of the names of escaped
slaves' family members and notes on their condition. In Ann Maria's
case, Still wrote of the heartlessness of Charles and Caroline Price, her
owners. He mentioned her love of freedom, which had eluded her up
until now. He wrote of her parents, one brother, and two sisters who
were free and also of her three brothers who were still enslaved in the
South. Of the fugitive herself, he admiringly described her as "a bright
molato, well grown, smart and good looking."[34] His accompanying
account book reminds us that there were costs associated with harbouring a slave: he records the cost for five and a half days' board for
"Jos. Wright (Ellen Capron)" as $2.75.[35]

After spending a couple of days in Philadelphia and meeting with
several members of the Vigilance Committee there, Dr. Harvey delivered Ann Maria to Charles B. Ray in New York City, who then quickly
brought her to the home of Lewis and Sarah Tappan.[36] Tappan, who
had taken over the administration of the Weems ransom fund, prepared
to pay the doctor the three hundred dollars that had been promised to
him for risking his own safety in bringing the girl from Washington. In
a cryptically written and unsigned note to Dr. Harvey, Tappan
expressed his regret in the third person that "Mr. T." did not have a
chance to see him and learn the details of the flight. However, he was
delighted with the "packet" that the doctor had delivered to New York.
It being Thanksgiving, the banks were closed, but the necessary
payment arrangements would be made the following day.[37]

As promised, the money was sent by express, along with a note that
"Ellen" was well and happy and that a daguerreotype had been taken.[38]

On receiving the money, Harvey returned to Philadelphia and purchased the mannequin for his college. In keeping with Tappan's businesslike way of managing his station of the Underground Railroad one of Harvey's letters included a receipt for his payment.[39] This contradicts the long-held view of many who have written about the Underground Railroad that the organization was so secretive that no one ever kept written records of its transactions.

That day, Tappan and his wife were preparing a large dinner for numerous friends and family. While the guests filled the downstairs, Ann Maria, still dressed as a boy, remained in an upper room. She had learned to be wary of strangers, but she displayed her gratitude with a smile when the trusted Tappan family members occasionally crept up to check on her or to bring her part of the feast of turkey and plum pudding that they were enjoying below. The master of the household confided in his diary that he was taken by the young lady, whom he described as tall for her age and "very pretty."[40] Mrs. Tappan agreed with her husband's assessment, stating that the girl "has a fine counte-nance, intelligent & bright."[41]

Some time earlier, Lewis Tappan had met a young girl about Ann Maria's age, at Sabbath school. She had just arrived in New York the day before and Tappan asked her how she came to make it there. "I was walking near the water when a white sailor spoke to me, and after a few questions, offered to hide me on board his vessel," she replied. He then asked if her parents were kind to her and if she loved them, to which she said, "Yes, I love them very much." His next question was about the treatment that the girl had received from her master and her mistress: "They treated me very well." The somewhat perplexed Mr. Tappan then asked how the girl could leave the gentle treatment of her owners and the parents she loved and who loved her and go with this sailor, who was a perfect stranger. Her heartfelt reply was "He told me I should be free!" Perhaps the wisdom in these words had left an effect on Tappan that he now experienced again with the arrival of Ann Maria.

The Tappans secured clothing for Ann Maria and a fine carpetbag to carry it in, as well as five dollars for her pocket. The day after Thanksgiving, she was taken to the home of Amos N. Freeman, a Congregationalist minister of a coloured church in Brooklyn. It had been hoped that Charles Ray could accompany Ann Maria for the remainder of her journey, but he was not able to leave for several days.[42] Believing that any delay was too dangerous, Reverend Freeman agreed to go in Ray's place to Canada, where she could be reunited with her aunt and uncle and perhaps attend school at the Buxton mission. At that time she could read "a very little" and her unknown future would improve greatly if she acquired the quality education for which Buxton was rapidly becoming renowned. Tappan told Freeman and Ann Maria that her uncle Abraham Young had assumed the name William.[43] He withheld the surname for the time being. He also loaned Reverend Freeman his cloak and promised him five dollars per day plus his expenses, which would be taken from the Weems ransom fund.[44]

*The Reverend Amos Freeman, who accompanied Ann Maria Weems by train to Canada* (courtesy of Joe Duff)

The minister and his young charge climbed aboard an express train at five that Friday afternoon and headed toward Canada. Worries about slave hunters seeking the large reward being offered for her capture intensified as they approached the Niagara River separating the two countries. But they met with no obstacles, and their joy was immense as they rode the train over the suspension bridge and across the border, on Saturday night under the spray of the wondrous Niagara Falls. Slavery was now at their backs and freedom in their faces.

Black poetess and anti-slavery lecturer Frances Ellen Watkins later took a keen interest in Ann Maria and inquired of William Still: "How fared the girl who came robed in male attire?"[45] No doubt Ann Maria felt similar emotions to those of Watkins when she arrived:

> Well, I have gazed for the first time upon Free Land, and, would you believe it, tears sprang to my eyes, and I wept. Oh, it was a glorious sight to gaze for the first time on a land where a poor slave flying from our glorious land of liberty would in a moment find his fetters broken, his shackles loosed, and whatever he was in the land of Washington, beneath the shadow of Bunker Hill Monument or even Plymouth Rock, here he becomes a man and a brother. I have gazed upon Harper's Ferry, or rather the rock at the Ferry; I have seen it towering up in simple grandeur, with the gentle Potomac gliding peacefully at its feet, and felt that that was God's masonry, and my soul had expanded in gazing on its sublimity. I have seen the ocean singing its wild chorus of sounding waves, and ecstacy has thrilled upon the living chords of my heart. I have since then seen the rainbow-crowned Niagara chanting the choral hymn of Omnipotence, girdled with grandeur, and robed with glory; but none of these things have melted me as the first sight of Free Land. Towering mountains lifting their hoary summits to catch the first faint flush of day when the sunbeams kiss the shadows from morning's drowsy face may expand and exalt your soul. The first view of the ocean may fill

you with strange delight. Niagara – the great, the glorious Niagara – may hush your spirit with its ceaseless thunder; it may charm you with its robe of crested spray and rainbow crown; but the land of Freedom was a lesson of deeper significance than foaming waves or towering mounts.[46]

During a short delay, Reverend Freeman ran to the post office and sent a hasty note to Tappan to share the good news. He also had to collect a letter that Tappan had mailed to him in care of the faithful Canadian abolitionist Hiram Wilson, who had formerly lived at the Dawn Settlement but was now working among the fugitives in St. Catharines. Tappan's letter revealed that the full name of Ann Maria's uncle was now William Henry Bradley.[47] As Freeman was waiting for his change, the bell rang signalling that the train was about to continue on the two-hundred-mile route to Chatham.

By eight o'clock that evening, they had reached their destination. It was dark and the roads had turned to mud after a heavy rain, so they could not hire a carriage to take them to Dresden for another two days and were forced to rent a room at a boarding house. On the way there Reverend Freeman's guide asked if the young man was his son. "No," he replied. Freeman then asked the guide if he knew of a man in Dresden named Bradley. When the guide declared that he knew him very well, the Reverend stated that his young companion was a relation of Bradley's. He offered no further explanation.

Ann Maria kept a low profile at the house, which contained several boarders and some visiting neighbours. At eleven p.m., Reverend Freeman wrote his second letter of the day to Tappan to let him know "all safe."[48] But sharing the news by mail was not the same as sharing it directly. Freeman was no longer able to contain the secret that they had held so closely for the past week – and that Ann Maria had held even longer. He confided to the landlord that the "boy" who was staying in his home was in fact a girl, and that she had come dressed like that all the way from Washington. As the word spread quickly through the household, the residents were amazed. Chatham's black inhabitants were delighted to welcome another refugee who had found a safe haven from slavery. Reverend Freeman recalled that "the whole company were on their feet, shook hands, laughed and rejoiced; declaring that this beat all they had ever seen before."[49]

The roads were still impassable on Sunday and despite an early start on Monday, it was late in the afternoon when they approached Dresden. Along the way, they met two men, one walking, the other on horseback. Reverend Freeman asked if they could give him directions to Mr. Bradley's house. The rider replied that it was about one mile farther on – and that he himself was the very man! Hearing this response, Ann Maria turned her head. Despite not having seen his fourteen-year-old niece for several years, Bradley wasn't fooled as so many others along the way had been. He cried out: "My Lord! Maria, is that you? Is that you? My child, is it you? We never expected to see you again! We had given you up; O, what will your aunt say? It will kill her! She will die! It will kill her!"[50]

William Bradley could not contain himself. Not only was he reunited with his niece, but he could also ask about all of the friends and family members that he had left behind in Maryland. He even asked about the owners from whom he and his wife had fled. Running ahead to open the gate and to make sure that the fire was well stoked to welcome them, he met his wife, who was just returning from an errand, and shared the news with her. Her reunion with Ann Maria was no less touching. Unable to move away from the gate, with tears rolling down her cheeks, she asked, "Ann Maria, is that you?" Words were no longer necessary as the two women embraced and wept.

Reverend Freeman was jubilant at having arrived in a country where all men were free. He hurriedly wrote yet another note to Tappan to share his good news.[51] As he began his return journey to New York, he carried with him the memory of the scene, the likes of which he had never witnessed.[52] Before Freeman left, William Bradley told the minister that he intended to write to his sister-in-law Arabella to implore her and her husband to come to the safety of Canada.

Perhaps Arabella would later take his advice, but for now her work in the United States was not yet done.

❧

Ann Maria was now safely in the bosom of her uncle's family. Tappan, Ray, and Bigelow were ecstatic. To Dr. Harvey, Lewis Tappan wrote: "May the Lord bless you & all who have participated with you in a deed of humanity on which you will ever have occasion to reflect with satisfaction."[53] In a second letter to Harvey, Tappan promised to send the trusted guide "a daguerreotype of Joe – Joe no longer."[54] Sarah Tappan, Lewis's wife, was also caught up in the excitement, and shared the news in a letter to Henry Richardson. She included her husband's thoughts that it might be best not to give the rescue any publicity. She quoted the words of Frederick Douglass that "the Practice of publishing every new invention by which a slave escapes from slavery has neither wisdom nor necessity to sustain it. Had not Henry Box Brown & his friends attracted slaveholding attention to the manner of his escape, we might have had a thousand Box Browns per annum. The singularly original plan adopted by William & Ellen Crafts perished with the first using, because every slaveholder in the land was apprised of it."[55]

However, the Tappans were so invigorated, perhaps to the point of recklessness, by Ann Maria's successful escape that they were unable to take their own advice. Accurately recognizing that this affair would have a special place in history, Sarah mused that "the rescue of Ann Maria Weems is a thing which will ever be thought of with satisfaction and gratitude by all who have had any hand in it." A month later, Sarah sent an article to the editor of the *Frederick Douglass Paper* describing the details of the Weems family's tragedies and triumphs. The story appeared in the February 1, 1856 edition. It is uncertain whether Douglass, who had left his paper in the care of an assistant while he was on a lecture tour, was aware that it would appear in print or even whether he was aware of the article's existence. As are all editors at one time or another, Douglass was occasionally conflicted about the propriety of publishing certain articles. Lewis Tappan understood his dilemma and confided in a letter to fellow abolitionist and friend Samuel Rhoads in Philadelphia that Frederick Douglass's "position is peculiar. He finds himself obliged, I suppose to admit many articles he does not approve; and he is about so much that probably a good deal finds admission for want of a suitable co-editor to act judiciously."[56]

The Tappans believed that a carefully written story would garner sympathy and inspire hope among its readers. An excited Sarah Tappan wrote to Douglass and requested a dozen copies of the paper; she quickly dispatched one copy across the ocean to abolitionist Maria Webb, who was probably involved in collecting money for the Weems ransom fund in Dublin, Ireland.[57] Sarah was also eager to learn more about the rest of the Weems family, particularly about Stella. Douglass told Sarah that she could find out much more detail by contacting Reverend Garnet, who had a particularly intimate knowledge of the facts.[58]

Lewis Tappan continued to keep an eye on the larger picture. He wrote to Henry Richardson in England, stating that he was optimistic that they could do something to rescue one or two of the Weems boys who were still enslaved. Initially he did not care whether they were purchased or whether they could be induced to escape.[59] He recognized that a limitless amount of money was needed to do the work of the Underground Railroad and that "hundreds could be essentially aided in their flight by a sum that would be required to pay the slaveholder for a single individual."[60] No less a figure than Harriet Tubman also reminded Tappan of this fact. In November 1855, she approached Tappan for financial assistance. The thirty-five-year-old woman, who was a fugitive slave herself then living in Canada, had made two trips back to the Slave States to bring out friends and relatives. She was about to return yet again to bring out two or three others; she did not know these people personally, but they were relatives of friends she had made in Canada. Tappan asked her how she would feel if she were discovered and sold into perpetual slavery in the Deep South. "She replied calmly & instantly 'I should have the consolation to know that I had done some good to my people.'"[61]

In a letter to Jacob Bigelow, Tappan could scarcely conceal his joy at Ann Maria's rescue. His handwriting almost jumps off the page as he relays with delight the scene of Ann Maria being reunited with her aunt and uncle. With veiled language meant to throw off any spying eyes, Tappan urged Bigelow to act quickly with her brothers: "Those chickens, far away, must be purchased sent to the uncle also. Don't fail to do it." In keeping with the need for secrecy, he signed his name as "Ludwig Temple."[62]

# CHAPTER 8

WHILE ANN MARIA WAS PLOTTING her escape from slavery, her sister Stella and her adoptive family were facing yet another crisis in Jamaica. In the summer of 1855, Henry Garnet was struck with the intermittent fever symptomatic of cholera. Luckily, his wife, Julia, and their natural children – including a newborn son, whom they had named after their contact in Scotland, Presbyterian minister Andrew Somerville – had recently returned to the United States, barely avoiding the most severe onslaught of the disease.[1] Although Julia headed a Jamaican industrial school for women that was lauded by her husband's Scottish employers, the Garnets believed that their children, particularly eleven-year-old Mary, would benefit from the education and opportunities offered in America. They boarded the ship *Harriet Ann* at the port of Black River, Jamaica, and safely arrived in New York on August 21.[2] Soon afterward Julia developed a full-blown attack of the fever too. Gradually, over the course of seven months, she regained her health at the Nantucket home of her free sister, Ann Crawford.

The Garnets were looking forward to being reunited. But tragedy struck again, leaving another gap in their family circle. Their adopted daughter Stella had lived in Jamaica for three years. Despite her freedom, the separation from those she loved had weakened her body and stolen her joy, making her even more vulnerable to the tropical diseases that were a constant threat. She, too, fell victim to the fever, but was unable to recover. Henry Garnet poignantly relayed the news of her death in a letter to those who had tried to help the Weems family:

December 20<sup>th</sup>, 1855

Stirling, Grange Hill, Jamaica

I know that you will be grieved and surprised to be informed of the death of poor dear Stella. She left us for a better world on the 12<sup>th</sup> day of December, at four o'clock in the afternoon. Her complaint was bilious fever, which she endured with great patience for seventeen days, when congestion of the brain took place and she fell asleep, aged twenty-four years and six days. From the beginning of her illness she believed she would not recover, and began to make ready for the returnless journey, and committed herself to the blessed Redeemer. When I told her that her race was nearly run, she paused for a moment and said, "There is only one thing I wish for in this world – I want to see my mother."

She paused again, and then continued, "I do not wish to live, I want to go home. In my Father's house there are many, many mansions. This world is shallow – there's nothing to it." She was visited by four of our ministers, and conversed with them calmly with great faithfulness.

Her remains were followed to the grave by a large number of weeping friends, and they planted flowers around her lowly bed. She was a child of sorrow, but she will suffer no more. The cruelty and humanity of slavery exiled her far from her native land and doomed her to die far away in a land of strangers, but she is free now; and God has wiped all tears from her eyes. She is the happiest and the freest of all the Weems family, and in the heavenly world there are no slave-hunters – no mourning captives – no dear, dissevered ties of nature, and no necessity for making appeals for the purchase of God's children. Although John Weems and his wife must be deeply affected to

hear of the death of their beloved daughter, still they must rejoice
when they reflect that she is beyond the reach of tyrants. May God
bless those kind friends in Britain who so nobly contributed towards
emancipating that poor slave "mother" for whose sake her dying
daughter only wished to live.

Henry H. Garnet[3]

The optimism that Henry and Julia Garnet had once felt for future
happiness in the Caribbean had steadily eroded. Try as they might, they
could not escape a past so tightly interwoven with pain. They had already
lost two of their children, and now Stella. Henry continued to dream of
a true homeland and was being tugged by the desire to go to his ancestral
continent, where he might serve as a missionary in Liberia.[4] But for the
present he followed what remained of his family and left for the United
States in early April 1856, racked by illness and exhaustion. As on his original voyage to Jamaica, the steamship was caught in punishing weather
and rough seas. The perilous trip from Jamaica to Boston's harbour lasted
thirty-two days.[5] Garnet's fever subsided by the time the ship reached the
Gulf of Florida and he gave praise to God for sparing his life.

*Commander John Newland Maffitt,
the slave owner who later worked
for the U.S. Navy capturing ships
that illegally imported African
slaves into the Americas* (photo
# NH 66684, U.S. Naval Historical
Center Photograph)

Despite their relief at surviving the voyage, the Garnets were burdened by the news of yet another misfortune. Shortly after their
arrival in Jamaica, a man had approached them and innocently asked
where they were from. Upon learning that Julia Garnet was originally
from South Carolina, he asked about her maiden name, to which she
replied, "Williams." Coincidentally, the stranger was able to share
with them some melancholy information: Julia's youngest sister,
Diana, and Diana's daughter, Cornelia, had become the property of
a John N. Maffitt, a seaman who worked on the schooner *Galveston*
for.the United States Navy. But Maffitt no longer had any need for
these two slaves and had placed both mother and daughter up for sale.

Frantically, the Garnets wrote to Reverend James Crawford in
Nantucket, Massachusetts, who had married Ann, another of Julia's
sisters. A kind man, Crawford had "wonderful brown hair, and the
merriest blue eyes and dimples, and that large, humorous, lovely
mouth that spoke evil of no man."[6] With the help of a group of "distinguished gentlemen," Crawford began negotiating Diana's purchase.
Maffitt wanted seven hundred dollars for Diana, or $1,900 for the
pair. Apparently not without some humanity, the owner wrote

*Reverend James Crawford, who was
instrumental in freeing the sister and
niece of Julia Garnet* (Courtesy of
the Nantucket Historical Association)

142

that "nothing would give him greater pleasure than to confer upon them the blessings of liberty" – provided that the money was paid.

Maffitt was "a slight, middle-aged, well-knit man, of about forty-two; a merry-looking man . . . reedy, determined, and full of life and business; apparently the sort of man who is equally ready for a fight or a jollification, and whose preference for the latter would by no means interfere with his creditable conduct of the former."[7] True to his reputation, Maffitt's patience was short-lived. Within another month he advised the family that he had concluded a deal for Cornelia that very day and planned to sell Diana the next month. Crawford began a fundraising tour seeking donations in both the United States and Canada. Like his brother-in-law, he had little money, certainly not nearly enough for this undertaking. A local newspaper reported that he received no pay for being minister to the Pleasant Street Baptist Church and had to rely on the proceeds from other labour to support his own household. The Garnets, once back in the United States, also assisted with the fundraising but, as was the case with the Weems family, both money and time were short. Between the two families they could come up with only two hundred dollars, which was all raised by Crawford.[8]

The Garnet and Crawford families were faced with similar arguments to those encountered by the fundraisers for the Weems family a few years earlier. Reverend H. Garrett, a Baptist minister from London, Canada West, spoke at a meeting at Detroit's city hall on the controversial subject of raising money to "purchase the liberty of slaves in the Southern states." The *Provincial Freeman* newspaper, published in Chatham by Mary Ann Shadd, attacked the principle of that endeavour, stating that "we condemn (and we believe the colored people generally do) every scheme of emancipation which admits the right of property in man. Our firm conviction is that any man or government that recognizes for a moment, such a principle, is an enemy to Universal Freedom." Shadd's immediate family had never been slaves, and she no doubt saw that issue in a strictly theoretical light.[9]

Of course, the Garnets had been involved in a situation like this before. Their thoughts turned to their friends in Britain, who had so generously donated for the purchase of Arabella and her children. There was money remaining in the Weems ransom fund and some of it had sat unused for years. Why couldn't they use part of it to ward off their looming tragedy? After all, they had been instrumental in initiating the effort to help the Weemses. The Garnets contacted Lewis Tappan and pleaded their case. Tappan believed their request was reasonable, provided that both the British contributors and the Weems family consented.

Coincidentally, at almost exactly the same time, the Ladies Committee for Assisting Fugitives from Slavery, which operated out of the London offices of the British and Foreign Anti-Slavery Society, was discussing the fact that some of the funds raised for the redemption of the Weems family had not been sent to America; more had been raised than was originally estimated to be required, and the committee deliberated on how to use the money. Earlier that same year, on January 28, 1856, the Ladies Committee debated using the funds to assist runaways who had fled to England. Their discussion had a particular urgency, as they were moved by a case involving a young orphan girl who had accompanied her master from New Orleans to England. The master was going to return to the southern states with his slave. The ladies wished to prevent this by arranging the child's permanent freedom and placing her in the care of the Orphans' Asylum at Bristol, England.[10]

Unaware of these discussions taking place across the Atlantic, Tappan wrote to Henry and Anna Richardson in Newcastle and to Mrs. Lydia Edmund Sturge, the sister-in-law of the British and Foreign Anti-Slavery Society's leader, Joseph Sturge, in Birmingham, England and secured their blessing to help the Garnets. On January 21, 1856, Tappan also wrote to Jacob Bigelow to ask him to secure John Weems's written consent for the remainder of the fund "to be expended to aid fugitives."[11] Bigelow responded a week later. It appeared that Arabella and John were hesitant to give their permission – a natural response coming from parents who were clinging desperately to the dream of rescuing their three sons. And in a most unexpected twist of fate, Bigelow had discovered some vague intelligence that renewed the hope of redeeming Joseph, Adam, and Augustus. Tappan had given up any expectation of this happening, fearing that they had been lost forever to the remote south. A man of extreme conscience, he believed that John and Arabella's feelings should be respected, and had he known that it might be possible to locate the boys he never would have suggested that the funds be used to help other slaves. However, that was hindsight, and Diana Williams would be lost if her family did not act quickly. The negotiations for her liberation began in earnest.

Arrangements to consummate the deal were complicated not only by financial issues but also by geography and by physical illness and emotional exhaustion. John Maffitt was from North Carolina and James and Ann Crawford were in Nantucket, Massachusetts, where they had recently been joined by Julia Garnet and her children. The entire family was still shaken by the death of Stella Weems, but Henry Garnet was able to find some comfort: "Every thing looks very pleasant in my dear native land – old faces and familiar voices are indeed cheering."[12] However, as long as Julia's sister remained in bondage, their happiness was incomplete.

The distraught family were partially rescued by a friend who stepped up negotiations and arranged a ninety-day grace period to come up with the money. A plan was made whereby a Dr. Thomas C. Worth of Wilmington, North Carolina, would act as the go-between, perhaps as an agent or perhaps as a humanitarian. Another man named George W. Davis would act as an agent for Maffitt. Precisely who Davis was and what role he played are unclear. The larger traders had networks of agents throughout the countryside, and like a pyramid scheme the man at the top would take his cut, so Davis may have been taking some sort of commission. Several people with the surname Davis had been among the major slave dealers in Virginia and a John Davis was an agent of the Washington slave trader John C. Cook.[13] The editor of Washington's anti-slavery newspaper the *National Era* was no fan of at least one of the Davis families; he displayed some of his own prejudices when he informed his readers that "the Davises, in Petersburg, are the great slave-dealers. They are Jews, who came to that place many years ago as poor peddlers; and, I am informed, are members of a family which has its representatives in Philadelphia, New York, etc.! These men are always in the market, giving the highest price for slaves. During the summer and fall they buy them up at low prices, trim, shave, wash them, fatten them so that they may look sleek, and sell them to great profit."[14]

In Diana's case there was no need to enhance her appearance for market; her long-separated sisters would love her unconditionally. Worth met with Diana's master in Norfolk, Virginia, on the first day of August 1856 and purchased her for seven hundred dollars. The two hundred dollars Crawford had raised had been added to five hundred dollars that was appropriated from the Weems ransom fund.[15] If Arabella had ever acquiesced to using the money for that purpose, she had not done so willingly or whole-heartedly. It appears harsh that she should have felt that way; after all, Julia Garnet had taken in her daughter Stella at a time when she herself was powerless to help. And the almost unbelievable sum of five thousand dollars had been raised in Britain on her family's behalf, with the Garnets playing a critical role in that unprecedented fundraising effort.[16] Arabella understood that others wanted their loved ones to be free, but her own family had to come first.

Maffitt set his seal and signature to "sell, assign and deliver unto the said T.C. Worth my negro woman Dinah, And I do hereby warrant the title to said Negro Woman against the claims of all persons whatsoever."[17] Five days later George W. Davis gave Worth a receipt for $714, which included principal and interest for the purchase. Perhaps this was done to disperse any cloud that hung over the question of legal ownership. On

August 14, 1856, Henry Garnet and James Crawford arrived in Lewis Tappan's New York office. They were accompanied by Dr. Worth "and a colored woman Diana late slave of J. N. Maffit, U.S.N. [United States Navy]. Diana is sister to Mrs. Garnet and Mrs. Crawford."[18]

The subsequent redemption of Diana's daughter Cornelia would be even more complex. Reverend Crawford took a leave from his ministerial duties and set aside his business so he could devote all of his time toward fundraising. Henry and Anna Richardson, along with other members of the Society of Friends in Newcastle-upon-Tyne and a Miss Hildich of Shrewsbury, spearheaded the drive. Andrew Somerville from Scotland also joined in the effort, just as he had previously done for the Weems family.

Finally, armed with the necessary funds, Reverend Crawford bravely ventured to South Carolina, where Cornelia was then held, to make the transaction. Despite his being free, it was still extremely dangerous for a person of colour to travel in the South. The son of a slave and her master, Crawford was of a skin colour that was fair enough that he could perhaps pass for white. He succeeded in purchasing his niece and, pretending to be her master (which technically he now was), they began their harrowing way north. In a well-conceived attempt to avoid questioning, Crawford announced, upon boarding a train, that the girl who accompanied him would not be allowed to sit in the first-class car. Rather, she was assigned to ride in the one reserved for baggage – and for blacks.

By February 28, 1858, life was as it should be, with Cornelia reunited with her mother, Crawford with his parishioners, and the extended family getting to know each other, some for the first time. The appreciative family published a heartfelt letter in the popular Boston anti-slavery newspaper *The Liberator* thanking the many people, particularly the Richardsons, who made the reunion possible.[19]

Across the ocean, Anna Richardson proudly followed the progress of Diana and Cornelia, publishing a small booklet addressed "to the Friends

*Cornelia Williams blossomed in freedom, eventually marrying a Civil War veteran.*
*Together they raised a large family of their own, as seen in this photograph from the*
*late 1880s.* (courtesy Stanford University)

of the Slave" and entitled *Anti-Slavery Memoranda*. Anna informed her
readers that Reverend Crawford was widowed shortly after freeing his
niece and sister-in-law and had soon thereafter married Diana. Anna
Richardson took great pleasure in periodically receiving a letter of gratitude from Cornelia, who was happily living in Nantucket with her
mother and doing well with her studies.[20]

In an ironic postscript to the story, by the time of Cornelia's redemption, John Maffitt had received a commission by the U.S. Navy to
capture "slavers" – ships that illegally continued to import Africans into
the Americas despite the prohibition on the trade by Britain, Portugal,
Spain, France, and the United States. Conditions in which these newly
enslaved people existed in the "Middle Passage" defied description.
Maffitt was quite successful at interfering with this barbaric practice,
capturing four slavers in a single year.[21] In the same year that Cornelia
was restored to her mother, Maffitt was singled out by then U.S.

*Slaves faced horrific conditions on the trip from Africa to North America known as the Middle Passage.* (Library of Congress image cph 3a42003)

President James Buchanan in his second annual Message to the Nation for capturing the slaver *Echo* near the coast of Cuba with 306 Africans on board. A U.S. government agent described the slaves' experience on board the *Echo* and the period immediately after they were liberated:

> They had been huddled together closer than cattle, and slept at night in as close contact as spoons when packed together. Privation of every kind, coupled with disease, had reduced all of them to the merest skeletons, and to such a state of desuetude and debility that on entering the fort they could not so much as step over a small beam, one foot high, in the doorway, but were compelled to sit on it and balance themselves over. It is impossible for you to imagine their sad and distressed condition. Even now, on board our ship,

after one month of kind treatment, good food, and pure air, they appear ghastly in the extreme . . . One hundred and forty-one died on the passage, eight died after the capture, 35 died at Charleston, and 57 have died on board our frigate.[22]

Lewis Tappan was quick to write in the *New York Evening Post* that he hoped this group would be returned to Africa.[23] Thanks to the work of Lieutenant Maffitt and his crew, the 271 survivors were ultimately returned to their home continent and deposited with the Colonization Society in Liberia, whose members promised to care for their physical needs for one year.[24]

# CHAPTER 9

AFTER THE LONG, DEMORALIZING period of over three years following the redemption of Catharine, Arabella, and the two youngest Weems boys, John Jr. and Sylvester, events were now suddenly colliding. Lewis Tappan and Jacob Bigelow were by now exchanging a flurry of letters about Adam and Joseph Weems, who they had learned were being held in Alabama by the slave trader John C. Cook. Arabella, Augustus, Sylvester, and John Jr. may also at one time have been a part of Cook's stock before Arabella and the two youngest boys were freed and Augustus was sold to another master.[1] Tappan had misjudged Bigelow's determination to free the boys and became acutely aware that they had perhaps acted prematurely in spending money from the Weems ransom fund to free Diana. The fund had now been significantly depleted. The abolitionists could only hope that at least one boy if not both could be freed – either by purchase or by "self emancipation."[2] To further complicate things, Sarah Tappan wrote a story about the Weems family and Ann Maria's audacious escape that was going to be published in the *Frederick Douglass Paper* the very same week.[3] Should Cook, who certainly had no love for Underground Railroad agents, be informed of the details of the transatlantic interest in the Weemses' case and of the fund, he might greatly inflate the boys' price, just as had happened with the other family members.

Learning of the possibility of redeeming her sons, Arabella was not willing to accept half-measures. She pleaded for further assistance in a letter to Tappan. Tappan was uncertain what to do; he had received countless similar requests and he admitted that "I have never been drawn sympathetically toward her."[4] Like some of his British comrades, when it came to the institution of slavery Tappan usually tried to focus on forests rather than trees. He wrote to a friend who knew Arabella and asked confidentially if she was "deserving of such repeated aid?" Even this most charitable of hearts in the abolitionist movement, who had given so much to the cause, still had a lot to learn. However, no matter what his inner conflict may have been, Tappan would never betray the mission entrusted to him by his British friends.

❦

John C. Cook maintained his principal residence in the District of Columbia and another one in the town of Eufaula in Barbour County, Alabama. He had been enticed to Alabama by the cheap and productive land that had become available in the state in 1837, when the secretary of war ordered that all of the Creek tribes be removed from the state after a series of lengthy skirmishes and wars. In addition to several large parcels of land in the townships, Cook purchased forty acres for the unbelievably inexpensive price of $79.75.[5] About nine miles outside of Eufaula, Cook also had a large plantation of 1,040 acres. Enough of the oak, hickory, dogwood, and short-leaf pine had been cleared from the heavily timbered land to provide full-time work for thirty slaves. The land was "new" and ideal for the cultivation of cotton and corn. It was a beautiful setting, with the Chewalla Creek winding its way through the property. There was a solid house, two logs thick, suitable for a planter or an overseer, as well as ten new log cabins for the slaves, with a well nearby, plus fourteen stables for the horses and mules, a new barn, a pea house, and a corn crib. The cotton gin was housed in its own log building.

Eufaula was situated on a high bluff overlooking the Chattahoochee River, which separates Alabama from Georgia. An early resident eloquently described the town:

> Oh, the beauty of the bluff scenery. The yellow jasmine and woodbine climbing the trees nod their fragrant greeting to the newcomers, and then scatter their bright crimson and gold cups on the honey suckles and pink laurel and poison ivy and the glad little violet tumbles and splashes over moss covered rocks below. Then the silvery glittering silent river with its green fringed banks and magnificent curve, and the boats at the wharf, lowland and plantation beyond and Georgetown in the distance. Even then before the addition of the railroad and bridges and handsome residences, it is strange any true artist should wander farther for one of nature's choicest pictures.[6]

Eufaula was an excellent place to base a company that dealt in slaves. By the 1850s, a covered bridge had joined the two neighbouring states, making commerce between them convenient. The river provided an important highway for shipping cotton, some of which eventually made its way to the manufacturers of Liverpool, England – despite the best efforts of people like Henry and Anna Richardson and Henry Garnet to discourage them from using cotton that was raised from slave labour. Hundreds of planters from Maryland, Virginia, the Carolinas, and Georgia moved to that vast area of the cotton belt, lured by the affordable land. To raise their crops, they needed thousands of slaves. Between 1840 and 1850 the number of slaves in the county had nearly doubled, from 5,548 to 10,780.[7] By the end of the next decade, there were 16,150 slaves in the county, owned by 1,143 masters.[8]

Businesses sprang up. Thomas Cargile, who had dealings with Cook, was an experienced cobbler and advertised that his "NEGRO SHOES are unsurpassed by any to be found in this market."[9] Dr. William Flake opened a "large and commodious" infirmary in the forest just outside of town. He assured the public that visiting him there would be less expensive than a house call by the physician who made trips to the various plantations scattered around the countryside. He promised to treat slaves for five dollars per week or fifteen dollars per month, but it would cost more for him to perform surgery or to care for "syphilictic cases."[10]

In the words of twentieth-century historian Eugenia Persons Smartt, "Eufaula was a place of plenty: her citizens hospitable, her officials faithful, her slaves contented and happy," but her analysis is rather flawed.[11] The town council imposed a fine of one dollar on every slaveholder who did not do his part to patrol the countryside for those runaway slaves who did not see themselves as contented and happy. These five-man patrols had to inspect every street and alley to ensure that all blacks were in their appointed places by the ten o'clock curfew. Violators were to be whipped, not exceeding thirty-nine lashes. Among his duties, the town marshal was responsible for whipping slaves who were either disorderly or profane. Any black who preached to or "exhorted" any slave without being licensed by a local body of white Christians was subjected to thirty-nine lashes for the first offence and fifty lashes for each repeated transgression. Slaves "of good character" who were given written permission by their masters to hire themselves out had to apply to the town council for a permit and pay a fee of five dollars. Additionally, slaves or free blacks were restricted from doing business unless they were under the responsibility of a "good white man."[12]

There was little tolerance in Eufaula for those who did not subscribe to the prevailing pro-slavery sentiment. At a meeting of the area's citizens in 1847, several resolutions were passed unanimously, stating that Congress had no power to pass any laws affecting the institution of slavery; that any new state could organize its own domestic institutions; that they would not vote for any candidate for president or vice-president who would not pledge to oppose all attempts to pass laws or make treaties "affecting injuriously in any way the institution of slavery"; and that no matter which political party they supported, there would be no division of opinion on this matter.[13]

Captain Elisha Betts, an open-minded Eufaula resident, steered too far away from the popular sentiment. He made the mistake of subscribing to the anti-slavery newspaper *National Era* and was impressed by its contents, despite not having abolitionist leanings and despite having been "born and raised (being now in the $62^{nd}$ year of my age) admidst slavery." It was his opinion that the institution of slavery "has a tendency to vitiate and demoralize those who own them, and to degrade those who do not." Betts also felt that it had negative effects on the free white population in the northern states, which apathetically turned a blind eye to slavery. No southern member of Congress who knew the truth about slavery would dare to raise his voice against it for fear of being labelled a traitor. Despite his misgivings, Betts was resigned to the reality that slavery was both the law and the custom of the land, and that it could not easily be removed.

When Betts' copy of the *National Era* arrived at Eufaula, the postmaster refused to deliver it. He took it upon himself to contact the newspaper's editor in the Washington office and inform him that he would not deliver that or any other "incendiary sheet." The paper was neither returned to Washington nor delivered to Betts, and the *Era*'s editor later reported that he suspected the postmaster had shown it around to others in the area. As a result, a large public meeting was held in Eufaula. The angry crowd turned into a mob and ordered the aging Captain Betts to leave his home. He had been a local hero for his gallantry in the Indian wars years before, but his status was instantly forgotten.

After fleeing, Betts was contacted by a friend who warned him that it would not be safe to return. Betts then sent a written appeal to the newspapers, protesting that he was against extremist views from either camp, and supported the compromises that had been made in Congress that were intended to bring southern and northern perspectives more in line.

The federal government reacted by dismissing the postmaster for refusing to do his duties. This action provoked another mass meeting, where unanimous resolutions were passed supporting the postmaster and refusing to accept any replacement. Eufaula's residents were not about to passively accept any decree from Washington that they did not agree with. They argued that Alabama had its own laws prohibiting the circulation of "incendiary papers" and that state law was paramount.[14]

Like other southern newspapers, such as those in Montgomery, Eufaula's *Spirit of the South* warned its readers against abolitionists. The August 5, 1851 edition carried an article reminding postmasters to be on the lookout for the anti-slavery paper *The Liberator*. The editors also watched the distant Canadian papers for news about runaways. With apparent glee, they carried an article on May 8, 1852, from Windsor's *Voice of Liberty*, about a Milly Banks who, along with her parents and two children, had successfully fled to Canada from Kentucky and was struggling. After arriving, Milly discovered that she could make only four dollars per month for doing "female labor" full-time. In Kentucky, she had been able to make that same amount by taking in washing at night.[15]

It was against Alabama state law to teach any slave or free black to read, write, or spell. The penalty was between 250 and five hundred dollars. Free blacks were not allowed to enter Alabama. If caught, they had thirty days to leave or were to receive thirty-nine lashes. If they did not leave after the lashings, they were to be sold at public auction. Anyone who assisted in the escape of a slave could be imprisoned for two to five years.[16]

In this pro-slavery setting, John C. Cook had a good thing going. Only minor conditions were attached to his type of business in Eufaula. On March 29, 1852, after dealing with a pressing social issue by passing a by-law "prohibiting the practice of bathing in the River in the daytime," the town council turned to more serious tasks and passed a tax on slave traders and speculators and created certain guidelines for that particular business. Despite these petty inconveniences, the demand for Cook's "product" was large and the collateral seemingly secure. In the event that a customer could not pay for "goods" bought on credit, slaves or land could be seized. When Cook sold a slave, he sometimes drew up a mortgage specifying terms of payment and registered it at the county courthouse.[17]

Cook was quick to take advantage of the opportunities that arose when local planters sold their land. When William De Witt sold his 1,370-acre farm to Alpheus Baker, the sale included fifty slaves. Baker apparently had no need for them and immediately – on that same day – sold the entire lot to Cook for $29,000. Coincidentally, only fifteen days previously, Cook had purchased 1,620 acres from the Bakers.[18] The world that those slaves knew would have come to a dramatic end that day. Their only hope of staying together was if the new owner wanted to keep them all. In the hands of a slave dealer they would certainly be separated.

The slave trade had brought Cook and his family great riches. The census of 1860 listed his occupation as "trader" and his assets as worth

*A slave cabin in Barbour County, near Eufaula, Alabama* (Library of Congress image mesnp 010000)

$55,000. His wife Cecilia was worth another $16,000. Incredibly, their five-year-old daughter, Florence, was listed as owning $10,000 in personal possessions. The family's total wealth amounted to $27,000 in real estate plus $54,000 in "personal property."[19] The latter no doubt mostly comprised their large holdings of human flesh. Cook was well known not only throughout Alabama but also in the District of Columbia and throughout Maryland. He was among the group of guards and deputies who had been rewarded by the government of Maryland for his role in capturing William Chaplin in 1850. As a close associate of Washington's Auxiliary Guard, whose job it was to patrol the streets at night looking for runaways, he saw little consequence in rounding up and imprisoning a few free blacks by mistake.

It is probably more than coincidence that others in the Auxiliary Guard also re-established themselves in Eufaula, likely maintaining a business connection to the slave trade. That was certainly the case of Hatch Cook, who directly followed in his older brother's footsteps.[20] William Smitha, another of the night watch who was involved in William Chaplin's capture, was also attracted to Eufaula, presumably as an agent of Cook's.[21] Smitha eventually went into the livery stable business, with Cook acting as guarantor to his loan to purchase the business.[22]

John Cook's partnership with Charles M. Price appeared to be a minor sideline to John and Hatch Cook's main slave-trading operation. The brothers, who conducted their business at various times under the names J.C. Cook & Co. and J.C. Cook & Brother, used a tavern in Eufaula's newly constructed Exchange building as their headquarters. Hatch had moved to Alabama to oversee the business, but John often travelled there as well. The Cook brothers opened for business by mid-September of 1851 and took out a notice in the *Spirit of the South* to advertise. They offered a free lunch every day and assured all gentlemen that they could "always find a choice assortment of wine liquors and cigars." They promised to add a new eating house by November where "oysters and the best of everything that the market affords will

be prepared at all hours and on the shortest notice." As a further entice-
ment they wrote, "It is the intention of the proprietor to keep a first rate
house, where gentlemen, either citizens or strangers, can at any time
pass a pleasant hour in the enjoyment of every luxury which the most
fastidious appetite could desire."[23] The advertisement does not make it
clear whether they were still speaking about food.

The business was an immediate hit. Complete with billiard table and
other amenities, the tavern became a favourite male gathering place.
After attending the grand opening, the local newspaper editor nearly
swooned with admiration and perhaps from the aftereffects of sampling
the refreshments:

> Cook's new establishment, we know not by what name it is called,
> but it ought to have a first rate one, for it can't be beat, was opened to
> the public with a free lunch on Saturday last and the number of those
> who 'smiled' approvingly through their glasses on the enterprising
> proprietor, on that interesting occasion was not small. It is a first
> class house, and would do credit to a town of larger pretensions than
> Eufaula. The proprietor is a clever fellow and understands his busi-
> ness. His stock of liquors and cigars is A No. 1. He has provided the
> most ample means of amusement for his visitors, and those who
> happen to have something of Falstaff's repugnance to their potations,
> will find a tall gentleman behind the bar, one Benjamin, by name,
> who will take pleasure in putting them through in the latest style and
> or the most approved principles.[24]

The Cook brothers were clever businessmen. They guaranteed that
their human wares were in a "sound and healthy condition." In at least
one case, they gave a one-year warranty, declaring that if the slaves that
they sold died or became "unsound" within the year, two arbiters would
be selected to decide upon proper financial recompense for the purchaser.[25] The brothers also regularly advertised in the *Spirit of the South*.

*This ad appeared regularly in the Eufaula newspaper* Spirit of the South *in the early months of 1852.* (Alabama Department of Archives and History)

The "well selected stock of Maryland" no doubt included Joseph and Adam (since renamed Addison by the Cook brothers) Weems. Perhaps, as was not uncommon, this was done to avoid Adam's being confused with someone else on the plantation. The likelihood of multiple slaves having the same name was high because John Cook bought and resold so many slaves.

By early 1855, the lustre had faded from the Cook brothers' partnership. The land boom had subsided. Much of the region's economic fervour earlier in the century had been based on credit, and debt had started to cripple many borrowers. The Cooks officially dissolved their business that year, and on February 20 they advertised that "all persons indebted to the late firm of J. C. Cook & Bro. will find their Notes and

Accounts in the hands of Cochran & Bullock for collection. Their immediate payments will save cost."[26] Not everyone could meet those terms, making the dissolution convoluted and prolonged. For example, the Cory and Barrington families were forced to sign over to Cook the rights to their lot and carriage warehouse if they could not meet the payment deadline. At that point Cook could sell their property and take one of their buggies, worth $150.[27]

By the end of the harvest season of 1855, John Cook had also decided to quit the farming business and had offered his land for sale. Perhaps one of the reasons he sold his land was that it did not measure up to the idyllic description that he had placed under the heading "Come Buy A Valuable Plantation" in the Eufaula newspaper: "To sum up all in a few words, it is a plantation that can't be beat in its productions, and in its many other advantages . . . It is useless to give more particulars, come and examine the Plantation and you will be satisfied to take hold if you want a good plantation."[28]

In fact, Cook had only acquired the land in February in a swap with another Barbour County resident, John Horry Dent.[29] The two men had frequently done business together. Dent periodically purchased slaves from Cook, who in turn purchased a piano from Dent.[30] The two also occasionally exchanged corn and fodder for the farm animals. When he initiated the land exchange in 1855, Dent confided to his diary that the land was inferior, the location remote, the buildings needed to be rebuilt and the fencing repaired. In all, he thought that the obstacles associated with getting the farm into a suitable state were not worth the cost or the effort. In addition, he wrote that it was not a healthy location, as it reminded him of another farm he had owned where he had lost twenty-five slaves to sickness over five years.[31] Whatever the true condition of the farm, when it was Cook's turn to sell he offered flexible terms to prospective buyers; he would be willing to divide the land into smaller parcels "to suit the purchaser." If desired, he would include "the corn, fodder, Plantation tools, cattle and hogs, horses and mules."

Furthermore, "the Negroes will also be sold, if desired." Inquiries could be made directly to Cook at his residence or business in Eufaula.[32]

The Cook brothers also decided to give up their tavern. The unlucky buyer, Samuel Burnett, fell behind on his payments and was forced to turn over "all the stock of Wines and Liquors and Segars of every description now on hand at the establishment known as *The Exchange*." Cook and Hatch reserved the right to take any of the tavern's stock at any time until the bill was paid.[33] In another agreement made the same day, Burnett and his partner, James Lucker, were forced to use additional items as collateral, including a billiard table, various glassware, "and many other items too numerous to mention." However, mentioned by name were the twenty-two-year-old slave Sophia and her three children, five-year-old Henry, three-year-old Ellen, and the infant Elizabeth.[34]

Along with the sale of his other properties, John Cook expressed a willingness to sell Addison and Joseph to the abolitionists, but demanded that the entire purchase price of $1,700 be paid in advance. In August 1856, Tappan sent the money to Jacob Bigelow, but negotiations fell through and it was returned to him on September 11.[35] It is difficult to determine what the problem was, but Cook was doing other strange things at the time.

In a document dated January 3, 1856, but not recorded at the Barbour County Courthouse until July 8, 1856, Cook played the part of a doting father: "In consideration of the natural love and affection which I entertain for my two daughters Mary D. Cook and Florence Cook have Given Granted bargained and conveyed . . . the following negro slaves . . . to have and to Hold all Said Slaves to the said Mary D. Cook and Florence Cook and their heirs forever to their own sale and separate use and behoof free from the debts liability or control of their future husbands." Further, when either daughter married or reached the age of twenty-one, the slaves were to be divided equally between them. All twelve of the slaves were children: Emanuel, Pompey, Russell, Dick, Susan, Lou, Sophia, Adeline, Marion, and Charlotte were all seven years old; Joe was three; and the oldest was a nine-year-old named Joseph. An odd caveat to the transaction was that John C. Cook reserved the right to take back Joseph at any time and "substitute another slave of equal value in his place."[36]

Although the age attributed to Joseph is off by one year, the timing plus the curious caveat leads one to speculate that this could have been Joseph Weems. (At fifteen Addison would have been too old to be on the gift list.) Could Cook have been attempting some legal manoeuvring to avoid sending the boy to Tappan and his supporters while still creating a loophole so he could regain ownership of Joseph if necessary? This may help to explain why Bigelow's first attempt to purchase the boys had failed. Perhaps Cook used the same tactic as had the financially troubled Henry and Catharine Harding some years earlier when they turned property over to their son Charles so that creditors could not seize their assets. Something was certainly amiss. The fact that at the time of the transaction Florence Cook had just celebrated her first birthday added to the absurdity of the situation.

In another attempt to buy the boys' freedom, Tappan wondered if Cook would agree to deliver them to his agent in Alabama, along with a bill of sale. As part of the deal the slave trader would be expected to deduct the expenses of bringing them to Washington. Tappan also advised Bigelow that "we must take care in making further negotiations not to injure our claim already made."[37] Dealing with Alabama slave owners had been painful for Tappan in the past. He could not forget the occasion, many years earlier, when he had received a slave's severed ear in the mail. It had been sent by a Montgomery, Alabama slave owner who had expressed his hatred for the northern abolitionist with the sarcastic message to place "the specimen of a negro's ears" in his "collection."[38]

The demands of Tappan's humanitarian work were great, and dealing with the emotional roller coaster associated with freeing the Weems boys only added to the sixty-nine-year-old's load. Following the disappointment of his failed dealings with Cook, Tappan and his wife drew up their last will and testament "after having sought Divine direction in the matter" and made a trip to Niagara Falls to revitalize themselves.[39] Sarah and Lewis, both previously widowed, had been married only two years, and his busy schedule had not allowed for a proper honeymoon. At the Falls, they acted the part of typical tourists. They began with a trip on the little steamboat called the *Maid of the Mist* and marvelled at the view. They took a carriage ride over the suspension bridge onto the Canadian side and "called on the Curiosity Shop, the menagerie, museum, etc. Saw two Buffaloes, two wolves, etc."

A deeply religious couple, they travelled the next day to the "colored" British Methodist Episcopal Church, which was central in the lives of hundreds of fugitive slaves and many generations of their descendants. The chapel was part of a larger conference in Canada West that had recently changed its name from African Methodist Episcopal to British Methodist Episcopal, in tribute to the nation that had granted them their freedom and guaranteed their rights. After some trouble locating the building, the Tappans finally found it but were disappointed to find that the congregation was not there. They contented themselves by travelling throughout the area, hoping that Lewis might recognize some things he had seen when he had visited as a young man in 1815.

Much had changed over the forty-one intervening years and signs of the great battle of Lundy's Lane in the War of 1812 were no longer evident. Tappan was nearly overcome "by the sublime views that are before us [that] are a sermon & an anthem more impressive than any discourse or hymn from human lips. We hear continually the 'voice of many waters' and our thoughts ascend to Him who created, upholds & blesses us – all creatures – and the magnificent scenery that greets our eyes."[40] Thus inspired, Tappan returned to his calling, including his dealings with Cook, with renewed vigour.

Cook's reputation among the abolitionists was already darkly stained by virtue of his occupation and his unscrupulous character. It was widely known that a couple of years before, the marshal of the District of Columbia had been ordered to arrest Cook and a fellow slave dealer, Benjamin O. Sheckells, for trespassing and stealing "one negro slave named Amstead of great value." Repeated requests to produce the slave were ignored and presumably he was sold south.[41] Cook became even more despised by Tappan with the breakdown of negotiations for the redemption of Addison and Joseph.[42] He did nothing to elevate his trustworthiness by offering to have the infamous William H. Birch act as his guarantor for the transaction. Tappan would not consider accepting the security of Cook, Birch, or any of their ilk.[43]

Cook promised to deliver the boys to his private slave prison in Washington within several weeks. Tappan refused to take any chances

The arrest warrant for slave traders John Cook and Benjamin Sheckells for unlawfully possessing another man's property, in this case a slave named Amstead (RG21, Entry 6, D.C. Circuit Court, Box 865, NARA)

with the slaveholder's pledge and in October of 1856 engaged the services of trusted attorneys Radcliffe & Kennedy, who years earlier had attempted to secure William Chaplin's freedom, to investigate whether Cook's property could be seized should he fail to release the brothers. Tappan also made sure the lawyers asked whether Cook used any agent whose property could be seized. Also, "if the money should be paid to Cook in Washington & a bill of sale delivered would there be any risk in John Weems or some friend of his going to Alabama & bringing the young men to Washington?"[44] Tappan advised his attorneys to employ a "first rate lawyer" near Cook's residence in Alabama to warn the slave trader that a law suit would be launched against him if he defaulted on the agreement. Tappan proposed to deposit the money in a bank or with a "responsible person known to be such by both parties, to be paid on the delivery of the boys in Washington & free papers." Experience had taught him to have no faith in Cook's promises or in those of any of his friends.[45]

It is quite possible that Tappan had some inside information on Cook's financial situation. As a merchant, Tappan had long been wary of extending credit and began to keep extensive files on people to evaluate their credit-worthiness. By using his extensive connections with the nation's abolitionists, he developed a network of contacts (including a young Illinois lawyer named Abraham Lincoln) who could offer credit information and character assessments on people from across the country.[46] By 1841 Tappan had developed America's first commercial credit-rating business, known as the Mercantile Agency. Ten years later, the agency had two thousand full-time employees. Still today, it remains the world's largest credit-reporting agency, operating under the name of Dun and Bradstreet.

John Cook was indeed deeply in debt. He and his wife, Cecilia, approached Justice of the Peace John H. Goddard, an old friend and former head of the Auxiliary Guard, to draw up papers to authorize Hatch Cook and a man named John Colby to sell all of the couple's

Alabama properties. Hatch could more easily handle the sales because he had put down permanent roots in the Deep South after his marriage to Elizabeth Brown on December 15, 1853.[47] In an attempt to satisfy the "divers and sundry persons" to whom John Cook owed "divers and sundry amounts," Goddard and another justice of the peace took Cecilia aside and questioned whether she fully understood the proceedings and willingly went along with her husband's decision.[48] Satisfied that she was freely giving her consent, they signed and sealed the document on December 29, 1856. Five days later the document was recorded at the Barbour County Courthouse and the process to liquidate all of John Cook's Alabama assets began.

Tappan felt a special obligation to the fundraisers to take as little risk as humanly possible and sought their counsel on his proposed actions. They were willing to do whatever they could to garner publicity that would help restore Addison and Joseph to their parents.[49] Despite the passage of four years since the fundraising for the Weems family had first begun, they were still very much on the minds of the British. Anti-slavery societies sent clothing to the United States to be sold at fundraising bazaars and made special mention of certain items being earmarked for the beleaguered Weems family.[50]

However, Cook would budge little with his terms. He demanded that a bond be posted to ensure that he would receive his money. Tappan worked feverishly to arrange it, along with Ezra Lincoln Stevens, who was a lawyer; former editor of the *True Democrat*, a Cleveland newspaper with anti-slavery leanings; former Oberlin collegemate of Sylvanus Boynton; as well as an associate of Jacob Bigelow in the Washington branch of the Underground Railroad.[51] Tappan asked Gamaliel Bailey, who was the editor of the *National Era* and who was financially indebted to him, to post the bond. Bailey agreed and planned on giving the bond certificate to John Weems. Tappan was alarmed at the suggestion and demanded that he receive it to ensure that all of the transactions be conducted in the most fiscally responsible and businesslike manner, again making reference to his obligations to the British fundraisers. Feeling that the passage of time was against them, he admonished his colleagues to act in haste and quickly make whatever arrangements were necessary.[52]

While the Cooks were selling their southern properties, Ezra Stevens and Major Benjamin B. French, a D.C. businessman who had founded the Washington Gas Light Company along with Jacob Bigelow and others, stepped forward to guarantee that the money would be returned to the Weems ransom fund should Cook default on his promise.[53] Their humanitarian gesture, taken at great personal risk, turned out to be unnecessary. Lawyers Radcliffe and Kennedy advised Cook to honour his previous commitment.[54] As 1856 drew to a close, Tappan once again authorized the payment of $1,700 and, with consideration for Joseph and Addison's comfort, asked that the boys be furnished with warm clothing as they made their way from Alabama to the winter climes of Washington. He also beseeched Stevens to send him a full account of the boys' journey and their arrival in the capital.[55]

Like their mother, their sister Catharine, and their two youngest brothers, John and Sylvester, Addison and Joseph had been purchased with funds raised primarily by British supporters. They arrived safely in Washington on February 4, to the delight of all involved. Tappan immediately shared the news with Anna Richardson in England.[56] He also urged Stevens to consult with Jacob Bigelow and quickly register the boys' emancipation. When he did not get an immediate reply, an impatient Tappan wrote again.[57] He wanted to ensure that there would be no legal loose ends, no potentially tragic oversights.[58]

On February 9, 1857, John Weems, who was now the legal "owner" of his two newly redeemed sons, had their manumission papers drawn up before a justice of the peace in Washington. The reason given for their freedom – "from motives of benevolence and humanity" – hardly needed to be expressed.[59] Addison was now sixteen, Joseph only twelve.[60] The papers read:

Know all men by these presents That I, John Weems of the City of
Washington in the District of Columbia from motives of benevolence
and humanity have manumitted and hereby do manumit and set free
from Slavery my two boys Addison Weems aged sixteen years and
Joseph Weems aged twelve year.

In testimony where of I have here unto set my hand and affixed my
seal this ninth day of February in the year of our Lord one thousand
Eight hundred and Fifty-seven.

His˙

*John X Weems*

mark

Signed Sealed and
Delivered in presence of
Samuel Grubb
John S. Hollingshead[61]

John and Arabella had one more child still in slavery. Augustus,
whose youth was snatched away from him, had suffered more than any
twenty-two-year-old should have to experience. After nearly five years
of being separated from his family, he must have been tempted to
abandon hope many times. But somehow he had managed to get word
to his father as to his whereabouts. His owner had agreed to sell him for
exactly what he had paid – $1,100.[62] The Washington and New York
Underground Railroad prepared for another passenger.

Tappan hoped that the newly emancipated Addison and Joseph
would immediately enter into trades and help raise enough money to
free their brother. The reunited family could then purchase a piece of
land in a free state or in Canada, where Arabella had travelled in that
spring to visit her family and friends, including Ann Maria, who

*The manumission document John Weems signed registering the freedom of his sons Joseph and Addison*

had recently written to Tappan and reported that she was doing well. Nevertheless, Tappan worried for the Weemses' future and hoped that in their innocence they would stay clear of any dishonest men.[63]

John Weems already had some land and was good at farming. But he wanted to move away from a slave community to a place where he could gather all of his children around him and they could receive a good education and prosper. Perhaps that dream would reach fruition, if only Augustus could be redeemed.[64]

CHAPTER 10

FORTY-TWO-YEAR-OLD Dr. James David Rumph owned a large plantation in the Eufaula area whose crops were watered by the sweat of
fifty-one bondsmen – including that of Augustus Weems.[1] He also
had property in other parts of Alabama, including in the town of
Union Springs in Macon County and in neighbouring Pike County,
where he had another seventy-three slaves at work.[2]

The doctor's wife of sixteen years, Caroline Margaret, died on
August 25, 1856, just months before the effort to free Augustus began.
She was only thirty-six, and left several young children. The widower
returned his loved one to the home of her youth, the Orangeburg
District of South Carolina, where the two had been born and joined in
marriage.[3] Of Swiss and German heritage, James and Caroline came
from the same prominent family, as they were first cousins. Caroline
was laid to rest in the Rumph family cemetery on their grandfather's
farm, about one hundred yards from his old homestead.[4]

For the first years of their marriage, the couple had continued to live
in South Carolina, where James, who had graduated from the medical
college at Charleston, had a successful medical practice as well as a farm
and twenty-two slaves.[5] Several of their ancestors were large planters.[6]
Their grandfather Rumph, on whose land the cemetery was established,
was a Revolutionary War hero who had achieved the rank of colonel.

His home was a frequent gathering spot for members of the state legislature. Most of the family were active in political and social affairs, and the doctor continued that tradition.

In the autumn of 1848 Dr. Rumph had been a member of a committee of twenty-five who met at the Orangeburg District Courthouse to express their anger at the northern states, which they felt were interfering with their rights to own slaves and to carry them into other parts of the country. Much of their outrage was directed at the anti-slavery advocates, but Rumph and his peers realized that public sentiment was gradually changing against them. In their report they wrote:

> The agitation of the subject of slavery commenced in the fanatical murmurings of a few scattered abolitionists, to whom it was a long time confined; but now it has swelled into a torrent of popular opinion at the North; it has invaded the fireside and the church, the press and the halls of legislation; it has seized upon the deliberations of Congress, and at this moment is sapping the foundations, and about to overthrow the fairest political structure that the ingenuity of man has ever devised.[7]

This expression of resentment would be a harbinger of things to come when thirteen years later South Carolina became the first to secede from the Union. The committee resolved that while they agreed (reluctantly) to the terms of the Missouri Compromise, which established a boundary between the slaveholding and the free states, they would not submit to any further restrictions of their rights on the matter. Protesting the unbearable slights that they suffered, they resolved with righteous indignation, "That the continued agitation of the question of slavery, by the people of the non-slaveholding States, by their legislatures, and by their representatives in Congress, exhibits not only a want of national courtesy, which should always exist between kindred States, but is a palpable violation of good faith towards the slaveholding

States, who adopted the present Constitution 'in order to form a more perfect union.'"[8]

Despite Rumph's distrust of and alienation from the national government, he was paid for his having provided medical care to U.S. soldiers several years earlier in the Florida Seminole War, thanks to an act passed by Congress. An acquaintance said he was "always a staunch democrat, an ardent Methodist, and was universally recognized as a man of erudition and as a genial gentleman."[9] Carrying these sentiments with him, Dr. Rumph and his family pulled up roots in 1854 and moved into the more westerly slave state of Alabama, near Mount Andrew in Barbour County. Like John C. Cook, he acquired large tracts of land there; in fact, the two had farms within the same lot.[10]

Rumph kept a journal to record his medical treatments and the activities on his farm. He wrote that in his first year in Alabama he had only ten "hands," his preferred term for slaves. When his family arrived on November 22, his overseer and slaves were already concluding the year's harvest. They had produced twenty bales of cotton and one thousand bushels of corn. The next year was busy, with two more "hands" joining in to help cultivate and plant an additional eighty-five acres. Three acres of potatoes and a small crop of rice were added to the staples of corn and cotton. When not busy in the fields there was fencing to repair, a negro house and chimney to build, and a well to be dug. By the next season, even more land was put into use. Despite a dry spell that retarded the growth of the plants, the cotton harvest yielded fifty bales.

Rumph also carefully recorded the month and year, but not the date, of the birth of all of his newborn slaves. He listed the mother's name, but not the father's. Little regard was given to slave unions, and the law dictated that children assumed the status of the mother. There are also some notes about more personal issues. When the "patriarchal dog, Diamond, breathed his last between the hours of four and five p.m.," the obviously emotional owner entered the details. The faithful pet died at the age of sixteen years, three months and nine days.[11]

Like most large land owners, the doctor had to rely on an overseer to run the day-to-day operations on the farm. It was a constant headache for many to find a satisfactory candidate for the job who was motivated and trustworthy, and who could get the most out of the workers. In his first four years in Alabama, Rumph had four different overseers. In an attempt to clearly lay out his expectations, he crafted a job description:

Rules for Overseers

1st   To make and mind plow stocks & assist about the Gin works & see it is kept in Order.

2nd   Weigh all the cotton and assist in packing.

3rd   To go regularly around the plantation & see that no stock gets in the fields & put up any fence that may be accidentally down.

4th   Pay special attention to feeding all the stock and count them regularly, night & morning.

5th   The hands to be put to work early in the morning and the work well attended to.

6th   To attend to allowancing of the negroes.

7th   Not to leave the premises only on business of the employer, or such as may be required by law unless by permission of the employer.

8th   To sell & trade by direction of employer.

9th   In feeding, see that everything is well fed, but no food wasted.

10th   The whole concern to be regarded by the overseer as his own farm for the time being.

11th   Sobriety strictly enforced.

12th   The negroes to be managed strictly but not cruelly.[12]

The rules on the Rumph farm were not so different from those Augustus had learned in Maryland. But everything else in Alabama was foreign and intimidating. Robbed of all his loved ones, he was very much alone.

❧

Arabella was determined to get her son away from the clutches of any overseer. She knew that there had been enough money raised to buy Augustus, but felt betrayed when five hundred dollars was given to purchase Diana Williams, Reverend Henry Garnet's sister-in-law.[13] That expenditure had left only $781.58 in the fund and Dr. Rumph demanded $1,100 for Augustus.[14]

No doubt still grieving for Stella and perhaps envious that Julia Garnet was there to comfort her daughter when she could not be, Arabella's long-held frustrations began to surface. She, along with John and Catharine, asserted in a private conversation with Mrs. Tappan that several years ago John had given Jacob Bigelow – one of their most courageous and ardent longtime supporters – $130 of his own money, which should have gone toward the purchase of Augustus.[15] When word of this reached Lewis Tappan and Ezra Stevens, Tappan immediately wrote to Bigelow in his no-nonsense style and demanded answers.

Bigelow defended himself by stating that "some years ago J.W. put into my hands a piece of money (the amount I have since forgotten) but a large amount I know was utterly worthless & was returned to him."[16] The silver and gold pieces were fine but some of the paper money was of no value. During the nineteenth century some banks issued paper notes but lacked the gold reserves to support the notes, and notes from one bank could not always be exchanged for coins in another. The value of the notes varied from bank to bank, and occasionally they were totally worthless. Bigelow went on to state that the money had immediately gone toward the purchase of other family members – there had been so many that he could not recall who they were.

Tappan admonished Bigelow as if he were an errant schoolboy:

It is rather a loose way of proceeding, is it not? – to receive "a piece of money" without keeping a means of the amount; returning part, and keeping an account of that; applying a portion to the purchase of some of the family, and not retaining a minute of the same or being able now to state how much? If our English friends know that any of us received & paid money, for a charitable object, in that way, should be [illegible] their confidence! I hope you will be able to make an account for the satisfaction of all parties.[17]

Bigelow was naturally offended by both the accusation and its tone. How could he who had given his heart to this family be called into question? He replied to Tappan the same day, expressing his hurt feelings. Tappan, portraying himself as caught in the middle, and no doubt feeling that he had gone too far, weakly explained that "I have no controversy with you, my old friend."[18] He thought that when John Weems returned from Canada where the family was temporarily taking solace, presumably with the Bradleys, at the Dawn Settlement, they could amiably sort the whole business out to the satisfaction of the Weems family and their friend Ezra Stevens. In a language that he probably should have used in his earlier letter, Tappan concluded: "Your labours for this family have been great & you will have the satisfaction at last of seeing them all enjoying & having liberty."

As for Henry Garnet, who was now minister at Shiloh Church in New York City, Tappan felt that he had undoubtedly already done his part. Garnet had been instrumental in raising much of the money for the Weems ransom fund, and Tappan felt certain that some of the money raised in England deserved to be spent to purchase Garnet's sister-in-law. The Garnet family also were poor and suffering, and Tappan thought that they could not do much to assist Arabella in raising money in New York, whereas John Weems and his sons should surely be able to raise the relatively small amount that was necessary to buy Augustus in a short period of time.[19] Having been let down on many occasions after having loaned money to blacks who did not live up to their promises to repay, Tappan was coming to espouse the biblical passage that "God helps those who help themselves."[20]

Lewis Tappan suggested, given the shortage of money, that Augustus attempt to escape. Tappan kept "a little fund on hand for fugitives" and was prepared to use it to assist in Augustus's flight.[21] He distinguished between money reserved for escape or for purchase and did not mix the two. But it would be decidedly more difficult for Augustus to escape from the depths of Alabama than it had been for his younger sister, Ann Maria, who had been held in the border state of Maryland. Tappan had clipped a newspaper article from Montgomery, Alabama, that graphically spoke of the challenges involved in attempting an escape and placed it into one of his scrapbooks. This article had originally been on a placard that was posted outside the Montgomery County Courthouse:

Notice – The undersigned would respectfully inform the citizens of Montgomery and surrounding country that he is stationed one mile from the Court House, on the South Plank Road, with the well known Pack of Negro Dogs formerly owned by G. W. Edwards and will attend to all calls that he may be favoured with. Terms of hunting will be reasonable For Ketching. Ten Dollars if in or near the city and charges in proportion to distance and trouble.

N.B. – All persons forbidden to strik a Negro with a stick or any weapon while in my charge unless he mislist, and then with caution unless there is danger of damage being done. Information by any person of Negros lying about their primesis will be attended to without charge if they are not their own.

A.V. Worthy[22]

The effectiveness of the slave hunters was vividly illustrated in the diary of a prominent planter who went to see the master of an escaped slave near Dr. Rumph's and John C. Cook's plantations: "Mr Varner was in no business mood, having the evening before had a valuable Negro man killed by Daniel Stanley his overseer and John Lewis who was running him with hounds. The Negro was badly beaten and Stabbed in several places by Stanley."[23]

It became clear that purchasing Augustus was the only prudent option. Ezra Stevens, by now intimately and emotionally involved in the long saga, pledged one hundred dollars of his own money. Tappan himself pledged an additional forty, leaving $178.42 lacking.[24] Showing her fiery maternal instincts, Arabella left the rest of her family in Canada and returned to the United States to somehow raise the remainder.

Arabella had shared her gift of freedom unselfishly and had spent the past few years working with Jacob Bigelow and other members of the Washington Underground Railroad to help others find freedom, which earned her admiration of fellow workers. A gushing Ezra Stevens wrote: "If there is a person in the world, that deserves the hearty co-operation of every friend of humanity, that person is Arrah Weems . . . Never have I had my sympathies so aroused in behalf of any object as in behalf of this most worthy family."[25]

Even as Arabella was preoccupied with saving one of her children, she proved herself worthy of Stevens's praise, by taking in the baby of a fugitive woman. Emeline Chapman had been her name when she had escaped from Washington, D.C., on August 30, 1856. According to the runaway slave advertisement published in the September 23 edition of the *Baltimore Sun*, Emeline's mistress, Mrs. Emily Thompson, and her husband, Robert, offered a three-hundred-dollar reward for the twenty-five-year-old, who was "quite dark, slender built, speaks short; and stammers some." After Emeline was threatened with being sold on the auction block, she had fled with her two children: a crippled two-and-a-half-year-old daughter, Margaret Ann, and a seven- or eight-month-old son, named John Henry after her husband.[26] In a cruel twist of fate, her husband was sold to the Deep South, his master fearing that he would try to join his family.[27]

The wording of the reward advertisement suggests that the children had gone with their mother. Indeed that was the case in the initial escape;

**$100** REWARD.—RAN AWAY from the sub-
scriber on Saturday, the 30th of August,
1856, a NEGRO WOMAN named EMELINE
CHAPMAN, aged about 26 years; 5 feet 4 inches high;
rather slender; quite dark-colored; speaks quick and
short when spoken to and stammers some; with TWO
CHILDREN—the eldest a female, about 2 years and
4 months old, the same color of the mother; the other a
male, about 6 or 7 months old, quite bright colored. I
will give the above reward if taken outside the District of Columbia, or $50 if taken within he limits of
the District—in either case; to be secured in jail or
brought home to me, so that I get them again.

MRS. EMILY THOMPSON,
86-3t,                    Capitol Hill, Washington, D. C.

*The runaway slave ad for Emeline Chapman, whose baby, Willie, Arabella Weems
transported to her (Baltimore Sun, September 6, 1856, courtesy of Maryland State
Archives' "Beneath the Underground")*

however, circumstances forced Emeline to leave both children behind in
the care of blacks who could conceal them. When she reached the office
of the Vigilance Committee, William Still unofficially christened the
"genteel, tall, slender, dark complected" woman with the new name of
Susan Bell.[28] She travelled the Underground Railroad as far as Syracuse,
New York, but would go no farther without her children. The agent there,
Reverend Jarmain W. Loguen, wrote to William Still on her behalf on
October 5, 1856, imploring him to contact Jacob Bigelow in Washington
to see if he knew anything of her family. Fate in this case was simultane-
ously cruel and kind: Arabella Weems would travel from Washington to
Philadelphia on July 13, 1857, to raise money for Augustus, and to deliver
baby John Henry Chapman – known by the Underground Railroad code
name "Willie" – to the Vigilance Committee there.[29]

Arabella had long been aware of the tragedy that had befallen Susan
Bell, and the two may even have been related. Susan Bell had escaped
nearly a year before Arabella went to Philadelphia, and she feared that
both of her children were dead; she had heard a rumour that John Henry
was no longer alive. But both children had been hidden away by

unknown black friends for those many months.[30] Arabella collected the baby but left the older girl behind in Washington; taking both at the same time might have aroused suspicion. Washington Underground Railroad conductor Ezra L. Stevens later suggested to William Still that Arabella or someone else return to Washington to retrieve Margaret and take her to Philadelphia as well. From there the child would be sent to New York and then on to Syracuse.

Arrabella arrived from Philadelphia at Tappan's home in New York at noon on July 15, 1857, with her charge. Tappan remarked that she was very attentive to the child and gave all of her time to him, day and night, for nearly a week, forcing her to neglect her own personal affairs. The original plan, devised by William Still and Ezra Stevens, was that she leave the child in the care of a Mrs. Babcock and that Reverend Loguen would come immediately and take the child on to Syracuse. However, the planning was poorly executed and Mrs. Babcock knew nothing of the arrangement. Faced with this dilemma, Arabella was forced to keep the child in her care. The Tappans graciously allowed them to stay in their home, but a disturbed Lewis fired off letters to both Stevens and Still, berating them for handling the affair so badly – for not making proper arrangements to relieve Arabella of this duty, for not arranging for the older child to also come north, and for the unnecessary delay in reuniting both children with their mother. However, Tappan's anger was softened when he admitted to being quite taken with the "the beautiful boy of 15 months old."[31]

Tappan and Stevens laid out a plan for Arabella – now with Willie in tow – to collect the money for Augustus's freedom. She would carry a subscription booklet while she was travelling to record the names of those who promised to donate toward freeing her son. Tappan and Stevens advised her to go to Syracuse, where Loguen would lend assistance. From there she should travel to Rochester and meet with Frederick Douglass, who was well acquainted with the case. After exhausting her efforts in western New York, she was advised to return to New York City, then to see William Still in Philadelphia, and finally to return home to Washington. Tappan calculated that at best it would take at least two weeks for Arabella to raise the funds. At worst, she would be unsuccessful because it was especially difficult to raise money during the summer season when many philanthropists were out of town. He was also perplexed at why Arabella's own family and other relatives in Canada could not come up with the amount, when it appeared to him that they were perfectly capable of doing so. He deemed that it would be convenient for her to approach them when she was in Syracuse, as there she would be close to Canada.[32]

Arabella did not feel that her family could help financially, so she turned to other proven friends. Reverend Amos Freeman, who had accompanied her daughter Ann Maria to Canada, again jumped in to help and spent a considerable amount of time appealing for aid. He was somewhat disappointed in being able to raise only sixty-eight dollars in New York City, blaming the small amount on the fact that many sympathizers were away from home.[33] Feeling that her supporters had accomplished all that they could, Arabella, along with Willie, boarded the express train for Syracuse on the morning of July 25. She arrived safely, although she was very frustrated at losing the subscription book that contained the names of those who had pledged money. Her hurried letter to Tappan upon her arrival in Syracuse shared that disappointing news along with details of Susan Bell's elation at being reunited with her youngest child.[34]

Clearly displaying his affection for the child, Tappan fired off a reply requesting that Arabella have two copies of a daguerreotype of Willie taken at his own expense, as a remembrance.[35] Tappan also joyfully shared details with his British friends in the anti-slavery cause, writing of Arabella that "'feeling for those in bonds as bound with them,' she determined, while in quest of means for the liberation of the last of her own children, to run the hazard of liberating another woman's child. Without consulting any one, therefore, she took this baby & brought him off, and after 534 miles travelling had the joy of restoring him to his mother."[36] Tappan included an admonition in the letter to keep the details secret, as Arabella would suffer repercussions under strict laws against helping a slave of any age escape if her heroism became publicly known.

Two months later, Tappan broke his own code of silence after receiving ten British pounds from Julia Griffith, who was active in organizing fifteen ladies' anti-slavery societies in England, Scotland, and Ireland. He proudly shared the story of Willie and the child's mother and sister and hoped that perhaps the money could be used to return young Margaret to her mother.[37] Tappan also wrote to Reverend Loguen as 1857 drew to a close, enclosing a one-dollar bill and thirty-two cents' worth of stamps that a lady had sent to him for Willie.[38]

Despite all of the joy of her reunion with her son, Susan Bell's heartache would continue for another year, until July 10, 1858 when Ezra Stevens could make final arrangements in Washington to send "ten packages," including one belonging to Susan Bell.

Continuing now alone, Arabella's fundraising was challenging and disappointing. Few contributed and Tappan believed that some who had subscribed to donate would never pay. Unlike Gerrit Smith, who had pledged to pay one-third of the expenses up to one thousand dollars, not everyone could be relied upon to deliver on their promises.[39] While all of this was going on, plans were made for Ezra Stevens to prepare to leave for Alabama to retrieve Augustus as soon as the money was collected.[40] On August 3, 1857, Smith's initial cheque for two hundred dollars arrived at Tappan's office right on cue.[41] Unfortunately Ezra Stevens, who had been so passionately involved to this point, was unable for some reason to use those funds himself to travel to Alabama to attempt to negotiate a lower price.[42]

*

Plantation owner Dr. James David Rumph was preoccupied that summer, having travelled to Knoxville, Tennessee, to attend a convention for southerners that began on August 10. One of the representatives from Alabama, he was among a delegation that numbered around one thousand men. The delegates listened to arguments that included proposals to deny the northern anti-slavery press access to the convention and to restore the African transatlantic slave trade to bolster the southern workforce. A representative from Mississippi voiced chilling words that no doubt resounded in the minds of many: "In the opinion of this Convention slavery is neither a moral, social, nor political evil, and therefore is not a proper subject of prohibition by legislation." He continued: "That we recognize, in the domestic institutions of the South, that form of Government best adapted to the African race, most conducive to the permanency of our republican institutions, and the great commercial interests of the world, and that as such it is the duty of the Christian and the patriot to improve and sustain them."[43] The delegates expressed diverse opinions on several issues, and discussions were sometimes heated. It was clear (in retrospect if not then) that the North and the South were on a collision course and the bonds that maintained the Union were being stretched to the breaking point.

On a more personal level, Dr. Rumph's slaves who were then working under the direction of the latest overseer, G. W. Kelly, faced recurring challenges resulting from adverse weather. They had cleared an additional twenty-five acres of forest and had begun planting corn in early March and cotton in early April. But the temperatures repeatedly and dramatically turned against them, freezing the tender corn shoots on three different occasions. The peaches in the orchard were killed by the frost and ice. When not frozen, the land remained wet and cold, threatening the farm's mainstay crop and causing Dr. Rumph to enter in his journal the words "no stand of cotton." Prospects for making money that year looked bleak, and without a crop to tend to Rumph would not need as many hands. He might have to turn to another source to make up the shortfall: the sale of his surplus slaves.

Dr. Rumph had recently inherited additional slaves following his father's death on December 13, 1856. In his will, John Rumph had specifically bequeathed to his son "a negro fellow named Ishama, son of Tena." An additional twenty-five slaves were to be divided among Dr. Rumph and his six siblings, "share & share alike." A particularly bittersweet clause included a stipulation that "it is my will and desire that my negroes Adam, Moses, Taft, Richard & Eva be sold at public outcry by my Executor and Executrix and after ample provision shall be made from the proceeds of said sale for the support and maintenance of my old negroes Priss and the two old Jocks who are too old to maintain themselves during their life time, that the balance of the proceeds of said sale be equally divided between the children and the children of such of my children who are dead."[44]

⬧

Before the summer ended, Arabella had found a way to claim what was hers. Both Tappan and Stevens agreed to advance her the shortfall she needed to purchase Augustus, with the expectation that the entire family would eventually repay them.[45] In a letter to Arabella dated August 1, 1857, the day that much of the English-speaking world celebrated the anniversary of Emancipation throughout the British Empire, Tappan expressed his regrets that he would not be in New York on her return journey, and said that he would leave the belongings she had left in his home at the Vigilance Committee offices. He wished her a safe and pleasant journey, and that she would "have the pleasure of seeing all your children free – industrious – happy – and grateful to God who has done so much for them."[46] The irony of the date was not lost on Tappan who, although not a British subject, noted that it was an "Auspicious anniversary."[47]

Two days later, a jubilant Tappan could be found busy at his desk writing to his old friend Lydia Sturge in England. After committing words of praise to the page about Arabella and Willie, he shared the news that someone was leaving for Alabama on that very day, August 3, with $1,100 in his pocket to redeem Augustus.[48] But nothing to do with the Weems family came easily, and it would be another month and a half before Arabella was finally able to share some good news with those who had helped her and her family:

Washington D.C.

September 19, 1857

Wm. Still Esquire, Philadelphia, Pa. Sir: – I have just sent for my son Augustus, in Alabama. I have sent eleven hundred dollars which pays for his body and some 30 dollars to pay his fare to Washington. I borrowed one hundred and eighty dollars to make out the eleven hundred dollars. I was not very successful in Syracuse. I collected only twelve dollars, and in Rochester only two dollars. I did not know that the season was so unpropitious. The wealthy had all gone to the springs. They must have returned by this time. I hope you will exert yourself and help me get a part of the money I owe, at least. I am obliged to pay it by the 12th of next month. I was unwell when I returned through Philadelphia, or I should have called. I have been from home five weeks.

My son Augustus is the last of the family in slavery. I feel rejoiced that he is soon to be free and with me, and of course feel the greatest solicitude about raising the one hundred and eighty dollars I have borrowed of a kind friend, or who has borrowed it for me at bank. I hope and pray you will help me as far as possible. Tell Mr. Douglass to remember me, and if he can to interest his friends for me.

You will recollect that five hundred dollars of our money was taken to buy the sister of Henry H. Garnet's wife. Had I been able to command this I should not be necessitated to ask the favors and indulgences I do.

I am expecting daily the return of Augustus and may Heaven grant him a safe deliverance and smile propitiously upon you and all kind friends who have aided in his return to me.

Be pleased to remember me to friends, and accept yourself the blessing and prayers of your dear friend.

Earro Weems

P.S. Direct your letter to E. L. Stevens, in Duff Green's Row, Capitol Hill, Washington, D.C.

E.W.[49]

One wonders if Ezra Stevens ever had the opportunity to discuss his experiences with former congressman Abraham Lincoln, who had once been his fellow tenant at Duff Green's Row.[50]

Nearly six weeks after Arabella sent the above letter to Still, at the end of what must have seemed like an interminable delay, the last of the Weems children was finally restored to his parents. Their son's body was weak with what was feared to be consumption, a disease that was often fatal at that time, but at least he was in the loving care of his parents rather than in the slave quarters of Alabama. The sickness had made the sale easier, as his master feared that the ailing Augustus would be of no further use to him as a slave. Dr. Rumph had purposely concealed his knowledge of the illness while the negotiations were going on. Although when healthy Augustus was valued at two thousand dollars, Dr. Rumph accepted $1,100. The money in hand was a much surer bet.[51]

Lewis Tappan sent word to England on September 30, 1857, to Henry and Anna Richardson at Newcastle-upon-Tyne, that all of the money from the Weems ransom fund had been spent. Although he had once questioned whether Arabella Weems was worthy of all the attention that she and her family had received, he reflected that now that he had met her he considered her to be "an interesting & good woman."[52]

The long saga of redeeming the Weems family finally came to an end, but the abolitionist's work showed no signs of abating. Still the requests for aid flowed in, as yet another heartbroken family member cried out for help. But it was impossible to save them all. On Christmas Eve 1857, Tappan could do no more than give cool advice and even cooler comfort in response to someone who found themselves in the same position as John and Arabella: "Why don't he run away? It appears to me that every man worthy of freedom should make the attempt. If he don't succeed the first time let him try again. Better die than be a slave. Have you faith to believe that God will answer your prayers by granting deliverance to your son? Let us pray."[53]

Ezra Stevens was ecstatic that the family had been reunited. But the financial challenges associated with Augustus's purchase weighed heavily upon him. He had paid $125 toward a loan and another seventy-five dollars was due on March 10, 1858. The overwhelming need to secure the money had forced him to agree to a usurious interest rate of 2.5 percent per month. As the time approached for repayment, he had no idea how he could settle it. In a letter to Tappan he wrote that "the family [Weems] had all they can do to support themselves & therefore the whole burden of meeting these payments has rested with me." Emotionally and financially spent from the experience, Stevens expressed the toll that such work exacted from dedicated abolitionists and vowed that "it will be the last time I shall involve myself in such matters to the extent I have in this."[54]

Augustus soon received medical treatment. What had originally been feared to be a lung infection was now diagnosed as dyspepsia. His health was improving and it was hoped that he would soon be able to help support the family.

As he had done with Addison and Joseph nearly a year and a half earlier, John Weems manumitted his eldest son, now a young man, on August 7, 1858:[55]

To all whom it may concern be it known that I John Weems of the City of Washington District of Columbia for divers good causes and considerations me thereunto moving have released from slavery, liberated, manumitted and set free and do by these presents hereby release manumit and set free my son Augustus Weems a Negro Man being of the age of 22 years and able to work and gain a Sufficient livelihood and maintenance: and him the said Negro Man named Augustus Weems I do declare to be henceforth free, manumitted and discharged from all manner of Servitude or Service to me my executors or administrators forever.

In Testimony Whereof, I have hereunto set my hand and affixed my seal this Seventh day of August in the year of our Lord one thousand eight hundred and fifty eight.

Signed Sealed and delivered              his
In presence of                    *John X Weems*
John S. Hollingshead                mark
Jas. St. Durham
District of Columbia
County of Washington

On this Seventh day of August, 1858 before me the Subscriber a Justice of the Peace in and for the County Aforesaid, personally appeared John Weems to me well known and acknowledged the within and foregoing deed of manumission to be his free act and deed.

Witness my hand and Seal this
7ᵗʰ day of August, 1858
*John S Hollingshead*

CHAPTER 11

FINALLY, AFTER SO MANY YEARS of heartbreak and elation, being separated then reunited then separated again, the Weems family was free to
be together. However, there were many others in the antebellum United
States who did not appreciate the former slaves' freedom. The Weemses'
erstwhile owners, the Hardings, were probably not pleased that the
family whose sale they had ordered to happen away from the vicinity of
Washington was now free and living in the nation's capital, where they
would serve as a constant reminder to other slaves that the master did not
control all things. Newspaper accounts of Ann Maria's daring escape
would only have thrown salt into the wounds of Charles Price and hundreds of others who had suffered a loss of their wealth due to the
meddling of abolitionists. Any slave's escape was an extremely courageous act of defiance, and many owners were left not only angry but
also bewildered that their property could be so ungrateful after the
"benevolent care" that they had received.

   The Weems family had once been part of their own community in
Montgomery County. It was a community of slaves whose members
could be removed at any time, but it was a community nonetheless.
They worshipped together, they witnessed each other's weddings, they
took joy in the births and baptisms of each other's children. It could
never be that way for the Weems family again – not in Maryland, not in

Washington, not even in the northern states, where freedom could be as elusive as a mirage. Canada offered their only tangible refuge. Ann Maria was there, as was Arabella's sister, Annie, and her family and other friends. But many others who had been an important part of their lives were still in the same position that they themselves were once in. How could the Weems family ever be content elsewhere when so many loved ones were left behind? Freedom was precious, even more so when shared. Arabella had first tasted freedom five years earlier, but before she could fully enjoy it, she had to help introduce its pleasures to eleven other people from her community. Unlike Arabella's, their cases had not ignited great abolitionist fires, and they were forced to emancipate themselves by flight.

The underground agents with whom Arabella was by now intimately involved, together with the slaves themselves, carefully laid out a plan of escape. Experience had shown that everything had to be well thought out, the details precise. A mass escape of this magnitude was fraught with pitfalls at every step. Other runaways over the years had guarded their secret so closely that they did not tell their friends, parents, or even spouses of their plan, fearing that all might come unravelled. But with so many people involved in this case, secrecy was not possible.

Among the slaves Arabella was going to help escape were little Willie's sister, Margaret Chapman, and Mary Jones, with whom she had a special relationship. Both had been owned by Adam Robb and, following his death, by his daughter Catharine Harding. Like Arabella, Mary was "quite above the average" intellectually and was attractive.[1] However, she was still a slave, and she found the Hardings oppressive and their children unbearable. Mary had been allowed to live on her own in Washington and to seek out work, provided that most of her pay went to her owner in Rockville, but she had been separated from her husband, Lewis, for most of their marriage. They had been married October 26, 1837, in a Catholic ceremony when he was about twenty-eight and she about twenty-four. Sixteen-year-old Ann Maria Talbot, now Ann Maria

Bradley, had served as witness to the union.[2] Mary would not leave without Lewis, nor he without her.

Lewis was a natural leader and solid in body and mind, "a man of superior stature, six feet high, with prominent features, and about one third of Anglo-Saxon blood in his veins."[3] His owner, Nancy (also known as Ann) Lyddane, had been lame for twenty years, and she relied heavily on Lewis for physical support and to serve as foreman on her farm, which included supervising six young slaves. Her husband had been an alcoholic and his uncontrollable love for rum had killed him fifteen years earlier. If the widowed mistress wished to travel, Lewis would pick her up and gently place her in the carriage. When she was sick and bed-ridden, it was he who attended to her.

Following Nancy Lyddane's death, Lewis fully expected that he would receive his freedom as a reward for his devotion. But her sons only laughed and refused to entertain the thought. The mistress had made no provisions to manumit Lewis and had in fact given her three sons title to all of her slaves, her "negro man Lewis, negro women Mary and Henny, negro boy Bob negro girl Caroline." The final straw occurred when Lewis's aunt, his last surviving blood relative, died and he was refused permission to attend her funeral. It was then that he confided in others his desire to flee and helped to organize his and their extremely hazardous escape.

The Joneses were instrumental in carefully orchestrating the connections with everyone who were to accompany them. Childless themselves, they were used to being looked up to as surrogate parents, and Mary was the godmother of fourteen children.[4] The plan was that three days after his wife's escape on July 8, 1858, Lewis and the others were to follow.[5] Mary and Lewis were by far the senior members of the group. The Auxiliary Guard was still at work, and Mary knew of their skill at manhunting from her own bitter experience in the slave jail at Washington. The sheer audacity of this large-scale escape and the reward money that would be offered would bring much attention to them and great risk to all of the Underground Railroad agents who were involved, including Jacob Bigelow, Ezra Stevens, and William Still.

Finally, in July 1858, at the appointed time, the operation began. A determined group, they had resolved to suffer any consequence because in their opinion anything was better than slavery. As expected, the escape was difficult. Their absence was soon discovered and a public cry raised. Reward advertisements were quickly placed in Washington's *National Intelligencer* and in the *Baltimore Sun*. The Auxiliary Guard was already on heightened alert. During that month thirteen other slaves had been placed in the district jail either as runaways or "for safe-keeping" by owners who feared that they too might try to escape. Slave dealers like John C. Cook, who acquired two of these unfortunates, rubbed their hands with glee at the prospects of quick profits.[6] Cook and Charles M. Price had recently resumed their partnership and pur-chased Alexandria's notorious Franklin and Armfield slave pen on Duke Street and, along with their other partners, George Kephart and William H. Birch, sought to pack the three-storey building with captives. They could handcuff fifty prisoners to the wall, twice that if necessary. Captured runaways were an important part of their lucrative business.

The Joneses' accomplices were Jake and Mary Ann Dade, John Dade, Henry Dade, Oscar Payne, Moses Wood, Joe Ball, David Diggs and a young crippled girl who had never learned to walk who was given the code name "Susan Bell." Each had his or her own unique and com-pelling story, with fragments recorded in runaway slave ads as well as in the journal of Underground Railroad agent William Still. Jake Dade, twenty-two and full of the vigour of youth, could not think of leaving his young bride, Mary Ann, in the clutches of slave owner Elias Rhoads, despite the fact that he was kind and treated her well. The son of Jake's own master was of a different ilk and was looking forward to putting Jake on the auction block as soon as the old man passed on. Jake's brothers John and Henry Dade were treated tolerably well, but their situation was no substitute for freedom.

*John C. Cook and Charles Price's slave pen at 1315 Duke Street, Alexandria, Virginia. The building still stands.* (Library of Congress image cph 3a28447)

The case was similar for thirty-year-old Oscar Payne. He considered his own experiences to be not unduly harsh, despite having had three brothers and one sister who had been sold south. He had no idea where they were, or if they still lived. Nor did he know the whereabouts of two other brothers, Brooks and Lawrence, who had escaped.

Moses Wood, who at age twenty-five "looked like he had been exceedingly well cared for, being plump, fat and extra smart" had no particular quarrel with his owner, General George Briscoe, except that he hired Moses out to N. Rice, Esquire of Washington and collected all of his pay. Moses did not, however, have any affection for his mistress, whose treatment he considered to be "pretty rough" – strong words from the polite and refined Moses. The cost of Moses's escape included leaving four sisters behind. Briscoe offered five hundred dollars as a reward for anyone who delivered Moses to the District of Columbia jail so that he could "get him again."[7] Moses had already once been committed to the District of Columbia jail. Curiously, his owner had committed him for being a runaway and had released him on the same day.[8] Perhaps Briscoe had taken him there to be whipped, which was one of the services jail workers offered. Of course, after Moses's second attempt to flee, Briscoe would have little use for the runaway and would hope to be reimbursed for his trouble by selling him off to a slave trader. Two other slaves, Cornelius and John Henry, had also previously tested Briscoe's patience by trying to run away.[9]

Joe Ball, whose father was white but whose mother was black, was thirty-four. He belonged to an aging spinster, Miss Elizabeth Gordon, who lived in Alexandria. Her young nephews and nieces, who would inherit her estate, saw Joe as a source of ready cash. One of those nephews, Thomas Gordon, got a bit ahead of himself, using his name as owner in the runaway slave ads. Joe's wife, Mary, and four children belonged to another owner, the widow Irwin, who had promised to free all of her slaves upon her death. Mary and family presumably tried hard not to let their anticipation show. Providing that Joe's escape was successful, they hoped to be reunited soon.

Two of Miss Gordon's other slaves had decided to escape a year earlier. Joe Ball's brother, Oscar, had been her "pet," and she had raised him from childhood: "When he was a little 'shaver' seven or eight years of age, she made it a practice to have him sleep with her, showing that she had no prejudice."[10] When Oscar reached manhood he asked his mistress if she would consent to allow him to purchase himself. She agreed to his request and placed the price at eight hundred dollars. Because of their friendly relationship and her deeply held religious views, Oscar proposed to her that seven hundred might be a more equitable price. Apparently subscribing to her own unique style of negotiating, the widow decided that one thousand dollars would be better. Oscar modestly declined the compliment that he was worth that much. In taking his departure, he would leave a wife and child behind.

Montgomery Graham had also belonged to Miss Gordon. She described him as "a very bright mulatto, about five feet, six inches in height, of polite manners, and smiles much when speaking or spoken to."[11] She seldom gave him much to smile about. Among other things, he begrudged her stinginess in allowing him "passes" to leave the farm. She offered one hundred dollars reward for each of them if they were taken in a slave state and two hundred dollars if captured in a free state. By the time she placed her ad it was becoming apparent that Montgomery Graham and the Ball brothers were part of a larger escape attempt, but she had not yet grasped its magnitude. The ad concluded that "one or more slaves belonging to other owners, it is supposed, went in their company." Oscar and Montgomery stopped short of their intended destination of Canada, and found work in Oswego, New York, changing their names to avoid detection. From there, Oscar, now known as John Delaney, exchanged letters with Joe as they conspired to reunite in the North. Oscar wrote to William Still, who had helped him and Montgomery, to ask his sage advice. The brothers thought it prudent for the runaways to wait until the next spring so they would avoid frostbite. Joe sent a list of the names of those who wanted to accompany him.

Also included in Joe's group was David Diggs, the slave of Josiah Harding and son of George and Hester Diggs, who had belonged to Adam Robb. After the escape Harding offered three hundred dollars if David was captured in a free state or two hundred dollars if he was taken in a slave state. Like most of these runaways, David was described as being "very polite and pleasant when spoken to." He was thirty-five and tall for the times at five foot ten or eleven inches. His runaway ad in the July 17, 1858 *National Intelligencer* noted that he had a "light copper color, prominent cheekbones, sunken eyes, whiskers around his face and under the chin." Diggs was probably aware of how effective those advertisements and efforts of the Auxiliary Guard could be: nine slaves who bore his surname had already spent time in Washington's slave jail.

There was one final member of this group of runaways. In a letter from Washington dated July 11, 1858, Ezra Stevens alerted William Still that "*ten packages* were sent to your address last evening, one of them belongs to Susan." Stevens's letter displayed the influence of Jacob Bigelow. It was full of subterfuge intended to deceive anyone other than its intended recipient. Cleverly conceived, the letter avoided the use of any name other than that of "Susan Bell," and the wording was unclear on whether Susan Bell was the runaway or the anxious recipient of "the package." After taking a circuitous route to Harrisburg, "Susan" intended to arrive in Philadelphia in a few days. From there she would travel to meet a servant who cared for disabled children at the New York State Asylum for Idiots in Syracuse.[12] Sympathetic by nature, Ezra Stevens took a special interest in Susan's case, as he had in Arabella's. The plan was to pretend that the child was being sent for treatment to Dr. Harvey Wilbur, who was the director of the asylum. Continuing to write in veiled language, Stevens referred to "a most excellent nurse" who worked for Dr. Wilbur who "would take a deep interest in the child, which, no doubt, will under Providence be the means of its complete restoration to health."[13] The abolitionist was rightfully certain that this "nurse" had the special healing power that only a mother could administer. After having been separated from her daughter for two years, the mother would equally benefit from the powers of the child. The smallest of "the packages" that Stevens referred to was Margaret Ann Chapman, the four-year-old crippled girl whose mother had escaped to Syracuse under circumstances that had compelled her to leave quickly without her daughter. From a distance, the mother had spent the intervening time trying to have her child, if she was still alive, brought to her. Just as Arabella Weems had done with Willie the year previously, Mary Jones, a relative of Susan's, carried the young Margaret to her mother, Susan Bell, aka Emeline Chapman.[14]

Clearly, the members of the mass escape attempt had so far eluded the intense manhunt that followed them. After leaving William Still in Philadelphia, they had been forced to separate into smaller groups and so far the tactic had worked. But when they reached New York State, the Great Lakes presented a barrier between themselves and Canada. The docks and bridges would be closely watched by slave hunters, with runaway slave ads in their hands and visions of rewards in their minds.

CHAPTER 12

WILLIAM AND ANNIE BRADLEY WANTED Arabella and her family to join them in Canada, which they found to be a cold and strange land. They felt the pain of separation from their family and friends and "nothing but the dread of slavery could reconcile them to the change."[1] The poignant desire to see loved ones again was echoed by other former slaves. The famous fugitive Harriet Tubman, who was from the same state as the Weemses and the Bradleys, spoke the words that they and thousands of others no doubt felt: "I had crossed the line. I was free; but there was no one to welcome me to the land of freedom. I was a stranger in a strange land; and my home, after all, was down in Maryland; because my father, my mother, my brothers, and sisters, and friends were there. But I was free, and they should be free. I would make a home in the North and bring them there, God helping me. Oh, how I prayed then."[2]

Unlike Harriet Tubman, Arabella Weems had loved ones to welcome her and to shelter her family until she and John could get a home of their own. By 1861, after eleven years in Canada, Arabella's sister and her husband had a fine one-and-a-half-storey frame house in the Dawn Settlement near Dresden, while most of their neighbours were still living in log cabins. Their home was a showpiece for what people could achieve, if only given the opportunity. The family was well respected and an important part of the community and of their neighbours' lives.

In 1863, when the managers of the British-American Institute, which was the heart of the Dawn Settlement, were charging and counter-charging one another with administrative improprieties, William Henry Bradley was both wealthy and respected enough to serve as a guarantor for one thousand dollars to Her Majesty's Court of Chancery for Upper Canada that he would be one of two people who would collect the moneys and rents due for the land, which had not been done with any regularity over the years.[3] Any revenue from lumber, crops, or other enterprises from the three hundred acres of Institute lands was supposed to be used for the benefit of the black community.

Mary and Catharine, the Bradleys' two daughters, who were just infants when their parents escaped with them, now had a houseful of siblings who had never known slavery: Elias, William, Annie, Jane, Alice, and Abram, who was the first to be born in Canada. Their parents had originally christened him "Abraham," a reminder of the name Abraham Young that their father had held when he belonged to William Pearce.[4]

Their niece, Ann Maria Weems, who had become like a daughter to them, must have been flattered when she was asked in 1861 to be the godmother of a neighbour's infant son, a role that her mother had so often taken in Maryland.[5] Ann Maria was by then a blossoming young woman, eighteen years of age. She had returned to Dawn after living up to the hopes of those who had helped her escape, having studied to be a teacher at the Colonial Church and School Society in London, Canada West.[6] The school, appropriately enough, was funded by some of the same British abolitionists who had only a few years before taken such a special interest in all of the Weems family, and the decision to found it was made in the wake of the fervour caused by the publication of *Uncle Tom's Cabin*.[7] It opened its doors in the same year that Ann Maria had taken her first uncertain steps away from a Maryland slave trader and toward freedom. If she had been present at the public meeting held in October 1856, she would have applauded her schoolmaster's words referring to *Uncle Tom's Cabin* and paying tribute to the mother country: "It was in England it met with response. It is English hearts that are beating for our oppressed colored brethren."[8]

English law protected Ann Maria in Canada, but her home state of Maryland never tired of demanding that fugitive slaves like herself be returned. In 1855, the General Assembly of Maryland had passed a resolution requesting that her representatives at Congress "take measures to obtain a treaty with the government of Great Britain, relative to restitution of slave property, belonging to American citizens, which may be found in her provinces. Whereas, Slaves held to labor in the South are constantly escaping to Canada where large numbers of them are now collected, and where they are protected by the British Government."[9] This resolution got them no further than it had in 1847, when two representatives of the governor of Maryland travelled to the governor general's office in Montreal demanding the return of a fugitive slave and were rebuffed. Upon meeting the abolitionist who had accompanied the slave and his family to Canada, the Maryland envoys were told that he thanked God that Canada was out of the slave hunters' reach. At this the men "became as fierce and ravenous as wild beasts, and said that they would lynch him if they had him in Baltimore."[10]

But slaves who had reached Canada, including Ann Maria Weems, needed to have no fear of southern lynch mobs or of extradition back into a life sentence of bondage. The "land of Canaan," sung about by thousands of black voices, offered a safe refuge. Living with family members in a broader black community added to the feeling of security. Ann Maria lived with her aunt, uncle, and cousins, but the 1861 census taker marked her as a non-family member, failing to understand how an extended family with slavery in common would grab hold and cling to one another when they could.

The large group of extended family and friends who were part of the mass escape in July 1858 were, almost miraculously, successful in reaching Canada. Upon arriving, the members of the group had many choices of where to put down new roots. In the large black community at St. Catharines, John Dade found a friend whom he had known in Washington. John, who was described as "a slave but a free dealer," no doubt had many friends. While still in Washington, he had assisted others to make their escape and had made connections with both William Still and the Canadian missionary and Underground Railroad agent Reverend Hiram Wilson. Through this friend he immediately got a job at the Willard Hotel, which paid eight dollars per month plus a room. This was a godsend, as during his escape John had exhausted the little bit of money that he had. Penniless, he was forced to walk the final distance from the suspension bridge at Niagara Falls to his destination in St. Catharines. Despite having no money, no change of clothes nor any personal possessions, he was optimistic and pleased with his situation. He only wished that his brother, Henry, who had fallen ill and was still in the United States, could join him.[11]

Joe Ball travelled farther on to Toronto. He wrote to William Still to thank him for all that he had done and to ask one last favour. He could not bear to continue to be separated from Mary and their children. When he left Alexandria, the couple had four children and a fifth had been born after his flight. Could not Still and his friends lend some assistance in that regard? Within three years of his arrival in Canada, Joseph was working as a brick maker, supporting his wife, Mary, and their children, Ann, Elizabeth, Maria, Melissa, and Eugene, still a toddler. He delighted in the fact that in Canada all of the children were able to run to embrace their father every night when he returned from work.[12]

Others who made their way to Canada chose to move farther inland and were drawn to areas of large black settlement such as in Chatham, Buxton, and Dawn, which were all in Kent County. Surrounding the Bradleys in and around the Dawn Settlement were several familiar faces from "back home," such as the elderly John Henson, with whom Arabella and her oldest children had once shared a master. He was a fairly new immigrant to Camden Township. Nearby also lived

*Josiah Henson, a former slave of Adam Robb's who was one of the founders of the Dawn Settlement* (New York Public Library image 1239121)

Josiah Henson, who as a child of five or six had briefly belonged to Adam Robb, although Robb had sold Josiah away to be reunited with his mother before Arabella was born. Josiah had been free for many years but had always been tormented with the thought that his brother, John, remained a slave, despite William Chaplin's best attempts to rescue him. As with so many slaves, Chaplin reported to Josiah that he "found [his] brother's mind so demoralised or stultified by slavery, that he would not risk his life in the attempt to gain his freedom." Chaplin made a second attempt to entice John to escape, with the same negative result.

Years slipped away. William Chaplin had been jailed following his famous failed rescue attempt, and Josiah continued to dream of seeing his brother again. Josiah had himself returned to the United States to rescue others, but had found no way to save his own family. Finally the opportunity presented itself when he received word that John's mistress, Jane Elizabeth Beall, the unmarried granddaughter of Adam Robb, was willing to sell him for four hundred dollars. This may have been the same John Henson who had been committed to the D.C. slave jail as a runaway on June 22, 1858, and released to John C. Cook.[13] Perhaps he had also attempted to participate in the larger escape involving his old friends Mary and Lewis Jones. At any rate, Jane Beall needed little more incentive to sell John, who was now in his sixties and past the age where he was of great value to her as a slave. Josiah became determined to find a way to raise the required amount.

Like several other former slaves, Josiah Henson had published an autobiography, in 1849. The abolitionists knew that there were few things as powerful as the testimony of those who had lived the horrors of slavery. By this time, Josiah was widely associated with Harriet Beecher Stowe's title character Uncle Tom. Stowe had noted in her *Key to Uncle Tom's Cabin* that there were parallels in Henson's life that substantiated the underlying truth in her famous novel. Josiah believed, and rightfully so, that a new and enlarged edition of his autobiography would have great public appeal and would sell enough copies to allow him to purchase his brother. Anti-slavery friends in Boston agreed to publish the book and Mrs. Stowe wrote the introduction. The money was soon raised and on September 8, 1858, Josiah purchased his brother John for $250. He travelled from Rockville, Maryland, to the port of Baltimore, then by sea to Boston. There he was met by his brother, from whom he had been separated for most of a lifetime. The brothers continued on to the Dawn Settlement in Canada West and enjoyed a reunion unencumbered by slavery's real or figurative chains.[14]

A few miles away in the neighbouring township of Chatham, along the banks of the Thames River, two other families from Montgomery County had settled into their own little log homes, which stood side by side. Ironically, the houses were on the lands of a United Empire Loyalist who had fled to Canada following the American Revolution so that the family could remain loyal to the British crown. Nearby was a small settlement of blacks that had grown up at the river crossing known as Gee's Ferry, later to be renamed Kent Bridge. The religious needs of these former slaves were served by a missionary paid through the philanthropy of the American Missionary Association, whose leaders included Lewis Tappan, Ezra L. Stevens, Charles Ray, and Jacob Bigelow.[15]

Mary Jones, now in her sixtieth year, shared one of the log homes with her husband, Lewis, who would soon be sixty-four. Despite her age, Mary was still tall and strikingly intelligent and had a demeanour that aroused the sympathies of those who met her. Lewis had recovered from his eventful escape, about which William Still wrote, "The suffering on the road cost Lewis a little less than death, but the joy of success came soon to chase away the effects of the pain and hardship which had been endured." Still went on to write: "The apparent solidity of the man both with respect to body and mind was calculated to inspire the idea that he would be a first-rate man to manage a farm in Canada."[16] Freedom had come late in life for the Joneses, but it had came nonetheless. Their home stood on a small parcel of land – only one acre, one-quarter of which was orchard. Their belongings were few. Mary no doubt had to leave behind the items – the tea canister, the oven, probably even the brass candlesticks – that she had purchased with hard-earned pennies over a decade before at the estate sale of her late master, Adam Robb. But she had friends who had helped her along the way, some of those same friends who had temporarily turned Ann Maria into a boy and carried her to Canada three years earlier. Mary knew something about happy reunions, and she would finally see Annie Bradley, who had served as witness at her wedding many years earlier.[17]

Next door to Mary and Lewis Jones lived the Weems family, with whom they had shared much in their former life, including standing as sponsors at the baptism of one of the Weemses' children a few years earlier.[18] John Weems, now sixty-two, was struggling to make a living in a new country. Last year's crop had been poor, and he had only been able to plant one acre of Indian corn and half that of potatoes on his thirty-five-acre farm. The wheat suffered from winter kill and from a disease called "midge." The spring crops had been attacked by wireworm and by frost. But they did have a small orchard and its yields were plentiful. While in no way could his compare with the property or livestock of William and Annie Bradley, John could boast of having a pig, a "milch cow," a calf and two horses. Their garden produced some carrots and beans and they had a two-hundred-pound barrel filled with pork to see them through lean times.[19]

No doubt the family carried the scars from their former life. Lewis Tappan had given them his blessing in a letter, but had stepped away to encourage them to be independent. He wrote to a friend: "What will become of the poor family I can not say. The times are such – so much want and distress on ever side – that nothing can be done for them from this quarter."[20] Unlike her husband, Arabella had learned to read and write. Like her neighbours Mary and Lewis Jones, she was Roman Catholic and listed her children as such. Her husband could not bring himself to profess any religion. Perhaps his faith had been too badly shaken by the many hardships he had endured. But Arabella and all of her family were finally free, and whenever she wanted she could make the short trip to Dresden to see her sister and her daughter, Ann Maria, or travel the few miles to Chatham to visit her son, Joseph, who had found work and was earning sixteen dollars per month as a live-in servant of a well-to-do white tailor.[21] Her two youngest children were also thriving. John Jr., the godchild of Mary and Lewis Jones, would be thirteen his next birthday and Mary, her only child who had never been a slave, was six. Slavery had robbed the family of years of togetherness, but that was behind them now. The morning sunlight had found its way through the shadows.

# EPILOGUE

JUNE 13, 1891 was to be a day of memories. There could be little doubt that Arabella Weems was in her eleventh hour, with the minute hand racing around to twelve. Before the day was over, any remnants of the weights she had carried for a lifetime would be lifted. There would be no tomorrow here, but for the faithful there was the promise of happiness elsewhere. Her second son, Dick, would be waiting for her. How could he not be? Perhaps his imperfect body would be healed, allowing him to join in with the other children as he never could in life. Stella, whose final wish was that she could see her mother again, would be there too – her request at long last answered. And also little Sylvester, whose time had been cut far too short by the aftereffects of a slave coffle under an unforgiving Alabama sun. Had he lived, he would now be forty. Instead he would be forever three.

Just as she had previously rejoiced over being reunited with the remainder of her boys, she had once more felt the pain of separation from each of them: first Augustus, then Addison, then John Jr., then Joseph. Augustus, like Sylvester, had died in the first year of his freedom. Medical treatment at the time was no match for his affliction, initially thought to be consumption. He was only twenty-two. Dr. Rumph had indeed made the financially wise decision to sell while he could. *Caveat emptor*: Buyer beware. John and Arabella Weems, who had been cheated out of spending five years with their son, were at least able to spend his final days with him. Despite their having had a bit of time to prepare for the upcoming grief, it was not enough – it never is. On November 24, 1858, less then three months after John Weems had registered the free papers for Augustus in Washington, and one day after his death, his parents buried him in an unmarked Canadian grave. Father Jaffre of St. Joseph's Catholic Church in Chatham officiated at the funeral.[1]

For the next decade, the remainder of the family, with the exception of Catharine, struggled on in Canada, revelling in their freedom, despairing at their losses, and often thinking of home. They were uncertain how the election of Abraham Lincoln would affect the United States but would have been delighted to learn that Jacob Bigelow, who took life-long pride in his role in freeing Ann Maria, had been selected as an assistant marshal to escort the president elect to the Executive Mansion at his first inauguration.[2]

Bigelow's appointment was in recognition of his role as a prominent delegate and permanent committee member for the Republicans as the party campaigned for justice and for the end of slavery.[3] He had found additional happiness in his marriage on July 25, 1859, to Rebecca M. Ogden, who looked upon her husband with immense pride as he passed in the colourful procession wearing a pink scarf with white rosettes, aboard a horse adorned with white saddle covers trimmed in pink and carrying a pink baton tipped in white.[4] Sadly, Jacob Bigelow died during Lincoln's first term in office and was denied the opportunity to witness the greatest of the president's accomplishments.[5] However, his widow carried on Bigelow's charitable legacy as an officer and donor to the National Association for the Relief of Colored Destitute Women and Children.[6]

John and Arabella watched the War of the Rebellion, as the Civil War was originally called, from the vantage point of British North America, which sent fifty thousand of its sons to southern battlefields – some for adventure, some for profit, others for larger ideals. But in the end they all went to settle the issue of slavery, whether they consciously knew it

*As soon as blacks were allowed to enlist, dozens of men from the area where the Weems family lived returned to the United States and joined the Union Army. Several fought with the Fifty-Fourth Massachusetts Regiment at the bloody attack of Fort Wagner. Many were killed in battle, but their bravery quieted the stereotype that blacks had neither the will nor the ability to serve as soldiers.* (courtesy of Buxton National Historic Site and Museum)

or not. Even President Lincoln acknowledged that one of the people most admired by the Weems family, Harriet Beecher Stowe, had played an important part in taking the first steps to remove the stain of slavery from their country, when he reportedly greeted the author by saying, "So this is the little lady that started this big war."

Arabella and her sister Annie surely devoured any information they could find about how the war was affecting their homeland. During the first two years of the war, the news was not comforting, with mounting Union Army losses to the Confederate forces. Familiar names were in the news that wafted its way to the small Canadian black settlement.

In 1861, at the outbreak of hostilities between north and south, slave owner Dr. Charles A. Harding – for whom the Weems family no doubt felt that Hell must hold a special place – was part of a delegation of the Maryland legislature who travelled to Montgomery, Alabama, the first capital of the Confederacy, to meet with President Jefferson Davis and his cabinet. They were cordially welcomed. Davis greatly appreciated receiving the assurance that the "State of Maryland sympathises with the people of these States in their determined vindication of the right of self-government." Even though the state had not yet seceded from the Union, Davis expressed his hope that Maryland, "whose people, habits and institutions are so closely related and assimilated with theirs, will seek to unite her fate and fortunes with those of this Confederacy."[7]

Maryland officially remained loyal to the Union but many – including Harding, who joined a Confederate regiment – made no secret of where their true loyalties lay. Indeed, of 653 ballots cast in the 1860 presidential election, Abraham Lincoln had not received a single Rockville vote.[8] Harding had been appointed assistant surgeon for the Union Army's First Maryland Infantry, but declined, instead enlisting as a private in Company C of the Second Maryland Cavalry before eventually achieving the rank of major and quartermaster for the Confederate States of America.[9] His brother-in-law, Robert W. Carter, had spent some time in the Capitol Prison in Washington during the war for providing aid to the enemy.[10]

Lieutenant John Newland Maffitt, who had accepted the money for Diana Williams that had been originally intended for Augustus Weems, feared that he might be called upon to bombard his home state of North Carolina after war was declared. He resigned his commission in the United States Navy and became infamous as a Confederate Navy commander who patrolled the Atlantic and the Gulf of Mexico, running the Union blockade of southern ports and capturing and sometimes destroying her ships. Maffitt even ventured into the English Channel to capture a ship laden with coal that was bound for the northern United

States, putting both the vessel and her cargo to the torch.[11] By summer's end of 1863, he boasted of having captured seventy-two ships worth fifteen million dollars.[12]

The war was costly on all fronts. It would cause Dr. James Rumph to feel acutely the anguish that the parents of his former slave, Augustus Weems, had suffered. Three of Rumph's sons fought for the Confederacy. Langdon, the youngest, was struck by typhoid fever. An embittered Dr. Rumph never forgave those whom he thought were responsible for the misery caused by the war, confiding to his journal: "Mr. Lincoln and his cabinet are responsible for all the sufferings, cruelties, carnage, murders, and deaths of this fratricidal war; yes every drop of blood spilt, wound received, sickness received in camp and hospitals where so many languished and died for want of freedom and food, peace and home and liberty."[13]

Not all of the disturbing Civil War reports that reached the Weems family came from the battlefront; some hit closer to home. When the draft was instituted in the North, the city of New York erupted in riots to protest the increasingly unpopular war. Blacks were the objects of the rioters' wrath. The "colored" orphanage was burned to the ground, several people were killed, and many more were left battered and homeless. The high-profile abolitionist Reverend Henry Garnet was targeted. Fortunately Mary, his quick-thinking daughter, had removed the brass nameplate from their front door with an axe, leaving the mob uncertain who lived there. White neighbours concealed Garnet and his family until the trouble passed.

Some good news also floated north to Canada's freed slaves. Justice was finally taking notice of the hated slave traders Cook & Price. Newspaper accounts showed that John Cook was up to his familiar tricks: he had recently preyed on the soft hearts and generosity of abolitionists by demanding nine hundred dollars for nine-year-old Sally Maria Diggs, affectionately known as "Pink," so that the little girl would not be separated from her grandmother.[14]

A later news item, printed after the Civil War disrupted the coastal voyage of the slave ships to New Orleans and other southern ports, was unconditionally satisfying. John Cook had placed a slave named Jane Coucy in a Baltimore slave pen for "safekeeping" for a period of sixteen months, apparently to ensure that she would not be freed if the rumours that President Lincoln might free the slaves in the District of Columbia proved correct. In an unexpected development, soon after the bloody battle of Gettysburg, Union soldiers arrived at the high wall that enclosed the two-storey brick building with orders to free everyone held within the slave pens of the city. Besides Jane Coucy, they found fifty-five men, women, and children, including infants who had been born there. The army commander ordered a blacksmith to remove the shackles of those who were in chains. As the suddenly freed slaves walked out onto the street, many were met by surprised and jubilant loved ones. The men in the group followed the soldiers to the colonel's headquarters and enlisted in the Second United States Colored Regiment, thereby helping to close all of the southern slave pens.[15]

John Cook's misfortunes paled in comparison to what happened to Charles M. Price. Cook & Price continued to advertise "Negroes wanted" in the *Gazette* well into 1861, even though Price had purchased Cook's interest in their Alexandria slave pen on January 17, 1860, for $2,500 and the business had been renamed Price & Birch.[16] The August 11, 1862 edition of the *Gazette* carried an advertisement that Price & Birch had relocated to a slave pen in Culpeper, Virginia.[17] Charles Price very naturally supported the Confederacy, which represented the only hope of his maintaining his lifestyle and business. Doing his part, Price allowed the rebel cavalry to occupy his fortified slave pen in the early days of the war, but their occupation would be short-lived. On the morning of May 24, 1861, while having breakfast, the southern soldiers were surprised by the Union Army, which captured both the building and its inhabitants. Price fled deeper into the heart of Virginia, outraged at the loss of his property to the enemy.[18] At times during the Civil War, Confederate prisoners of

**NEGROES WANTED.—**We wish to purchase any number of NEGROES, of both sexes, for cash. All letters addressed to us, at this place, will receive prompt attention. Having bought the establishment, lately occupied by Millan & Grigsby, West end Duke street, and having refitted it to make it one of the most healthy and comfortable Depot for NEGROES, we will receive them on board on the usual terms.
aug 30—eotf. **PRICE & COOK.**

*Charles M. Price and John C. Cook revived their slave-trading partnership from the previous decade, as witnessed in this* Alexandria Gazette *ad from November 1, 1860.* (Library of Congress microfilm)

war were held in Price's cells, once reserved for slaves destined for the auction block. Newly freed men took pleasure in pointing out to prisoners that their positions had been reversed.[19]

In a disingenuous attempt to seek compensation for his loss, Price drew up a bogus deed dated June 1, 1861, turning over the property to his brother-in-law and fellow slave-trader, Solomon Stover, who feigned his support for the Union. The pair also registered a deed in Montgomery County, Maryland, recording that Price had sold eight slaves, six horses, a buggy, and several household articles to Stover.[20] Seeing through this ruse, the Senate committee that reviewed compensation claims for properties seized or damaged by the Union Army firmly rejected the application, stating: "You allowed the organized military forces of the enemy to occupy and use this property; it was captured from them within enemy's lines. You yourself was a rebel, abandoning your home in a loyal State, and seeking the protection of the enemy and sojourning with him. You have no standing in court; you can claim no compensation for your property, either its use or damage."[21]

None of the news that arrived from Washington would have been as eagerly sought by Arabella and Annie as word about their mother. At

times, Cecilia would have been right in the middle of the unpredictable
and rapidly unfolding events. During the Civil War, Cecilia's owner,
Jane E. Beall, remained staunchly in favour of the Union; this despite
the fact that she and her sisters were large slave owners. Of course,
President Abraham Lincoln had made it very clear that it was not a war
to end slavery but rather a war to save the Union. In the fall of 1862, the
Northern Army of the Potomac set up their headquarters near
Rockville. Major General George B. McClellan wrote to his wife telling
her of his progress and letting her know that he had found a room in the
house of Jane Beall, whom he described "as an old maid of strong
Union sentiment, who refused to receive any pay" for her hospitality.[22]
However, she had recently had no trouble accepting money from the
federal government in other ways.

*A woman standing beside the Alexandria slave pen that at one time belonged to
Charles M. Price and John C. Cook* (Library of Congress LC-B811- 2300[P&P])

Earlier that same year Congress had passed "an act for the release of certain persons held in service or labour in the District of Columbia." The act was extremely controversial. All slaves in the District were to be freed and all of their owners were to be compensated from the public treasury. Word spread like wildfire. On April 16, 1862, Harriet Beecher Stowe's brother, Henry Ward Beecher, hastily fired off a telegraph to Abraham Lincoln: "The *Independent* goes to press at 2 oclock PM this day Wednesday. May I say that the district of Columbia is free territory?"[23] It was so.

Jane Beall and her sisters were among those who applied under that act for compensation for her slaves who had been hired out and were then living in Washington. Among them was the grey-haired Cecilia

*A Union soldier reads the Emancipation Proclamation to newly freed slaves.*
*After Lincoln signed the proclamation, celebrations took place across the country.*
(Library of Congress image cph 3a08642)

Talbot, who had long ago been estimated as past the age of usefulness. Because of her advanced years she was evaluated on May 15, 1847, at fifteen dollars. On Christmas Eve, two years later, at the time of the re-evaluation and distribution of Robb's estate, her value had declined to ten dollars. On February 2, 1852, her age was estimated at seventy-eight and her value had further depreciated to one dollar. Ten years later, when the federal government agreed to compensate slave owners for freeing their slaves in D.C. Cecilia had miraculously gotten eighteen years younger and was now listed at about seventy years of age in the petition for compensation. Her owners, who had shamelessly fudged her age by nearly twenty years, maintained that she was still a good cook and active and healthy.

Associated with the practical side of administering the payments was an irony to beat all ironies. Bernard Campbell, the owner of one of the largest slave-trading empires, was hired by the federal government to use his considerable expertise in determining the proper amount of compensation.[24] Among the slaves that he evaluated were those of the Beall sisters. No fools when it came to business dealings, the Beall women contended that although they lived in Maryland, which was not included in the offer for compensation, they had hired out some of their slaves to people in Washington. And they could certainly attest that their slaves had not "borne arms against the United States in the present rebellion, nor in any way given aid or comfort thereto." Therefore they should collect any money they might be entitled to under the law. On July 11, 1862, when Jane Beall appeared before Campbell, seven of her slaves, including Cecilia, were absent.[25]

By October 30 Cecilia still had not appeared and the commissioners wanted to know why. The commissioners finally brought in an impartial gentleman named Henry Busey and questioned him about Cecilia's whereabouts, age, abilities, and general health. They must have been satisfied with Busey's account, because the Beall sisters were granted fifty dollars in compensation for Cecilia and $9,350 for

*Black citizens in Washington, D.C. celebrated the abolition of slavery in a march outside the White House in 1866.* (Library of Congress image cph 3a34440)

an additional seventeen slaves that they owned.[26] Mercifully, Cecilia did not have to suffer the indignity of being examined by the much-despised slave trader. She had already experienced far too many degradations in her lifetime.

The former owner of Cecilia's son-in-law William Henry Bradley also tried to get compensation for the loss of his slave. In 1864 a new Maryland constitution freed that state's slaves. Three years later, William Pierce joined with other Marylanders who claimed to have remained loyal to the Union during the Civil War and were therefore entitled to payment for their slaves. After hearing complaints that many slaves had been induced to leave their owners and enlist in the Union army, the General Assembly ordered that a listing be made of all slave owners and their slaves as of November 1, 1864. Pierce deviously listed

"Abraham Young," even though Young had been free in Canada for fourteen years by then. Pierce was unsuccessful in this deceit, and no reimbursement was granted.

Despite some foreboding hints that the racially intolerant status quo was being maintained, there were some promises of equal rights and opportunity. But no inducement to return to the United States was stronger than the desire to be reunited with family. Even though in Canada they were surrounded by relatives and friends, the Weemses had left many other loved ones behind. Cecilia was among those still there and Arabella longed to see her again.

As more settled conditions descended upon the U.S. capital, the lure of home eventually became too strong, pulling John, Arabella, their surviving sons, and Mary, along with Lewis and Mary Jones, back to the familiar surroundings of Washington by 1868.[27] They were a part of that great black migration from Canada that came after the Civil War ended. The northward exodus had reversed, just as Reverend Thomas M. Kinnard, a Toronto-based abolitionist and former slave, predicted in 1863: "If freedom is established in the United States, there will be one great black streak, reaching from here to the uttermost parts of the South."[28] The Underground Railroad that had been such an important part in their history was beginning a final journey into the realm of legend.

The Weems family and their friends returned for many reasons. There had been several years of crop failures in Kent County, where they lived. The climate was harsher than they were used to. The winds blew colder there, partly because of latitude, partly because it was not home. Some Canadians had only begrudgingly accepted the former slaves, and once slavery was abolished their discrimination encouraged the blacks to leave. There was also a prevailing feeling that those who had acquired new skills and independence in Canada had an obligation to return to the United States and help with Reconstruction. After all, even old friends in Britain like Anna H. Richardson had answered Lewis

Tappan's appeal to provide woollen worsted and cotton garments for the newly freed but destitute blacks.[29] Those who had prospered in freedom should do no less.

And there was a prevailing optimism that there would be new beginnings for all blacks in the United States, with their rights assured and their futures bright. This hopefulness came from some of the Weemses' old friends who were leaders in the movement for civil rights. Lewis Tappan and Henry Garnet had shared the stage before a large, adoring crowd at an "Emancipation Jubilee" held in January 1863 to celebrate the issuance of the Emancipation Proclamation that declared "all persons held as slaves" within the rebellious states "are, and henceforward shall be free." On February 12, 1865, Garnet became the first African American to preach at the Capitol Dome in Washington. Tappan continued to fight for even the most basic rights for blacks, including ending their exclusion from riding on railroad cars, a ridiculous practice he thought must excite "the loudest laugh in hell."[30]

*Slavery was completely abolished in the United States of America in December 1865.* (Library of Congress image cph 3a06245)

The Weemses would not have been naïve enough to believe that society would immediately change or that all those in positions of power would be sympathetic to their rights. John H. Goddard, who had been the captain of the Auxiliary Guard and the captor of Mary Jones, would still be a force to be reckoned with, after the executive session of the United States Senate confirmed his appointment as justice of the peace for Washington County in the District of Columbia on May 18, 1864. Some progressive senators were opposed to his appointment and appealed to the president to rescind it, but Lincoln, ever the conciliator, declined, stating that the resolution was already "a part of the permanent records of the Department of State."[31]

Of course, there were many uncertainties following the traumatic assassination of Abraham Lincoln on Good Friday, April 14, 1865. "Father Abe," as he was affectionately called by many blacks, was mourned and eulogized at countless memorial services by former slaves on both sides of the border. The Weems family would have been appalled that John C. Cook was chosen to be one of the marshals to march in Lincoln's funeral procession.[32] John and Arabella might have found it more fitting that Cook, as part of D.C.'s murky slave-trading subculture, was called as a witness during the assassination conspiracy trials to testify about the character of one of the suspects.[33]

Following the Civil War and Lincoln's assassination, Arabella's mother lived in D.C.'s shanty town district known as Swampoodle with the widowed Charlotte Branham, another former slave of Henry and Catharine Harding's, who very well could have been one of Cecilia's daughters. Dependent upon Charlotte's meagre income as a washer-woman, these two ladies, who had also taken two young children into their home, would have appreciated any assistance that the Weems family could offer.[34] The sketchy records leave us to wonder if the children, Charlotte Tompkins aged seven, born in Louisiana and eleven-year-old Fannie Warren from Alabama, might be Charlotte Branham's granddaughters born to her daughters who had been separated from their mother during slave days.

John and Arabella's immediate family were confident that they would fare reasonably well in Washington. There were jobs to be had and Addison and Joseph, forever close because of shared blood and experience, worked together there as labourers. The pair initially shared a home on Sixth Street with the rest of the family, and chose to remain together the next year after their parents and siblings moved to John Jr.'s nearby home. However, pitiless fate again stepped in. Addison died on May 17, 1871, at age twenty-eight, after suffering a long illness. He had made a gesture to regain his personal identity by retaking his birth name, Charles Adam Weems. His funeral took place at his residence, 228 New Jersey Avenue.[35]

John Jr. had certain advantages over Addison and Joseph: he had acquired his freedom at a much younger age, he had never been separated from his mother, he had been apart from his father for only a relatively short time, and he had learned to read and write. John had taken up the carpentry trade and prospered at it. He would have been excited on April 12, 1869, the day that he purchased his first home, thanks in part to the generosity and financial backing of Sylvanus Boynton. He would share it with his parents, younger sister, Mary, and William Saunders, who was a young carpenter originally from Alabama. John Jr. paid one thousand dollars for a property on New Jersey Avenue and within a year it had nearly doubled its value.[36] By 1871 he had expanded his carpentry business, basing it from an additional property on Q Street.[37] On October 1, 1872, the family moved into a new home at 205 Tenth Street. Just when John Jr.'s future looked promising, he was stricken with a long and painful illness that, according to the local newspaper, he "bore with Christian fortitude."[38] Early in the morning of October 25, 1872, he succumbed. His family and friends gathered for a funeral service for their twenty-two-year-old loved one at St. Joseph's Church on Capitol Hill two days later.

*The Weems family lived in this house on
Tenth Street SE in Washington, D.C., when
they returned to the United States from
Canada.* (courtesy of Sandy Harrelson)

Of the six sons born to Arabella and John, Joseph was now the only
one remaining. He had risen to the highest social status of the boys,
having been appointed by Frederick Douglass to the prestigious position of sergeant-at-arms of the District Council. Young and determined,
Joseph fought for the rights that had for so long been denied to him. On
one occasion, when he was refused first-class accommodations on the
*Lady of the Lake* because of his colour, he took the boat's owners to court
rather than quietly acquiesce to the injustice.[39] He, too, was the recipient
of the kindness of Sylvanus Boynton, who loaned him money to purchase a home. Displaying his consideration for the family, Boynton
established easy terms, charging no interest and setting up a legal trust so
that if Joseph should default on the loan and the land had to be sold at
public auction, Joseph would still get whatever money was left after
the expenses were paid.[40] But everything started to come undone with the
death of Addison and the long illness and subsequent death of John Jr.
Joseph tried to come to his parents' aid, moving into the family home on

Tenth Street and putting money toward the payment of their mortgage. But yet again it fell to the family's guardian angel, Sylvanus Boynton, to come to the rescue and hold the house in his trust for the Weemses' use.[41]

The Weems family was still reeling with grief from the deaths of Addison and John when Joseph was swept up in the smallpox epidemic then ravaging Washington. Under order of the board of health, Arabella and John would have placed a yellow flannel flag on the house's exterior, warning all passersby of the disease within. They were expected to fumigate with sulphur three times a day and to disinfect every part of the home with chlorinated soda, carbolic acid, or another approved chemical. They were to hang a one-square-yard cloth in the afflicted person's room, saturated with disinfectant. No clothing or bedding could be removed from the room that had not been cleaned and disinfected. Only a nurse who had previously had smallpox or a family member (most likely Arabella) was allowed into the room.

Joseph died within eight weeks of his younger brother, John, on December 20, 1872.[42] No church service was allowed, and according to city policy Joseph's body was to be buried within six hours of death. No one other than an ambulance driver, an appointed representative of the board of health, and the immediate family could accompany his body to its final resting place in the Small Pox Cemetery situated near the banks of the eastern branch of the Anacostia River on the grounds of the Washington Asylum.[43]

At some point in the previous decade, Ann Maria had also died, although it is unclear if her death occurred in Canada or in the United States. After leaving her mark for a brief time in the 1861 books of Dresden's Anglican church, she slipped away from the surviving public record as stealthily as she had at one time eluded the slave trader who mistakenly thought he owned her for life. Her name does not appear in the 1870 D.C. census with others of her immediate family or in the 1871 Canadian census. Confirmation of her passing came from Mary when she later swore in a legal document that at the time of Joseph's death in 1872, she and Catharine were the only surviving sisters.[44] None of the Weems boys had married and neither they nor Ann Maria lived long enough to celebrate the marriage of their baby sister, Mary, on October 24, 1873.[45]

In 1872 William Still published his groundbreaking book *The Underground Rail Road: A Record of Facts, Authentic Narratives, Letters, &C., Narrating the Hardships, Hair-breadth Escapes and Death Struggles Of the Slaves in their Efforts of Freedom, As Related by Themselves.* It brought public focus back to the family's dramatic histories, including the bravery of Arabella in restoring little Willie Chapman to his mother, the daring flight of Lewis and Mary Jones, the redemption of Augustus, and the clandestine help of Jacob Bigelow, Dr. H., Anna Richardson, Ezra Stevens, and Lewis Tappan. It was unfortunate that none of the family was fully able to enjoy their renewed celebrity. They would not have known that Tappan, partially paralyzed after a stroke that left him unable to write, dictated a letter to Still encouraging him to include "one of his most interesting 'underground' experiences" – that of the thrilling escape of Ann Maria Weems.[46] Most of the Weems family would also never get to enjoy reading their story in a small biography, *Sketch of the Life of Rev. Charles B. Ray,* that was written by Ray's daughters. The Weems episode had a very special significance in Ray's life, and was featured prominently in his biography, which also contained copies of the letters that he had exchanged with Jacob Bigelow and Anna Richardson, as well as mention of Ray's life-long friendship with Reverend Amos N. Freeman, who had accompanied Ann Maria to Canada and who later aided Arabella in raising money to purchase Augustus.[47]

The crushing weight of so many bereavements caused John Weems's health to deteriorate, as it did for Cecilia, who also suffered the infirmities associated with advanced age. When her son-in-law tried to have her cared for, the *Evening Star* provided its readers with an insensitive chuckle at John's expense. The headline sarcastically blared, "OVER THE HILL TO THE POOR HOUSE; A Centenarian Mother-in-Law Sent Down to It." The article said the "colored man" John Weems, who appeared to be about seventy-five years old, had travelled to police headquarters to appeal for the admission of his mother-in-law to the poorhouse hospital. He stated that she could not walk or look after herself in any way. Little wonder, as John told the officials that to the best of his knowledge she was 126 years old! When asked what her name was he replied that it was "Cecilia something" – he did not recall her last name, because, in his words, so far as he knew, she had never been married. John was sent away with the instruction to return only after he could provide her surname. John came back later armed with the name: Talbot. With that, Cecilia was admitted to the hospital, commonly referred to as the "almshouse."[48]

Cecilia lived another four months before succumbing to old age and "senile debility" at the Freedman Hospital on September 16, 1875. No one seemed to know her exact age; her death certificate recorded it as one hundred years. There was no disputing that Cecilia had lived long enough to see herself and all of her descendants finally and forever free.[49] Many of the loved ones who had been in and out of her life while she was enslaved had returned to her.

Arabella and John had many wounds in their lives, but their pain was partially soothed by the arrival of grandchildren. Mary and her husband, James, remained living in their tiny house, where their children filled the rooms with life. The couple thoughtfully paid tribute to Mary's father and brothers by naming their first son John Albert Savoy, born on March 26, 1875, and their second Charles Sylvester Savoy, born October 15, 1877. The baptisms of the children at St. Peter's Church were particularly special because the children's aunt, Catharine Weems, was able to attend and serve as godmother both times.[50]

John Weems spent his final days working as a gardener, raising plants from the soil as he had always done.[51] He and Arabella probably walked the few short city blocks to be a part of a huge assembly at the emotional speech given by Frederick Douglass at the unveiling of the Lincoln Emancipation statue and to remember Henry Highland Garnet, who had been active in the fundraising.[52] But John's time was growing short. At seventy-seven years, seven months, and four days, he had lived a long and eventful life. He passed over at eleven-thirty in the morning on May 30, 1878, in the Washington home that his son and namesake had purchased nine years before. John's final suffering, from gastritis, was lengthy and painful. But the *Evening Star* indicated that he had regained his faith and had borne his agony "with a Christian fortitude." A requiem mass was celebrated in the basement of St. Peter's Church.[53] The lower part of the church was reserved for black members who were barred from the main sanctuary.[54] John was buried in the same hallowed ground as Cecilia, at the District of Columbia's Roman Catholic Mount Olivet Cemetery.

Now without her life's partner, Arabella needed to be around her remaining family more than ever. As an unselfish expression of the love that they bore for Catharine Weems and all of her family, the Boyntons brought Arabella into their New York City home for a short time, so that she could finally live and heal her grief under the same roof as her daughter. She surely found some measure of joy in the births of more grandchildren: Augusta Weems Savoy, born November 16, 1879, Joseph O. Savoy, born November 21, 1881, and Lydia Savoy, born November 23, 1882.

When she returned to Washington, Arabella was perhaps able to spend some time with her extended family, Charlotte Branham and Mary and Lewis Jones, who were all living in D.C. Since coming home from Canada, the Joneses had moved around considerably, sometimes living apart from each other, as their work demanded. Lewis had various jobs: as a labourer, driver, and janitor. Mary found work as a servant, doing the work she had been trained to do as a young slave. Made of sturdy stock, they both worked at the D.C. Temperance Hall – he as a cook, she as a washerwoman – when they were in their late seventies.[55]

When the mulatto couple's age finally caught up with them, they moved together into a home for the aged run by the Little Sisters of the Poor, an order of nuns from the Motherhouse in St. Pern, in Brittany. The home on H Street was opened in February 1871. The Sisters, who were unable to speak English, quickly busied themselves with begging missions for food and supplies and were amply rewarded for their efforts by the generous Washington public. It was another nine years before the Sisters, after consultation with the archbishop, decided that blacks were as entitled to their charity as whites. However, in keeping with the times, it was decided that blacks should live in a separate building. On June 30, 1881, the Sisters, thanks to generous donations, purchased an adjacent small frame house and opened it as an asylum for African Americans. Mary and Lewis Jones were among the first inhabitants after the "colored" home opened in November of that year. To celebrate, a day of feasting and blessings was held for the inmates of both races. Being Catholic, Mary and Lewis would have been able to receive the sacrament of confirmation that was administered by Archbishop Gibbons to thirty of the residents. The Joneses would have cheered in 1882 when Congress ordered that an alley separating the white and black homes be opened to allow a covered passageway to be built to join the two.[56]

The aged couple enjoyed the comforts of the home and the care of the devoted Sisters. Both died of heart disease after illnesses that lasted six months, Lewis at age eighty-four, on April 25, 1882, and Mary, aged seventy-eight, the next year on September 16, 1883.[57] Charlotte Branham's constitution was more remarkable than either of the Joneses' or even Cecilia Talbot's. Charlotte also later spent her final months at the Little Sisters of the Poor, surviving Mary Jones by eighteen years and living until the ripe old age of 104.[58]

Arabella spent her final years surrounded by her daughter Mary and her many grandchildren. Unfortunately Arabella did not get the chance to see her last grandchild. Mary was pregnant with the fittingly named James Raymond Boynton Savoy when her mother was stricken with her final illness, breast cancer. Arabella joined her host of loved ones who had gone before on June 13, 1891, at the age of eighty-four.[59] The *Evening Star* made no mention of her remarkable life, only that a requiem mass would be held at St. Peter's Church, and that she had borne, as had her late husband and son, her painful, year-long illness "with Christian fortitude."[60] No one who had known Arabella would expect anything less. She too was buried at Mount Olivet Cemetery, with no stone to mark her spot.

Annie and William Bradley spent the rest of their lives in Canada. At the time of Arabella's death, Annie, then widowed since the mid-1880s, was living in a Dresden home with one of her sons. The sixty-eight-year-old woman was now raising three of her daughter's children. Granddaughters Viera and Elva Smith were twelve and eleven respectively; grandson William was ten. Although raised a Roman Catholic, Annie converted shortly after arriving in Canada. She joined the British Methodist Episcopal Church, so renamed from the original African Methodist Episcopal Church in honour of the British government, which had afforded a place of refuge for thousands of freeing slaves like herself. In her final three years, she suffered from chronic heart disease until a sudden heart attack took her at ninety-two. Annie had outlived her elder sister by twenty-two years. At the time of her death on Friday April 18, 1913 she was survived by three daughters, two sons, twenty-two grand-children, and twelve great-grandchildren. The funeral cortege left her home the following Monday, taking her to the funeral service at the BME church, then on to the cemetery of the former British North American Institute on the old Dawn Settlement grounds, where she was laid to rest.[61]

Catharine Weems, who had been the first of the family to be redeemed by the largesse of abolitionist supporters, spent most of the remainder of her life in the household of Sylvanus Boynton, where she had been taken "temporarily" so she could get used to freedom. The mutual affection that grew between her and the Boyntons was genuine and deep. Loyal and profoundly religious, Catharine repaid the family's kindness. She remained with Sylvanus through good times and bad – when he was falsely accused of stealing money from the treasury department, after the death of his first wife, Eliza, and through years of emotional and financial disappointments when stonewalling politicians prevented him from establishing a railway in Panama. Catharine stayed devoted to him during Boynton's brief and disastrous second marriage to a neglectful woman "who constantly associated with people of bad character . . . drank intoxicating liquors to excess . . . abandoned her home and spent time in dissipation . . . has been guilty of adultery."[62]

Later the aging Sylvanus, whose investments had made and lost him fortunes, turned over to Catharine the legal title for the Weems family home in Washington. In a shaky hand, he wrote that he did this "especially for over forty years of continuous service rendered to the said party of the first part and to his family, for which no adequate compensation has been or can be made, and in consideration of the fidelity, loyalty and devotion of the said Catharine Weems to the party of the first part, and, especially as the nurse and God Mother of Henry D. Boynton, recently deceased, the son of the said party of the first part, and, for the love and affection the said Grantor herein bears and entertains for the said Grantee."

Catharine moved to the house in her later years, and considered it to be rightfully hers. Never married, Catharine left money in her will to the religious organizations that had meant so much to her in her lifetime, some of which she became associated with by virtue of her travels and her relationship with the Boyntons. To St. Mary's Catholic Church in Elyria, Ohio, she bequeathed three hundred dollars. It was in this church's cemetery that Eliza Boynton was buried in 1897 and her husband, Sylvanus, in 1912.[63] Catharine gave a similar amount to St. Cyprian's Colored Catholic Church in Washington, where she, Mary, her nieces and nephews worshipped in later years. She gave one hundred dollars to Washington's Little Sisters of the Poor for the Catholic home for the aged where her uncle, Lewis Jones, and two aunts, Mary Jones and Charlotte Branham, spent their final days. Two hundred dollars was directed to the Oblate Sisters of Providence, who ran St. Ann's Academy of Washington. Another three hundred dollars was given to St. Ann's Orphan Asylum.

St. Peter's, the Washington church where her parents' funerals were held, was given one hundred dollars "for the purpose of having Masses said for the Souls in Purgatory." Whatever was left in the estate was to go to St. Joseph's Male Orphan Asylum and to St. Vincent's Orphan Asylum. A bequest of one hundred dollars to St. Mary's Catholic Church in Rockville, Maryland offers an interesting insight into Catharine's soul. This was the church of her youth, where she and her siblings had been baptized, where her parents had been married and her grandmother confirmed, where they all, as slaves of Adam Robb and later of Catharine and Henry Harding, sat in the "negro pews."

Catharine must have been able to recall a thousand excruciating memories from that time in her life. The Harding family had been the source of many of them. Catharine and Henry Harding and their children bore the responsibility for separating the Weems family and changing their lives forever. But however bitter those memories were, they were the only ones that she possessed. As Josiah Henson had once written, his brother who was once held by the same master as the Weems family had his mind "demoralised or stultified by slavery." Yet another slave who had fled to the safety of Canada lived in dread of ever seeing his master again for fear the man had magical powers that could transport him back to the South. Those effects did not easily disappear with the Emancipation Proclamation or the passage of the amendment to the Constitution that permanently put an end to slavery.

Catharine Weems had been freed in 1853. Her mother, her sister Ann Maria, and five of her brothers had been sold to the slave traders by the Hardings a year earlier. A stipulation of the sale was that none of the family could be resold anywhere in the vicinity of Washington, D.C. This clause was intended to ensure that the family would never be together again or near other loved ones or familiar surroundings. One might have thought that any attachment that Catharine once had to the Harding family was severed forever as a result, but such was not the case.

Mary and Catharine had for several years shared the house that Sylvanus Boynton had purchased. Mary, the youngest Weems child, had experienced an unhappy marriage with James Savoy, whom she accused of being abusive and adulterous. James worked as a barber at the House of Representatives and, despite the fact that he made a respectable wage, he never established his own household for his wife and six children nor, according to Mary, did he contribute to the Weems household expenses, even when requested to do so by his father and mother-in-law before their deaths. Finally, after twenty-nine years of marriage and two years of desertion, Mary filed for divorce.[64]

Throughout her entire life, Mary never left the family home. Now unencumbered by a husband who could make any marital claim on the property, Mary contended that since she and Catharine were the only two surviving Weems children and that none of her siblings ever had children, not to mention that she had regularly contributed to paying the household expenses, she was the legal co-owner. But Catharine felt otherwise. Before dying, Catharine turned the house and property over to J. Maury Dove and Nannie C. Dove – the granddaughter of Catharine and Henry Harding. Mary, the only of the Weems children to have never been enslaved, fought this transaction in the courts for years. She contended that Catharine's mind had become unsound and that the Doves had used "undue importunities, persuasions and suggestions" to influence Catharine. Furthermore they employed "fraud, misrepresentation and artifice." Upon Catharine's death, the Doves demanded that Mary vacate the home. A defiant Mary, ultimately with the court's backing, refused to do so.[65]

A half-century earlier, Catharine and Henry Harding considered the Weems family and all that they may have possessed as theirs. Such was the law of the times. As the nineteenth century came to an end it would appear that the Hardings' granddaughter felt the same.[66] Perhaps little had changed. Slavery's shadow remained on the household long after its glow was extinguished.

# ACKNOWLEDGEMENTS

THIS BOOK COULD NOT have been written without the help of Charles Brewer, a remarkable historian and dear friend to all of my family. His familiarity with archives, libraries, archivists, and historians in Washington, D.C., Maryland, and many other parts of the United States was invaluable to my knowing where to go and with whom to speak about relevant records. Throughout the entire detective process of researching this book, Charles constantly retrieved and analyzed documents, followed yet another lead, and offered suggestions on what the next steps should be. I, along with everyone who enjoys reading the details of the remarkable Weems family's story, owe a tremendous debt of gratitude to Charles.

My wife, Shannon, who is also the curator of the Buxton National Historic Site and Museum, was a frequent companion and aide on research trips, as well as a proofreader, sounding board, technician for scanning documents and images, and a constant support for the many aspects of this project. Her portrayal of Arabella Weems at various speaking engagements over the years has given me an insight into what I imagine was Arabella's soul. Shannon has no idea how much she contributed to developing this book, and it is my pleasure to publicly acknowledge and thank her.

231

I also am indebted to many friends, both old and new. Foremost among the former is Elisa Carbone, author of an award-winning book on Ann Maria Weems entitled *Stealing Freedom*, who provided information and encouragement. Elisa was responsible for one of the most enjoyable experiences during the early stages of the research phase, when she took Shannon and me to the tavern that was once owned by the slave trader Charles Price, and introduced us to the delightful Williams family who now live there. Likewise I am indebted to Anthony Cohen, a Maryland historian, whose enthusiasm and expertise on Montgomery County makes him a joy to be with and to learn from. Patricia Andersen, librarian at the Montgomery County Historical Society in Rockville, and volunteers Diane Broadhurst and Jane C. Sween (whom the library is named after) were extraordinarily helpful in guiding us through area records and sharing their research, and helping to put perspective on historical figures and locations. Patricia has compiled an invaluable database of transactions involving slaves that are recorded in the Montgomery County land records. It was Diane who uncovered the sale of John Henson to his brother Josiah. I would also like to thank two employees in particular from the Montgomery County Circuit Court Law Library, Janet Camillo and John Cannon, who went the extra mile to try to find records that had seemingly disappeared. The staff at the Maryland State Archives in Annapolis, including Pat Melville, Chris Haley, Michael McCormick, and Kim Moreno, were very helpful and the Archives of Maryland Online is superb. The University of Maryland's McKeldin Library was a great place to seek out microfilm copies of newspapers, anti-slavery documents, and the American Missionary Association papers.

I always feel like a kid in a candy store when visiting the archival capital of the United States: Washington, D.C. The staff members at the National Archives, the Library of Congress, the D.C. archives, and the Family History Library of the Church of Jesus Christ of Latter Day

Saints were always helpful in directing us to various nuggets in the gold mines in which they work. Warmest thanks to Jerry McCoy at the Martin Luther King Jr. Memorial Library for his help on a variety of things. Thanks to Scott Taylor, manuscripts processor at Georgetown University Library's Special Collections division for providing a copy of a signed receipt from the Bulkley Southworth Griffin Papers for John C. Cook's sale of a slave; and to Lynn Freeman, the rectory manager for St. Peter's Church for the baptism records of Mary Weems Savoy's children. Jenny Masur, manager of the National Capital Region National Underground Railroad Network to Freedom, kindly forwarded background studies of two slave pens in Alexandria, Virginia. Howard University's Moorland-Spingarn Research Center manuscript department has its own Lewis Tappan collection and the library owns a rare copy of the biography of Charles Bennett Ray.

One of the most gratifying aspects of having a love for history is the many wonderful people one meets along the way. That is certainly the case with Mary Kay Ricks, a D.C. historian and author of *Escape on the Pearl*, who was generous with her knowledge and became an immediate friend. It was an unexpected pleasure to be contacted by Sandy Harrelson, who along with her husband, Barry, are the current owners of the D.C. home where the Weems family and their descendants lived well into the twentieth century. Sandy is herself an historian and is diligently researching the home and all who have lived in it. I would like to say a very special thank you to both Sandy and Barry for sharing their research and for inviting us into their home and allowing us to feel the lingering presence of the Weemses.

Our trip to Alabama to get a feel for the southern landscape and to research the owners of several of the Weems family was a fascinating experience. Thank you to the staff at the Eufaula and Montgomery public libraries, the Archives and Special Collections of Auburn University's Ralph B. Draughon Library, and the Montgomery County

Courthouse. The Alabama Department of Archives and History (which holds the Rumph Family Papers) was an enjoyable and fruitful place to research, made even more so by the help of Frazine Taylor.

New York State provided several rich repositories. Our visit to the Geneva Public Library and to the Geneva Historical Society's Prouty-Chew House and Museum was a great beginning to learn more about and understand the place to which Stella Weems fled and began her new life with the Garnet family. The University of Rochester's Rush Rhees Library has microfilm copies of the Rhodes House anti-slavery papers, which were critical in learning more about the British anti-slavery movement; Cornell University has the most impressive slavery and abolitionist collection that I have seen – and they have placed a great deal of it online. This is a must visit! Thank you to librarian Diane Cooter at the Special Collections Research Center at Syracuse University Library for helping me with the voluminous Gerrit Smith papers. I am grateful to Judith Wellman, the director of Historical New York Research Associates, for pointing me to the Sydney Howard Gay Papers at Columbia University and to Richard J. Hourahan, archivist of the Knapp House on Long Island, for providing information on the Underground Railroad in New York and on the family of Charles B. Ray.

Pennsylvania, with its long anti-slavery tradition, has many important places in which to research. The University of Pittsburgh's Hillman Library provided me the opportunity to view microfilm copies of records of the Pennsylvania Society for Promoting the Abolition of Slavery as well as those of the Maryland State Colonization Society. During the course of my research it was a treat to exchange information with Steve Harvey of Aston, Pennsylvania, the great-great-great-grandson of Ellwood Harvey (Dr. H.), a hilarious yet serious researcher who has done much to bring his ancestor to the fore of the Weems story, a position he so richly deserves. The pre-eminent Underground Railroad historian Charles Blockson, curator of the archives that bear his name at Temple University, and his assistant, Aslaku Berhanu, thoughtfully answered my questions about William Still and his surviving papers. It has been our good fortune to know and admire Mr. Blockson for many years and we applaud his pioneering work and continuing commitment to the field.

The Western Reserve Historical Society library – and the staff there – are jewels in Cleveland, Ohio. They hold many unique items that can't be found in other archives, including the Sylvanus C. Boynton Collection, which unfortunately did not include any references to Catharine Weems but did reveal more about the man who took her in when she first found freedom.

The Black Abolitionist Archives at the University of Detroit Mercy provided a great foundation and continuing source of information on the Weems family and the broader anti-slavery movement. I'd like to extend a heartfelt thanks to Roy Finkenbine for opening the archives, guiding me through the collection, and rolling up his sleeves and pulling and copying documents. The microfilm records of the Maryland State Colonization Society, the *Black Abolitionist Papers* and various anti-slavery newspapers continually lured me to the Purdy/Kresge Library at Wayne State University in Detroit, as did those of the British and Foreign Anti-Slavery Society at the Harlan Hatcher Graduate Library at the University of Michigan in Ann Arbor. The same campus has the Clements Library with a rich collection that includes the records of the Rochester Ladies' Anti-Slavery Society, the Weld-Grimké papers, and the African-American History Collection. The Burton Historical Collection at the main Detroit Public Library is another treasure trove that occupies a special place in my heart.

Further afield is the New Jersey Historical Society's Raritan Bay Union and Eagleswood Military Academy Collection, which houses the papers of the slave trader George Kephart. I am indebted to reference librarian James Lewis for providing a receipt of Adam Robb's for the sale of a slave. Thank you to Sabra Ionno and Michael Radice from the Harriet Beecher Stowe Center in Hartford, Connecticut, for allowing me to go through the correspondence in their archives and to

Meredith Evans, curator of printed materials at Archives and Special Collections at the Robert W. Woodruff Library of the Atlanta University Center, for sending me letters from Lewis Tappan to Ellwood Harvey as well as one from Frederick Douglass to Sarah Tappan that were contained in the Henry Slaughter Collection. Matthew Turi, the manuscripts reference librarian from the Wilson Library of University of North Carolina at Chapel Hill, kindly sent a copy of some of the contents of the John Newland Maffitt papers. It was good to chat with Stanford University's William B. Gould, whose book *Diary of a Contraband* sheds an important light on his ancestors, Cornelia and Diana Williams, who were freed from slavery in part with money from "the Weims Ransom Fund." Professor Gould graciously shared family photographs that were forwarded by Alba Holgado, the digital course management coordinator from the Robert Crown Law Library.

From the United Kingdom I would like to thank Denis Peel from the Society of Antiquaries of Newcastle-upon-Tyne; Julia Hudson, assistant archivist and records manager at the Friends House in London; and Pam Wilson, library and information assistant at Newcastle City Archives, for providing additional information on Henry and Anna Richardson; and Benjamin S. Beck (first cousin, four times removed from Henry Richardson), who also provided images of the Richardsons. Thank you to Derek Oliver in the manuscripts department of the National Library of Scotland for providing letters from Reverend Alexander Somerville to Henry Highland Garnet; and to the staff of Tyne & Wear Archives at the Blandford House in Newcastle for information on the Richardsons and James Clephan.

There are many authors whose work I consulted during the process of writing this book, and I am deeply grateful to every one of them. None more so than to Stanley Harrold, whose excellent book *Subversives: Antislavery Community in Washington, D.C., 1828–1865* and his article "Freeing the Weems Family: A New Look at the Underground Railroad," which appeared in *Civil War History* (volume 42), gave an in-depth look at the anti-slavery movement in general and at the Weems family in particular. I look forward to one day having the opportunity to meet Professor Harrold so I can personally thank him and praise his work, and so we can chat about the Weems family who have captured our imagination and to whom we have become so attached.

It was my pleasure to meet Hilary Russell many years ago when she investigated the workings of the Underground Railroad for Parks Canada. I could not have guessed at the time that her future work, *Final Research Report: The Operation of the Underground Railroad in Washington, D.C., c. 1800–1860*, which she wrote for the Historical Society of Washington and the U.S. National Park Service, would be so meaningful for my future work. I would express the same sentiments about Professor Loren Schweninger from the University of North Carolina at Greensboro, whose online project, Race and Slavery Petitions, included a case involving Adam Robb. Although our meeting was brief, I was taken by the sparkle in the eye of Gwendolyn Midlo Hall, Professor Emeritus from Rutgers University, and even more so by her work, the Louisiana Slave Database, which gave names to those forgotten people. Two telephone meetings – with Dorothy Provine, author of several works, including *District of Columbia Free Negro Registers, 1821–1861*, and with Jerry Hynson, who published *D.C. Department of Corrections Runaway Slave Book, 1848–1863* – were both educational and enjoyable. Ralph Clayton's *Cash For Blood: The Baltimore to New Orleans Domestic Slave Trade* illuminates that chapter of the domestic slave trade.

And, of course, where would we be in the twenty-first century without online collections at our fingertips, including Documenting the American South, Ancestry, the Godfrey Memorial Library, and an almost endless list of resources? Wow!

Closer to home in Ontario is the exceptional Dana Porter Library at the University of Waterloo, with its marvellous microfilm collection of anti-slavery society minutes, pamphlets, newspapers, the Lewis Tappan Papers, and seemingly endless other things. The University of Toronto's

Robarts Library has microfilm copies of anti-slavery newspapers and the Canadian correspondence in the American Missionary Association Papers. There was always something new and relevant to find in the Archives of Ontario. The Archives and Research Collections at the University of Western Ontario's D.B. Weldon Library has been my favourite research spot for many years, and I offer a particular expression of thanks to Theresa Regnier and John Lutman. Also at Western, Huron College, which includes the Anglican Diocese of Huron Archives, afforded information on the Colonial Church and School Society.

Research of the Bradley and Weems families in Canada was aided by the resources and friendly staff at the main Chatham-Kent public library in Chatham, which holds microfilm copies of early area newspapers and censuses. In the same building, the Kent Branch of the Ontario Genealogical Society, staffed by an amazing group of volunteers, has a large collection of regional research materials on individuals, institutions, and geographic locations. I would like to extend my appreciation to several of the Kent Branch members for their years of supplying answers to my questions: Robert Neil, Joan Griffin, Wilson Kerr, and Les Mancell. Also to Jay Smith and Joan Eckert for providing information about the employer of Joseph Weems. The Dresden library has microfilm copies of that town's newspaper, whose contents revealed more details on the Bradley family, as did mortgage and deed records at the Kent Land Registry office in Chatham. The Mormon Family History Center in Chatham has microfilm land, vital statistics, and area church records among its permanent collection. It was there, with mixed emotions, that I discovered the death and burial of Augustus Weems in the St. Joseph's Church Baptism, Marriages, and Burial Register. Even after months of painstakingly searching through records on both sides of the border for what became of every member of the family, discoveries like this brought me no joy.

Our connection to the historical community has grown much larger and our understanding of history much broader thanks to friends and associates Paul Lovejoy, Michelle Johnson, David Troutman, et al., at the Harriet Tubman Institute at York University; Diane Miller, James Hill, and the other directors at the U.S. National Park Service's Underground Railroad Network to Freedom; Carl Westmoreland, Angela Corley, former director Spencer Crew, former director of freedom stations Orloff Miller, and other staff at the National Underground Freedom Center; Tracey Weis from Millersville University, Pennsylvania; Renée Soulodre-La France from King's University College, London, Ontario; Shannon Ricketts, Derek Cooke, Owen Thomas, and others currently and formerly from Parks Canada; Paul Samson, Janet Jones, Eva Salter, Ghislaine Brodeur, Darren Winger, and Marie Cheesman from Ontario's Culture and Tourism ministries; James Walker from the University of Waterloo; Jennifer Bullock and Michelle Perry from Adam Matthew Publications in England; our comrades, such as Afua Cooper, Hilary Dawson, Donald Simpson, Jacqueline Tobin, and Jim and Lisa Gilbert, who are independent historians; and those at the many historical sites and museums in Ontario and in the United States, such as Wilma Morrison, Donna Ford, Steven Cook, Barbara Carter, Gwen Robinson, Bryan Walls, and especially the late Arlie Robbins, who are just the tip of the iceberg of those who have contributed in many ways to laying the foundation for this book.

It has been a pleasurable experience to work with the people from McClelland & Stewart. Former senior editor Chris Bucci was the first to champion this project, and Trena White has been wonderful with her editing skills, her patience, and her vision. I am grateful to Denise Bukowski for her part in making this project a reality.

And now back to special old friends. Joyce Middleton, Lori Gardner, JoAnn Hartley, and Karolyn Smardz Frost read various versions of this manuscript and, even when they wished to spare my feelings, shared impressions, suggestions, and encouragement as only real friends can. Years ago, Alice Newby, the late Margo Freeman, and I loved researching the story of Ann Maria Weems so that we could tell it to visitors at the

Buxton museum. Historians Dennis Gannon from D.C. and Marie Carter from Dresden, Ontario, could always be counted on to explore records and generously share their findings. Chicago's Tony Burroughs and Boston's Kate Clifford Larson are giants in the genealogical and historical community, and I thank them for their work, their help, their suggestions, and their friendship. I particularly thank Kate for taking the time from her busy schedule to travel to the Baker Library at Harvard Business School to scour the collection of R.G. Dun & Co. in search of credit reports on slave traders.

To my children, Christopher, Justin, Melanie, and Rebecca, I thank you for your uncomplaining support as you grew up in a household where history was perhaps too often the centre of our little universe. And I salute my father, Earl, who has for years jumped on the tractor at our farm when I should have been driving it, never discouraging me from following my historical pursuits. My mother, Corinne; sister, Cheryl; mother-in-law, Yvonne; and all of the members of both families have been constant sources of encouragement. And finally, to my home community at Buxton, which was once Canada's largest planned fugitive slave settlement, I thank you for being a place that values its history and for having allowed me the opportunity to be one of the voices to share it.

# NOTES

CHAPTER I

1. Marriage of George Judy to Ann Clements, March 21, 1823. Also Charles B. Jones and Jane Clements, October 4, 1836. In the case of the marriage of John Alvee to Elizabeth Ramsey, it was the bride who had to promise publicly to bring up the children as Catholics. Roman Catholic Marriage Records at Montgomery County, Maryland Historical Society Library.

2. "Married privately and secretly Ezechias Trundle and Emily Jones, with dispensation from the Archbishop, they being first cousins," May 1, 1836. Also, Oliver Clark to Catharine Cooper, April 12, 1851. Roman Catholic Marriage Records at Montgomery County, Maryland Historical Society Library.

3. Marriage of John Clements and Emily Livers, September 29, 1835. Roman Catholic Marriage Records at Montgomery County, Maryland Historical Society Library.

4. Henry Edmonson to Ann, property of William Gitting, August 7, 1827. Roman Catholic Marriage Records at Montgomery County, Maryland Historical Society Library.

5. Roman Catholic Marriage Records at Montgomery County, Maryland Historical Society Library.

6. 1850 U.S. census for Rockville, Montgomery County, Maryland, dwelling #295.

7. Sarah Tappan to Frederick Douglass, *Frederick Douglass Paper*, January 15, 1856.

8. Stanley Harrold, "Freeing the Weems family: A New Look at the Underground Railroad," *Civil War History*, vol. XLII, December 1996, p. 293.

9. Roman Catholic Baptismal Records at Montgomery County, Maryland Historical Society Library.

10. Roman Catholic Baptismal Records at Montgomery County, Maryland Historical Society Library.

11. *Daily National Intelligencer Press*, August 19, 1824. Maryland State Archives Online: http: //ww2.mdslavery.net/dsp_searchresults.cfm?fn=4&search=8 [accessed August 12, 2007].

12. Session Laws, 1805, vol. 607, p. 47. Maryland State Archives online.

13. Quoted in *Proceedings and Debates of the 1850 Constitutional Convention*, vol. 101, Debates vol. 2, p. 222. Maryland State Archives online. http://aomol.net/megafile/msa/speccol/sc2900/sc2908/000001/000101/html/am101de–222.html

14. E.S. Abdy, *Journal of a Residence and Tour in the United States of North America, from April, 1833 to October, 1834* (London, 1835), p. 89.

15. Jeffrey Brackett, *The Negro in Maryland: A Study of the Institution of Slavery* (Freeport, NY: Books for Libraries Press, 1969), pp. 79 and 80. Originally published 1889 in the John Hopkins University Studies in Historical and Political Science, ed. Herbert B. Adams.

16. Session Laws, 1839, vol. 600, p. 38, Maryland State Archives online.

17. Liber BS 11, book 37, Montgomery County Land Records, Montgomery County Courthouse.

18. Worthington G. Snethen, *The Black Code of the District of Columbia in Force September 1ˢᵗ, 1848* (New York: 1848), pp. 38-39.

19. Steven Doyle, "The Irony of Liberty: Origins of the Domestic Slave Trade," *Journal of the Early Republic*, vol. 12, no. 1, Spring 1992, pp. 37-62. Doyle quotes from the original letter from Mifflin to Adams, September 24, 1798 in the Adams Family Papers held at the Massachusetts Historical Society.

20. These names were extracted and published by Ralph Clayton in his valuable book *Cash for Blood: The Baltimore to New Orleans Domestic Slave Trade* (Bowie, MD: Heritage Books, 2002), p. 428. Pages 641-55 give information on the ships and details on individual trips, slave traders and captains.

21. *Twelve Years a Slave. Narrative of Solomon Northup, A Citizen of New-York, Kidnapped in Washington City in 1841 and Rescued in 1853, From a Cotton Plantation near the Red River in Louisiana*. Published by: Derby and Miller, Auburn, Derby, Orton and Mulligan, Buffalo, Sampson Low, Son & Company, London, 1853, pp. 44 and 45.

## CHAPTER 2

1. *The Centinel of Liberty and George-town Advertiser*, March 17, 1797, issue 84, p. 1. Also, the marriage of Adam Robb and Ann Lansdale on September 8, 1789 appears in "Prince George's County Marriage Record 1777–1789," p. 50. Copies of the index card registration available at Maryland State Archives online.

2. Information from the research of Eleanor M.V. Cook, January 2001, as attributed to an article entitled "Stage Coach Days in the District of Columbia" in Records of the Columbia Historical Society, vol. 50, pp. 15-16.

3. *Washington Federalist*, September 29, 1804, issue 683, p. 1.

4. Ibid., May 25, 1805, issue 749, p. 1.

5. *Federal Republican*, April 16, 1813, vol. VII, issue 956, p. 4.

6. *Daily National Intelligencer*, May 2, 1818, vol. VI, issue 1657, p. 3; *City of Washington Gazette*, May 24, 1820, vol. V, issue 770, p. 2.

7. Adam Robb was executor of the estate of James Suter according to the *Federal Republican* of March 22, 1816, vol. X, issue 1310, p. 1, and he was one of four commissioners appointed by the county court to dispose of the land of the late John Rabbitt, Sr. *Daily National Intelligencer*, November 19, 1819, issue 2139, p. 3.

8. *Washington Federalist*, November 16, 1803, issue 549, p. 3.

9. Ibid., June 8, 1804, issue 639, p. 3, and June 22, 1804, issue 645, p. 4; *National Intelligencer and Washington Advertiser*, October 9, 1805, p. 3.

10. *The Hornet, or Republican Advocate*, October 18, 1809, vol. I, issue 38, p. 4.

11. *Hagers-Town Gazette*, July 23, 1811, vol. III, issue 115, p. 3.

12. John Greenleaf Whittier, *The Conflict with Slavery: Politics and Reform, The Inner Life and Criticism*. Published online at Project Gutenberg http://library.beau.org/gutenberg/etext05/wit3610.txt

13. This information was made available by Eleanor Cook, who deposited her research on Adam Robb at the Montgomery County Historical Society in Rockville, MD. Ms. Cook notes that the purchase of Grace and child is recorded in Prince George's County land records, JJ1, folio 579.

14. 1800 census for Third District, Montgomery County, Maryland.

15. Josiah Henson, *Truth Stranger Than Fiction: Father Henson's Story of His Own Life* (Cleveland: John P. Jewett and Company, 1858), pp. 13-14.

16. *Federal Republican*, September 13, 1814, vol. VIII, issue 1153, p. 3.

17. Ibid., August 26, 1814, vol. VIII, issue 1149, p. 3.

18. John Hope Franklin and Loren Schweninger, *Runaway Slaves, Rebels on the Plantation* (New York and Oxford: Oxford University Press, 1999), pp. 28-29.

19. Sally E. Hadden, *Slave Patrols, Law and Violence in Virginia and the Carolinas* (Cambridge, MA and London, UK: Harvard University Press, 2001), pp. 162-65.

20. Liber V, book 23, Montgomery County Land Records, Montgomery County Courthouse.

21. Purchase recorded February 29, 1828 by Adam Robb (executor of estate of Upton Beall) from John Madden and Elias Madden, Liber BS 1, book 27, Montgomery County Land Records, Montgomery County Courthouse.

22. BS 11, book 37, Montgomery County Land Records, Montgomery County Courthouse.

23. BS 12, book 38, John Braddock mortgage from Adam Robb and Henry Harding, March 6, 1844, Montgomery County Land Records, Montgomery County Courthouse.

24. On July 27, 1839 Adam Robb received $900 from Pollard Webb for a "negro" man, William. Receipt is included in the George Kephart Correspondence, Manuscript Group 285, Raritan Bay Union and Eagleswood Military Academy, housed at the New Jersey Historical Society. Special thanks to James Lewis, reference librarian.

25. *National Era*, November 21, 1850 (reprinted a letter from Kephart's partner, Reuben B. Carlley, dated March 24, 1831 from Montgomery County, MD).

26. Frederic Bancroft, *Slave Trading in the Old South* (Columbia: University of South Carolina Press, 1996), pp. 64, 65 (reprint from original published by J.H. Furst Company, 1931).

27. Maryland State Archives, Montgomery County Court Equity Papers, MSA T415-3-35 (msa sc 4239-25 – Negro Charity, Mary and Kitty vs. Adam Robb, and Lansdale). This includes a bill in 1818, William Campbell's statement of 1818, Adam Robb's reply of May 19, 1819, and the Chancery decree of July Term 1820.

28. Inward Slave Manifests for the Port of New Orleans, Roll #1, 1818–1820 and Roll #2, January–March, 1821. Slaves included: Joshua, age 19; Peggy, 8; Lydia, 16; Airy, 19; Rachel, 9; Mary, 9; Abrams, 14; Lloyd, 13; Tom, 12; Sam, 18. Transcribed by Dee Parmer Woodtor, PhD and made available online at http://www.afrigeneas.com/slavedata/Roll.1.1818-1820.html and http://www.afrigeneas.com/slavedata/Roll.2.1821.html. Note that Henson's name was transcribed as "Fenson." Information on the sale of Hannah, Henson, and Leve to John Andrus dated December 15, 1820 has been made available through the Louisiana Slave Data project, undertaken by Dr. Gwendolyn Midlo Hall, http://www.ibiblio.org/laslave/fields.php

29. V, book 23, Montgomery County Land Records, Montgomery County Courthouse.

30. W, book 24, Montgomery County Land Records, Montgomery County Courthouse.

31. Maryland State Archives, Prince George's County Court (Chattel Papers), MSA C1174, 1818–1822, 40,233-205/221, C1174, available at http://ww2.mdslavery.net/dsp_searchresults.cfm?fn=4&search=13 [accessed August 11, 2007].

32. Court Minute Book, St. Landry Parish, Louisiana, submitted by Mike Miller to http://ftp.rootsweb.com/pub/usgenweb/la/stlandry/court/cbm3.txt

33. The new company "Osbourn & Childs" advertised such items in the *Daily National Intelligencer* on September 18 and October 10, 1817.

34. *Daily National Intelligencer*, February 13, 1817, April 12, 1817, August 2, 1817.

35. District of Columbia Land Records for Georgetown, Liber AL36, new folio 202, old folio 195. Indenture from Briscoe Davis to John N. Robb.

36. John Robb assessment for July, 1817. *Records of the City of Georgetown (DC) 1800–79, Assessment of Real & Personal Property, 1813–18* Microfilm publication no. 605, Roll 9, p. 171 of the assessment.

37. District of Columbia Land Records for Georgetown, Liber AQ41, new folio 280, old folio 390. Indenture from John N. Robb to Adam Robb dated April 17, 1818 and recorded April 30 of the same year. Slaves listed were John in his early 30s; Joe, about 32; Becky and Nellie, who were both about 50; Peggy, 18; Nellie, 4; and Charles, 14. Sale of Charles from Catharine Lansdale to John N. Robb provided by Eleanor M.V. Cook in an account of the Robb family in the Montgomery County Historical Society. Ms. Cook quotes from document in Montgomery County Land Records, Liber O, folio 21.

38. Joan M. Dixon, *National Intelligencer Newspaper Abstracts, 1818–1820* (Bowie, MD: Heritage Books), p. 196 (Tuesday, February 1, 1820 *National Intelligeneer*).

39. Mary C. Thornton, *A Complete Guide to the History and Inmates of the U.S. Penitentiary District of Columbia 1829–1862* (Bowie, MD: Heritage Books, 2003), p. 5.

40. Joan M. Dixon, *National Intelligencer Newspaper Abstracts, 1818–1820* (Bowie, MD: Heritage Books), p. 310. (Saturday, February, 15 *National Intelligencer*).

41. *Republican Star and General Advertiser*, April 22, 1823, vol. XXIV, issue 35, p. 4. Note that both the 1822 and 1823 taxes assessed to Adam Robb are listed in the same newspaper the next year on March 23, 1824, vol. XXV, issue 31, p. 3.

42. Session Laws of 1816, 1828, 1829, 1839, 1841, Maryland State Archives online. Also, S. Somervell Mackall, *Early Days of Washington* (Washington: Neale Co., 1899), p. 67.

43. The March 25, 1825 edition of the *Daily National Intelligencer*, p. 4, column 2 published an advertisement pursuant to a decree of the Circuit Court of the District of Columbia for a public auction of the property of John Robb to settle a dispute involving his heirs.

44. Montgomery County, Maryland Register of Wills, Liber HH 1,2, & 3. 1847–1851. Hall of Records CR 39, 627. Microfilm copy at Montgomery County Historical Society, Rockville, MD.

45. HH Orphans' Court (microfilm), Books 1, 2, 3. 1847–1848, Montgomery County Courthouse.

46. Ninian's wife was Sara Ann, and his daughters Ann Sophia and Mary Eveline Victoria. Ann Sophia, born September 13, 1837, baptized September 18, 1837. Daughter of Niny, of Mr. Robb's and Sara Ann of Mr. H. Harding's. Sponsor was Ester of Mr. Robb. Vital Records. St. John's Church (Catholic), Forest Glen, MD. Transcribed by Mabel Leonard Gibson and Edna Plummer Lines. Presented by the Janet Montgomery Chapter of Montgomery County, MD DAR 1924, pp. 54, 56.

47. Montgomery County, Maryland Register of Wills. Liber HH 1,2, & 3. 1847–1851. Hall of Records CR 39, 627, microfilm copy at Montgomery County Historical Society, Rockville, MD.

48. Montgomery County, Maryland Register of Wills HH3, folio 148. (Note that what appears to be Letton's name is almost illegible.)

49. *Baltimore Sun*, December 19, 1849, quoting from an article that had appeared in the *Journal* from Rockville, MD.

50. Montgomery County, MD Register of Wills HH3, folio 148.

51. Montgomery County, MD Register of Wills HH3, folio 149. Info courtesy of Diane Broadhurst, Montgomery County historian.

52. Transcription of the Inventory of Adam Robb's Estate, filed May 1847 in Montgomery County, MD.

53. Roman Catholic Baptismal Records at Montgomery County, Maryland Historical Society Library.

54. STS 4, book 42. Montgomery County Land Records, Montgomery County Courthouse. "The Hermitage" was bequeathed to sons Charles and Elias Harding by John Harding in his will, probated February 5, 1751. Recorded in Book A1, p. 74,

Frederick County, as noted in William Neal Hurley, Jr., *Harding Families*, Our Maryland Heritage, Book 39 (Bowie, MD: Heritage Books), p. 1.

55. BS 12, book 38, Montgomery County Land Records, Montgomery County Courthouse.

56. Proceedings of Orphans' Court in the case of Edward Harding, Sr. (deceased), February 3, 17 and December 29, 1829, microfilm wk. 352-353, 1827–1855, pp. 59, 61, 62, 112, 113, Wills Department, Montgomery County Courthouse. Josiah Harding's guardian was Erasmus Perry.

57. Last Will and Testament of Charles Adam Harding. Copy in the "Harding" file at the Montgomery County Historical Society, Rockville, MD.

58. STS 3, book 41, Montgomery County Land Records, Montgomery County Courthouse.

59. David Diggs, one-month-old son of "George, property of Mr. Robb & Hasety, property of Mr. Harding (Edward)" was baptized on November 4, 1821. Sponsor was "Ann (free woman)." Vital Records, St. John's Church (Catholic), Forest Glen, MD. Transcribed by Mabel Leonard Gibson and Edna Plummer Lines. Presented by the Janet Montgomery Chapter of Montgomery County, MD DAR, 1924, p. 7.

60. Henry Harding was appointed as one of the trustees by the Montgomery County Court of Equity to offer up for public sale some of the late Upton Beall's land. Instrument recorded September 26, 1846. STS 2, book 40, Montgomery County Land Records, Montgomery County Courthouse.

61. Proceedings of Orphans' Court, microfilm HH, 1847–1848, Wills Department, Montgomery County Courthouse.

62. In the 1850 census for the Fourth District (Rockville) for Montgomery County, Maryland the Household of Henry (68 years old) and Catharine A. Harding (58) included Charles A. Harding (29), Elizabeth A. Harding (35), Catharine F. Harding (25), and a female named Ellen R. Queen (16).

63. *Montgomery Sentinel*, July 29, 1856, and *Baltimore Sun*, July 10, 1856, p. 2. The Brannums – Charlotte, Ned Sr., and their son Ned Jr. – were among those slaves who were previously transferred from Henry Harding to his son Charles to avoid creditors. Possible relationship to Arabella surmised because Cecilia Talbot lived with Charlotte Brannum in 1870 after emancipation.

64. *DC Department of Corrections Runaway Slave Cases*. Special Collections microfilm M9597-1. Maryland State Archives.

65. Jerry Hynson, *District of Columbia Runaway and Fugitive Slave Cases: 1848–1863* (Westminster, MD: Willow Bend Books, 1999), p. 13. Also, George, 2 months old, was baptized July 2, 1826, son of "George, property of Mr. Robb & Ester, property of Edw. Harding." Vital Records, St. John's Church (Catholic), Forest Glen, MD. Transcribed by Mabel Leonard Gibson and Edna Plummer Lines. Presented by the Janet Montgomery Chapter of Montgomery County, MD DAR, 1924, p. 30.

66. William Still's handwritten notes in Pennsylvania Abolition Society, "Journal C of Station No. 2 of the Underground Railroad (Philadelphia, Agent William Still)

1852–1857" in the Historical Society of Pennsylvania Collections (microfilm). Entry dated September 25, 1854 for Chas. King & Robt White.

67. William Still, *The Underground Rail Road: A Record of Facts, Authentic Narratives, Letters, &C., Narrating the Hardships, Hair-breadth Escapes and Death Struggles Of the Saves in their efforts of Freedom, As Related by Themselves and others, or Witnessed by the Author, Together with Sketches of Some of the Largest Stockholders, and Most Liberal Aiders and Advisers, of the Road* (1871), p. 483, reprinted in 1970 by Johnson Publishing Company. January 17, 1826 baptismal record for George Edward Diggs naming "Mary, of Mr. Robb," photostat copy of Catholic Records Baptisms 1813–1856 at Montgomery County Historical Society, Rockville, MD.

68. *National Era*, December 23, 1858, p. 202.

69. *A Narrative of Thomas Smallwood, (Coloured Man) Giving an account of his birth – The period he was held in slavery – His release – And removal to Canada, Etc. Together with an account of the Underground Railroad. Written by himself* (Toronto: James Stephens, 1851).

70. Benjamin Drew, "Narrative of Francis Henderson" in *The Refugee: or the Narratives of Fugitive Slaves in Canada* (Boston: John P. Jewett and Co. 1856). The formation of the Auxiliary Guard in the city of Washington was approved by the U.S. president on September 10, 1842. The slave patrols referred to by Henderson had been operating prior to his escape from Washington in 1841.

71. "The Case of William L. Chaplin," Library of Congress American Memory website, http://memory.loc.gov/cgi-in/query/r?ammem/llst:@field (DOCID+@lit(llsto41div3)), pp. 21-22.

72. Jerry Hynson, *District of Columbia Runaway and Fugitive Slave Cases: 1848–1863*, p. 14.

73. Ibid., p. 65. (Note that by the time of Dorsey's escape in July 1857, Catharine Harding was married and had the surname Maddox.)

74. Adam Robb's ownership of George Diggs established by his son David's baptism on November 4, 1821 at the age of one month. Father recorded as "George, property of Mr. Rob [sic] and mother Hasety, property of Mr. Harding (Edward)." Sponsor was Ary of Mr. Edward Harding. A later entry of March 15, 1829 upon the baptism of another son named Henry, lists both George and Hasety as belonging to Mr. Robb. Source: "MD Counties Montgomery Fore," Maryland DAR Genealogical Records Committee report, series 1, vol. 38; Vital Records of St. John's Church (Catholic) Forest Glen MD, copied by Mabel Leonard Gibson with assistance of Edna Plumber Lines, 1924.

75. David and Harriet Diggs had their ten-month-old daughter, Elizabeth, baptized on October 16, 1847 in a Catholic ceremony. David belonged to Josiah Harding and Harriet to Mr. Dorsey. At the time of the marriage of David Diggs to Harriet Ross on December 1, 1844 she belonged to Remus Dawsin. Source: "MD Counties Montgomery Fore," Maryland DAR Genealogical Records Committee report, series 1, vol. 38; Vital Records of St. John's Church (Catholic) Forest Glen, MD, copied by Mabel Leonard Gibson with assistance of Edna Plumber Lines, 1924.

76. William Still, *The Underground Rail Road* (1871), p. 487. (Interestingly, David Diggs, property of Dr. J. Harding, married Harriet Ross, property of Remus Dawsin, on December 1, 1844 at a Catholic ceremony in Montgomery County. There is no mention of Diggs's wife in William Still's account.)

## CHAPTER 3

1. *Frederick Douglass Paper*, February 1, 1856.
2. Photostat copy of *Catholic Records Baptisms 1813–1856* at Montgomery County Historical Society, Rockville, MD.
3. Roman Catholic Baptismal Records and Marriage Records at Montgomery County, Maryland Historical Society Library. Note that Cecilia's name is variously spelled Cicely and Celia in some documents.
4. *The Letters of William Lloyd Garrison*, vol. IV, *From Disunionism to the Brink of War 1850–1860*, ed. Louis Ruchames (Cambridge, MA and London, UK: Belknap Press of Harvard University Press, 1975), no. 36 (quoting from a published letter dated July 12, 1845 that appeared in the New York *Herald*).
5. "The Case of William L. Chaplin," Library of Congress American Memory website.
6. W.L. Chaplin to Gerrit Smith, March 28, 1848. Gerrit Smith Papers, Box 6, Syracuse University Library, Special Collections Research Center. Also, Manumission of Mary and her child, James, "in consideration of good will Justice & humanity and in further consideration of $300 paid by W.L. Chaplin," in Dorothy S. Provine, *District of Columbia Free Negro Registers 1821–1861* (Bowie, MD: Heritage Books, 1996), Registration #2226, vol. 3, p. 538.
7. "The Case of William L. Chaplin – Appeal," Library of Congress American Memory website, p. 7. Also note that Chaplin had tried to encourage the brother of Josiah Henson to escape from slavery with his aid. However,

> he found my brother's mind so demoralized or stultified by slavery, that he would not risk his life in the attempt to gain his freedom, and he informed me of this fact. Still I could not rest contented, and Mr. Chaplin promised to make another effort, as he intended to visit the neighbourhood again. He laboured with my brother the second time, with no good result, and then he endeavoured to assist Mr Toomb's slaves, who had resolved to escape from Georgia to Canada. Mr. Chaplin was detected, and thrown into prison to await a trial.

(Josiah Henson, *"Uncle Tom's Story of His Life." An Autobiography of the Rev. Josiah Henson*, edited by John Lobb, London: Christian Age Office, 1876, p. 153).

8. W.L. Chaplin to Gerrit Smith, May 17, 1848. Gerrit Smith Papers, Box 6, Syracuse University Library, Special Collections Research Center.
9. Mention of Bradley's relationship with Chaplin is recorded in *Frederick Douglass Paper*, Rochester, NY. August 18, 1854, "Canada and the Colored People."

10. *DC Department of Corrections Runaway Slave Book.* Maryland State Archives microfilm M9597, entry dated August 9, 1850. Note that in Maryland State Archives, Session Laws 1853, vol. 403, p. 129, the General Assembly of Maryland passes an act to compensate the people who arrested William L. Chaplin. Those compensated included John H. Goddard, E.G. Handy, James F. Wollard, John Davis, and John C. Cook. In the *Runaway Slave Book* mentioned above, on August 9, 1850 J.H. Goddard and E.G. Handy committed Allen, slave of Stephens, and J.H. Goddard and J.F. Wollard committed Mary Jones, slave of Harding. (Note that John C. Cook later was the slave trader from whom Addison and Joseph Weems were purchased. John Davis was an agent of Cook. Also note that according to www.pbs.org website "Africans in America," William Chaplin was expected to bring six slaves to an anti-slavery convention at Cazenovia, New York but he was arrested; might they have been Allen, Garland (White), Mary Jones, Abraham Young/William Henry Bradley and family and/or Stella Weems?)

11. Reprinted in the *Geneva Gazette*, August 9, 1850.

12. W.L. Chaplin to Gerrit Smith, September 9, 1850. Gerrit Smith Papers, Box 6, Syracuse University Library, Special Collections Research Center.

13. *National Era*, September 26, 1850.

14. Ibid., November 21, 1850.

15. Stanley Elkins and Eric McKitrick, "Institutions and the Law of Slavery," *American Quarterly*, summer 1957, vol. 9, no. 2.

16. *Anti-Slavery Advocate*, December 1853.

17. William Pearce, like the Robbs, Bealls, and Hardings, was also a prominent Montgomery County citizen. On January 15, 1819 he was appointed a road commissioner. Laws of Maryland, Maryland State Archives online.

18. This law was designed to pacify the southern slave owners by making it illegal for anyone to assist in the escape or concealment of runaway slaves. The penalty was a fine of $1,000 or six months in jail. Also, United States marshals or special commissioners could demand that any citizen be ordered to assist in the capture of any runaway or be tried for treason. An added enticement was that judges or justices of the peace were paid five dollars if they found a black to be a free person and ten dollars if they found him or her to be a fugitive. Blacks were not allowed to testify in their own defence. As a result, blacks were kidnapped from the streets or from their own homes – even some who had been free for several generations!

19. Lewis Tappan to Joseph Sturge, April 1, 1851, Tappan Papers; *Anti-Slavery Reporter*, May 1, 1856.

20. *Anti-Slavery Reporter*, May 1, 1856 (article referring to the beginnings of the Dawn Settlement, up to 1856); *The Nonconformist*, October 8, 13, and 20, 1852.

21. *Anti-Slavery Reporter*, February 2, 1852. Reference to the Wilsons' work appears in a letter from Hiram Wilson to Miss Elizabeth Mountfort of the Ladies Anti-Slavery Society of Portland, ME, dated March 8, 1850, posted online by the Maine Historical Society, www.MaineMemory.net

22. Indentures from Chatham-Kent Registry Office, Township of Camden Gore, concession 5, east half-lot 3. Registration A19, #1162. Elizabeth Woods to William Henry Bradley and Ann Maria Bradley.

23. Benjamin Drew, *The Refugee: or the Narratives of Fugitive Slaves in Canada* (Boston: John P. Jewett and Co., 1856).

24. Sarah Tappan to Frederick Douglass, *Frederick Douglass Paper*, January 15, 1856.

25. *The North Star* (Rochester, NY), October 31, 1850.

26. *Geneva Gazette*, Friday, March 21, 1851.

27. *Anti-Slavery Reporter*, December 1, 1852, published letter by Henry H. Garnet.

28. Ibid., January 1, 1850.

29. 1850 census for the Town of Seneca, NY. (Note that Geneva was at that time listed as a part of the town of Seneca.)

30. Wilson Armistead, *A Tribute for the Negro: Being a Vindication of the Moral, Intellectual, and Religious Capabilities of the Colored Portion of Mankind, with Particular Reference to the African Race* (Manchester and London: William Irwin, 1848). Also "Eulogium on Henry Highland Garnet, D.D." delivered by Alexander Crummell to the Union Literary and Historical Association, Washington, DC, May 4, 1882. Other details on Garnet are included in William J. Simmons, *Men of Mark: Eminent, Progressive and Rising* (Cleveland, George M. Rewell & Co., 1887).

31. Connecticut General Assembly, "An Act in addition to an Act entitled 'An Act for the admission and settlement of Inhabitants of Towns'" May 24, 1833. (Complete act can be found on Yale University's Gilder Lehrman Center for the study of Slavery, Resistance, & Abolition website http://www.yale.edu/glc/crandall/02.htm)

32. *Christian Recorder*, January 22, 1870 (Philadelphia).

33. *Colored American*, August 21, 1841 (New York) contains the marriage announcement. *Christian Recorder*, March 23, 1882 (Philadelphia) gives account of Henry Garnet's residence in Troy at the time of his marriage.

34. George F. Bragg, *Men of Maryland* (Baltimore: Church Advocate Press, 1914), p. 122

35. *The North Star* (Rochester, NY), June 23, 1848; July 7, 1848; August 25, 1848.

36. *Gateshead Observer*, September 7, 1850. Also, the indication that young Mary accompanied her father appears in David E. Swift, *Black Prophets of Justice, Activist Clergy Before the Civil War* (Baton Rouge and London: Louisiana State University Press, 1989). Mr. Swift notes that this information came from "a handwritten account in the possession of Charlotte Mebane, Mary Garnet's granddaughter."

37. *Frederick Douglass Paper*, June 26, 1851, reprinted from the *British Banner*.

38. *Gateshead Observer*, September 28, 1850. Black Abolitionist Archives at the University of Detroit Mercy, McNichols Campus, document 10894a.

39. *Gateshead Observer*, September 21, 1850. Black Abolitionist Archives, document 10875.

40. Lewis Tappan to Julia W. Garnet, November 5, 1850 and April 1, 1851, Tappan Papers.

41. Samuel Rhoads to Lewis Tappan, 11 month 21st day, 1850, Gerrit Smith Papers, Box 31, Syracuse University Library, Special Collections Research Center.

42. Julia Garnet to Gerrit Smith, February 14, 1851. Gerrit Smith Papers, Box 19, Syracuse University Library, Special Collections Research Center.

43. Earl Ofari Hutchinson, *Let Your Motto Be Resistance* (Boston: Beacon Press, 1972), p. 64.

44. W.L. Chaplin to Gerrit Smith, November 2, 1848. Gerrit Smith Papers, Box 6, Syracuse University Library, Special Collections Research Center.

45. *Frederick Douglass Paper*, June 26, 1851, reprinted from the *British Banner*.

46. "Eulogium on Henry Highland Garnet, D.D.," delivered by Alexander Crummell to the Union Literary and Historical Association, Washington, DC, May 4, 1882.

47. *The Slave*, issue 10, p. 40, October, 1851.

48. H.H. Garnet to Gerrit Smith July 7, 1851. Gerrit Smith Papers, Box 20, Syracuse University Library, Special Collections Research Center.

49. *Christian Recorder*, January 22, 1870.

50. *Geneva Gazette*, March 7, 1851 and *Frederick Douglass Paper*, March 11, 1852.

51. *Frederick Douglass Paper*, January 16, November 13, December 11, 1851.

52. Ibid., February 19, 1852, reprinted from *Newcastle Advertiser*.

53. Ibid., March 11, 1852.

54. *The Slave*, no. 24, p. 93.

55. Rev. Somerville to E. Chappell, October 27, 1853, National Library of Scotland, Edinburgh, MS 7639, pp. 361, 362.

56. *The Slave*, no. 23, p. 92.

CHAPTER 4

1. Jeffrey Brackett, *The Negro in Maryland: A Study of the Institution of Slavery* (Freeport, NY: Books for Libraries Press, 1969) p. 179. Originally published 1889 in the John Hopkins University Studies in Historical and Political Science, ed. Herbert B. Adams.

2. *The Black Abolitionist Papers: Canada, 1830–1865*. Editors C. Peter Ripley, Roy E. Finkenbine et al. (Chapel Hill and London: University of North Carolina Press, 1986). p. 79.

3. *Voice of the Fugitive* (Windsor), December 16, 1852.

4. Harriet Beecher Stowe to Mary A. Estlin, December 16, 1852. Estlin Papers. (microfilm MIC R24 at Dana Porter Library, University of Waterloo, Ontario)

5. *Nonconformist*, November 3, 1852.

6. *Inquirer* (London), November 6, 1852.

7. *North American and United States Gazette* (Philadelphia), Thursday, November 11, 1852, issue 18,610, col. C.

8. *Boston Daily Atlas*, Thursday, November 11, 1852, issue 114, col. D. *Vermont Watchman and State Journal* (Montpelier), Thursday, November 18, 1852, issue 52, col. G.

9. *The Nonconformist* (London), November 17, 1852

10. Ibid., November 3, 1852

11. *The Slave*, November 1852, Number 23

12. Clare Midgley, *Women Against Slavery: The British Campaigns, 1780–1870* (London and New York: Routledge, 1992), p. 139.

13. Joseph Sturge, *A Visit to the United States in 1841* (Boston: Dexter S. King, 1842).

14. *Christian News* (Glasgow), November 11, 1852.

15. *Inquirer* (London), November 20, 1852.

16. Ibid.

17. Ibid., November 13, 1852, from a report that originated in a letter from Henry Highland Garnet to the *Christian News* (Glasgow).

18. Reprinted in the December 1852 edition of *Anti-Slavery Advocate*.

19. *Anti-Slavery Reporter*, February 1, 1856.

20. Reprinted in the December 1852 edition of *Anti-Slavery Advocate*.

21. *Anti-Slavery Advocate*, April 1853.

22. *Anti-Slavery Reporter*, April 1, 1853.

23. *The Nonconformist*, October 8 and 20, 1852.

24. The Sturge family's financial support for the Dawn Settlement is mentioned in the *Chatham Tri-Weekly Planet*, January 10, 1860.

25. Lewis Tappan to Joseph Sturge, April 1, 1851, Tappan Papers. Library of Congress, Washington, D.C.

26. *Anti-Slavery Reporter* reporting on a meeting held in London, July 5 and adjourned to July 12, 1852. Another letter of support for Henson appeared in the October 13, 1852 edition of *Nonconformist*.

27. Harriet Beecher Stowe to Mary A. Estlin, December 16, 1852, Estlin Papers (microfilm MIC R24 at Dana Porter Library, University of Waterloo, Ontario)

28. *Anti-Slavery Advocate*, no. 4, January 1853.

29. Reprinted in the *Anti-Slavery Advocate*, no. 1, October, 1852.

30. *Anti-Slavery Advocate* reporting on annual meeting held January 26–28, 1853.

31. *The Nonconformist* (London), January 5, 1853.

32. *New York Daily Times*, December 6, 1852 (reprint of article that previously appeared in the *London Daily News*).

33. *Anti-Slavery Advocate*, no. 6, March 1853.

34. Minutes of January 1853 meeting of the Bristol and Clifton Ladies Anti-Slavery Society, microfilm in the Alexander Lovell Murray collection at University of Western Ontario, London.

35. *The British Friend: A Monthly Journal, Chiefly Devoted to the Interests of the Society of Friends*, no. XII, vol. X, 1852.

36. Susan Edmonstone Ferrier to Helen Tennent, October 8, 1852, from *Memoir and Correspondence of Susan Ferrier, 1782–1854* collected by John Ferrier, ed. John Andrew Doyle (London: John Murray, 1898), p. 349; cited in "British and Irish Women's Letters and Diaries," copyright Alexander Street Press, LLC, in collaboration with the University of Chicago. Available at http://alexanderstreet4.com

37. Lewis Tappan diary July 27, 1855, Tappan Papers, Library of Congress. Note that

the British abolitionists consistently misspelled the Weems name as "Weims." Also, *The Slave*, issue 23, November 1852.

38. Henry Richardson to L.A. Chamerovzov (secretary of the British and Foreign Anti-Slavery Society), September 5, 1854. Microfilm in the Rhodes House Anti-Slavery Collection at the University of Michigan Harlan Hatcher Graduate Library, Ann Arbor, MI.

39. Memorial to Ellen Richardson, *Frederick Douglass Papers*, Library of Congress American Memory website: http://memory.loc.gov/mss/mfd/19/19018/0002.gif

40. Anna Richardson to Charles B. Ray, October 9, 1853, as cited in *Sketch of the Life of Rev. Charles B. Ray* (New York: Press of J.J. Little & Co., 1887), p. 45. Copy in the Moorland Spingarn Research Center Library, Howard University, Washington, DC.

41. *The Slave*, no. 24, December 1852, p. 93.

42. Ibid., no. 27, March, 1853, p. 11.

43. *Anti-Slavery Reporter* May 1, 1853, vol. 1, no. 5, New Series, p. 114 (letter is dated from Washington, DC, March 16, 1853).

44. Ibid.

45. *Personal Memoir of Daniel Drayton, for Four Years and Four Months a Prisoner (for Charity's Sake) in Washington Jail*, reprint of 1855 edition by Negro Universities Press, New York, 1969. This also appears in "Captains Drayton and Sayres" in *Slave Rebels, Abolitionists, and Southern Courts*, vol. 2, p. 440.

46. *Gateshead Observer*, December 18, 1852.

CHAPTER 5

1. *The Slave*, no. 24, December 1852, p. 94.

2. Letter from Rev. Garnet, *Christian News*, January 20, 1853, from *Black Abolitionist Papers*. Also *The Slave*, no. 25, January 1853, p. 4. Further details of the preparations for the trip are in an October 7, 1853 letter from Rev. Somerville to Rev. H.H. Garnet on pp. 321 and 322 of MS. 7639 from the National Library of Scotland, Edinburgh.

3. *The Slave*, no. 28, April, 1853, p. 16.

4. Ibid., no. 24, December 1852, p. 95.

5. Rev. Somerville to H.H. Garnet, November 5, 1852. National Library of Scotland, MS. 7639, pp. 364-366 and 429-431.

6. *The Slave*, no. 28, April, 1853, p. 16. Also *Inquirer*, April 23, 1853, from *Black Abolitionist Papers*.

7. *Daily National Intelligencer* (Washington, DC), Saturday, October 12, 1839, issue 8318, col. A, and Wednesday, November 8, 1843, issue 9586, col. C.

8. Barbour County Land Records, Casbar Jones to Cook & Price, Book K, pp. 181, 182.

9. *Papers of the American Slave Trade, Series D. Records of the U.S. Customhouses, Part 1, Port of Savannah Slave Manifests, 1790–1860*, ed. Robert E. Lester. These manifests are on microfilm in the Manuscript Division of the Library of

Congress. A finding aid is available online, courtesy of LexisNexis, at
http://www.lexisnexis.com/academic/Results1.asp?datasections=Communities%3A
Academic+Faculty+and+Librarians&query=manifests. Price's manifest dated
February 28, 1853 is on microfilm, reel 7; folder containing this begins at frame 0535.
Cook's was November 16, 1853, reel 8; folder begins at frame 0001. His brother and
additional partner, Hatch Cook, also used the *Metamora*, shipping a single 45-year-old
slave on September 1, 1853, reel 7; folder begins at frame 0815.

10. *Anti-Slavery Reporter*, February 1, 1849.

11. *Daily Cleveland Herald*, Monday, March 12, 1860, issue 60, col. A.

12. *Sketch of the Life of Rev. Charles B. Ray* (New York: Press of J.J. Little
    & Co., 1887). Evidence of Sylvanus Boynton attending Oberlin College
    is taken from *Oberlin College Name Index to 1850*.
    http://www.morganohiolibrary.com/OberlinCollege.html. Marriage of Sylvanus
    Boynton to Eliza N. Gibbs took place October 23, 1851, according to Marriages of
    Lorain County, Ohio 1824–1865, compiled by Elyria Chapter, Daughters of the
    American Revolution and the Genealogical Workshop, Lorain County Historical
    Society, Elyria, OH, 1980, printed by Unigraphic, Inc., Evansville, IN.

13. Benjamin Slight diary at United Church Archives, Toronto.

14. Autobiography of Reverend William King, *The William King Collection*, Public
    Archives of Canada.

15. Benjamin Drew, *The Refugee: or the Narratives of Fugitive Slaves in Canada*
    (Boston: John P. Jewett and Co., 1856) p. 30. Also Sarah H. Bradford, *Scenes in the
    Life of Harriet Tubman* (Auburn, NY: W.J. Moses Printer, 1869), p. 19, has quote:
    "I looked at my hands to see if I was de same pusson."

16. Interview with Mrs. Joseph Wilkinson in *The Freedmen's Inquiry Papers*, National
    Archives, Washington, DC.

17. *Gateshead Observer*, December 18, 1852.

18. Frederick Douglass, *Life and Times of Frederick Douglass, Written by Himself. His
    Early Life as a Slave, His Escape from Bondage, and His Complete History to the Present
    Time* (Boston: De Wolfe & Fiske Co., 1892), p. 329

19. Herman Freudenberger and Jonathan B. Pritchett, "The Domestic United
    States Slave Trade: New Evidence," *Journal of Interdisciplinary History*, Vol. XXI,
    no. 3 (Winter 1991), p. 474. These estimates are from 1830.

20. G.W. Featherstonhaugh, *Excursion Through the Slave States*, vol. 1 (London: 1844),
    pp. 119-121.

21. Anna Richardson to Charles B. Ray, December 10, 1852, as cited in *Sketch of the Life
    of Rev. Charles B. Ray* (New York: Press of J.J. Little & Co., 1887), pp. 41 and 42.

22. Ibid., pp. 42–43.

23. On July 12, 1852 Bernard M. Campbell sold a parcel of land in Montgomery to
    Camilla D. Gerald. Montgomery County Land Deeds, p. 505 (microfiche)
    Montgomery County Courthouse. On October 18, 1852, twenty-year-old Martha
    Weems was sent aboard the *Helen A. Miller* to New Orleans (Ralph Clayton,

*Cash for Blood*, p. 428). It is unknown whether Martha Weems was related to John and Arabella.

24. *Advertiser & State Gazette*, under the headline "Reply to the Noble Ladies of England," February 3, 1853.

25. William Still, *The Underground Rail Road*, pp. 54-56.

26. *The Slave*, no. 26, February, 1853.

27. *Frederick Douglass Paper*, December 16, 1853.

28. Code of Alabama, 1852, sections 2056-2057, as quoted by Frederic Bancroft in *Slave Trading in the Old South* (Columbia: University of South Carolina Press, 1996), p. 198 (reprinted from original published by J.H. Furst Company, 1931).

29. *The Nonconformist*, April 20, 1853, p. 321.

30. Andrew Somerville to H.H. Garnet, National Library of Scotland, MS. 7639, p. 531.

31. *The Slave*, no. 29, May, 1853, p. 24.

32. Ibid., no. 35, p. 44. Also *Sketch of the Life of Rev. Charles B. Ray*.

33. Anna Richardson to Charles B. Ray, October 9, 1853 as appears in *Sketch of the Life of Rev. Charles B. Ray*, pp. 44-45.

34. *The Slave*, no. 35, p. 44.

35. Sarah Tappan to Frederick Douglass, *Frederick Douglass Paper*, January 15, 1856.

36. Fredericka Brener, *The Homes of the New World: Impressions of America* (New York: Harper and Brothers, 1853), vol. 2, pp. 202-03.

37. *New York Daily Times*, September 14, 1853, p. 4.

CHAPTER 6

1. 1853 Slave Tax List for Montgomery County for Henry, Charles, and Josiah Henson. Original at Maryland State Archives.

2. JGH 2, Book 45, Montgomery County Land Records.

3. Isaac Cory was the unfortunate victim as reported in the Monday, April 18, 1853 edition of *Tribune*. This article is in Lewis Tappan's Scrapbook #1 at Moorland Spingarn Archives at Howard University.

4. This undated article is in Lewis Tappan's Scrapbook #1 at Moorland Spingarn Archives. The article cites its source as the Washington correspondent of the *Ashtabula* (Ohio) *Sentinel*.

5. Ulrich Bonnel Phillips, *American Negro Slavery: A Survey of the Supply, Employment and Control of the Negro Labor as Determined by the Plantation Regime*, 1918. (Digital copy available through Project Gutenberg at http://www.gutenberg.org/files/11490/11490-8.txt) The author quotes from a manuscript in the New York Public Library filed under "slavery."

6. *Anti-Slavery Reporter*, June 1, 1855; reprinted the article from the *Washington Star*.

7. Lewis Tappan to Henry Richardson, July 27, 1855 and September 1, 1855, Tappan Papers. (There is mention in this letter that Tappan "is willing to be united with Mr. Whiting and Mr. Lane in taking care of the money.")

8. *The Slave*, no. 46, p. 88.

9. Lewis Tappan to Henry Richardson, September 1, 1855, Tappan Papers.

10. *Anti-Slavery Reporter*, May 1, 1855, p. 116.

11. Lewis Tappan, diary July 19, 1855, Tappan Papers.

12. Tappan to Henry Richardson, July 21, 1855 letter book 1855–1856, Tappan Papers.

13. Tappan to Joseph Sturge, November 27, 1855.

14. Tappan diary, July 21, 1855.

15. Ibid., July 26, 1855.

16. Ibid., August 16, 1855.

17. Tappan to Henry Richardson, November 14, 1855.

18. Tappan to Joseph Sturge, November 27, 1855.

19. Tappan diary, August 23, 1855.

20. Tappan to Henry Richardson, July 27, 1855.

21. Ibid, October 9, 1855 and November 14, 1855.

22. *National Era*, October 9, 1851, vol. V, no. 249, p. 163.

23. Lewis Tappan to his cousin Mrs. Jona(than) Bigelow, December 1, 1847,
Tappan Papers.

24. Tappan to Henry Richardson, July 27, 1855.

25. Ibid., November 16, 1855.

26. Lewis Tappan diary, July 18, 1855; Tappan to Henry Richardson, July 21, 1855;
Tappan to Jacob Bigelow, July 20, 1855.

CHAPTER 7

1. Jerry M. Hynson, *District of Columbia Runaway and Fugitive Slave Cases: 1848–1863* (Westminster, MD: Willow Bend Books, 1999). Charles Price appears on pp. 18 and 47; John Cook, pp. 7, 24, 33, 73 and 88; George Kephart (misspelled as "Kephaus"), p. 31; John Davis on pp. 9, 10, 21, 22, 26, 32, 37, 49, 50, 66, 70, 80, 86, 92, 99 and 104; Solomon Stover, pp. 43 and 100.

2. Montgomery County Land Records, JGH3, pp. 32 and 189, Montgomery County Judicial Center, Rockville, MD.

3. 1853 slave census for Montgomery County, District 1. Originals are at Maryland State Archives, Hall of Records.

4. Charles M. Price of Unity is listed as a hotel-keeper in *Thomson's Mercantile and Professional Directory*, Maryland 1851–1852.

5. 1850 census for First or Cracklin District, Montgomery County, MD, dwelling #241; 1860 census for Fourth District, Montgomery County, MD, dwelling #491.

6. M.N. Work, "The Life of Charles B. Ray," *Journal of Negro History*, vol. 4, October 1919, p. 369. Also Lewis Tappan to Jacob Bigelow, July 20, 1855, Tappan Papers.

7. Lewis Tappan to Jacob Bigelow, July 20, 1855.

8. W.B. Williams to Wilbur Siebert, March 30, 1896, Siebert Papers, Ohio Historical Society (provided courtesy of Anthony Cohen).

9. Letter from Jacob Bigelow to William Still, Oct 6, 1855, in William Still, *The Underground Rail Road*, p. 180.

10. Bill of sale registered at Montgomery County Courthouse, JGH3 (1853–1854), Folio 245–246.

11. Letter from Jacob Bigelow to William Still, June 27, 1854, in William Still, *The Underground Rail Road*, p. 177.

12. W.B. Williams to Wilbur Siebert, March 30, 1896. Siebert Papers, Ohio Historical Society (provided courtesy of Anthony Cohen).

13. Letter from Jacob Bigelow to William Still, June 22, 1854, *Black Abolitionist Papers* microfilm, item #15302. Purdy/Kresge Library, Wayne State University, Detroit.

14. Letter from Jacob Bigelow to William Still, September 9, 1855, in William Still, *The Underground Rail Road*, p. 178.

15. St. Mary's Church (Rockville, MD) records. Montgomery County Historical Society, Box 4, folder 3, 1856–1870. Note that under the list of "colored" appears "Cecilia J. Talbot" and "Maria G. [sic] Wimm" (presumably another relative).

16. Francis Patrick Kenrick, *Theologia moralis* (1843).

17. Lewis Tappan diary, October 4, 1855, Tappan Papers.

18. M.N. Work, "The Life of Charles B. Ray," *Journal of Negro History*, vol. 4, October 1919, pp. 369-70.

19. *Evening Star* (Washington), October 3, 1855.

20. *Baltimore Sun*, September 24, 1855.

21. 1850 census of ward 4, Washington City, dwelling #413.

22. Letter from Jacob Bigelow to William Still, October 6, 1855, in William Still, *The Underground Rail Road*, p. 180.

23. Lewis Tappan diary, November, 1855, Tappan Papers.

24. William Still's handwritten account from records of the Philadelphia Vigilance Committee. Lewis Tappan described Ann Maria "as tall of her age & very pretty. She can read a very little." Lewis Tappan diary, November 30, 1855.

25. Reprinted in the *Anti-Slavery Reporter*, November 1, 1852.

26. Clara Marshall, *The Woman's Medical College of Pennsylvania: An Historical Outline* (Philadelphia: P. Blakiston, Son & Co., 1897). Available online at Harvard University website http://pds.harvard.edu:8080/pds/tmpimages/1881469.gif. *The Agitator*, July 5, 1855, p. 2. Thanks to Elisa Carbone's author's notes to her 2001 edition of *Stealing Freedom* for sharing the identity of "Dr. H." Further description of Dr. Harvey's Underground Railroad activities appears in John E. McDonough, *Idylls of the Old South Ward* (Chester, PA: Chester Times Department of Printing, 1932), pp. 77-78.

27. Harriet Beecher Stowe, *A Key To Uncle Tom's Cabin* (Bedford, MA: Applewood Books), p. 155. Reprint of original 1853 publication by John Jewett & Co.

28. Syracuse University Library, Special Collections Research Center, Gerrit Smith Broadside and Pamphlet Collection, Digital Edition: *To The People of the county of Madison*, http://libwww.syr.edu/digital/collections/g/GerritSmith/445.htm

29. Letter from Jacob Bigelow to William Still, November 26, 1855, in William Still, *The Underground Rail Road*, pp. 180-81.

30. Jacob Bigelow to Rev. Chas. B. Ray, November 17, 1855, *Sketch of the Life of Rev. Charles B. Ray* (New York: Press of J.J. Little & Co., 1887), p. 40.

31. Ibid., p. 41.

32. Session Laws, 1817, vol. 636, p. 81. Maryland State Archives online. http://www.msa.md.gov/megafile/msa/speccol/sc2900/sc2908/000001/000636/html/am636–81.html [accessed August 26, 2007].

33. *The Progress*, December 7, 1878. Also W.B. Williams to Wilbur Siebert, March 30, 1896. Siebert Papers, Ohio Historical Society (provided courtesy of Anthony Cohen).

34. Journal C of Station No. 2 of the Underground Railroad (Philadelphia, Agent William Still) 1852–1857, Papers of the Pennsylvania Abolition Society, the Historical Society of Pennsylvania.

35. *Accounts of the Vigilance Committee of Philadelphia, 1854–1857*, Papers of the Pennsylvania Abolition Society.

36. M.N. Work., "The Life of Charles B. Ray," *Journal of Negro History*, vol. 4, October 1919, p. 370, and Sarah Tappan to Henry Richardson, December 8, 1855, Tappan Papers.

37. Lewis Tappan to Ellwood Harvey, November 29, 1855, Tappan Papers.

38. Ibid., November 30, 1855.

39. Lewis Tappan diary, December 4, 1855, Tappan Papers.

40. Ibid., November 30, 1855.

41. Sarah Tappan to Henry Richardson, December 8, 1855, Tappan Papers.

42. Ibid.

43. Lewis Tappan diary, December 1, 1855 and Lewis Tappan to Jacob Bigelow, December 3, 1855, Tappan Papers.

44. Tappan diary, November 30, 1855.

45. William Still, *The Underground Rail Road*, p. 792. Letter from Frances Ellen Watkins, September 12, 1856.

46. Ibid., p. 789.

47. Tappan diary, November 30, 1855.

48. Tappan to Jacob Bigelow, December 3, 1855.

49. Excerpt from letter from Amos Freeman to Lewis Tappan, as related by Mrs. Sarah Tappan in an article published in *Frederick Douglass Paper* and reprinted in William Still's *The Underground Rail Road*, p. 686. Also appeared in Sarah Tappan to Frederick Douglass, *Frederick Douglass Paper*, January 15, 1856.

50. Lewis Tappan to William Still, n.d, reprinted in *The Underground Rail Road*, p. 711.

51. Lewis Tappan diary, December 3, 1855, Tappan Papers.

52. Excerpt from letter from Amos Freeman to Lewis Tappan, as related by Mrs. Sarah Tappan in an article published in *Frederick Douglass Paper*, January 15, 1856 and reprinted in William Still, *The Underground Rail Road*, p. 688. Further details of the reunion in Dresden appear in letter from Lewis Tappan to Jacob Bigelow, December 6, 1855, Tappan Papers.

53. Lewis Tappan to Dr Ellwood Harvey, December 4, 1855, Tappan Papers.
54. Lewis Tappan to Dr. E. Harvey, December 6, 1855. Henry P. Slaughter collection, Box 37, folder 3, Robert W. Woodruff Library, Archives & Special Collections, Atlanta University.
55. Sarah Tappan to Mr. (Henry) Richardson, December 8, 1855, Tappan Papers.
56. Lewis Tappan to Sam'l Rhoads, January 2, 1855, Tappan Papers, Library of Congress, letter book 1854–1855, p. 97.
57. Lewis Tappan to Maria Webb, March 1, 1856, Tappan Papers, Library of Congress, letter book 1852–1857, p. 105.
58. Frederick Douglass to Mrs. Tappan, March 21, 1856, Henry P. Slaughter Collection, Robert W. Woodruff Library, Archives & Special Collections, Atlanta University.
59. Lewis Tappan to Henry Richardson, February 12, 1856, Tappan Papers.
60. Ibid., September 1, 1855.
61. Ibid., November 14, 1855. (Although Tappan did not identify the woman by name, there can be little doubt that he is referring to Harriet Tubman.)
62. Tappan to Jacob Bigelow, December 6, 1855, Tappan Papers.

CHAPTER 8

1. Andrew Somerville to H.H. Garnet, July 30, 1855. National Library of Scotland, MS. 7640, pp. 174-175.
2. New York Passenger Lists Record for Henry Garnet, age 5, as listed on Ancestry.com; quoting from Microfilm Serial M237, Roll 155, List number 797. Details of Julia Garnet's Industrial School appear in a letter from Andrew Somerville to H.H. Garnet, National Library of Scotland, MS. 7639, pp. 608–09.
3. *Missionary Record*, March 21, 1856, *Frederick Douglass Paper*, March 21, 1856; *Voice of the Fugitive* portions reprinted in Joel Schor, "Henry Highland Garnet: A Voice of Black Radicalism in the Nineteenth Century," *Contributions in American History*, no. 54 (Westport, CT and London, UK: Greenwood Press).
4. Andrew Somerville to H.H. Garnet, July 30, 1855. National Library of Scotland, MS. 7640, pp. 174-175.
5. Henry H. Garnet to Gerrit Smith, March 25 and October 3, 1856. Gerrit Smith Papers, Syracuse University.
6. William B. Gould IV, *Diary of a Contraband: The Civil War Passage of a Black Sailor* (Stanford, CA: Stanford University Press, 2002), pp. 35-37. Also Nantucket Historical Association website, www.nha.org/pdfs/otherislanders/ OceanIslanders3.pdf. Description of James Crawford was given by Arthur C. Brock of Nantucket on Nantucket Historical Association website www.nha.org/history/hn/HNracerelations.html with notation that this originally appeared in the Spring 2002 issue of *Historic Nantucket*. Mention of assistance given by Anna Richardson and other British sympathizers appears in William Still, *The Underground Rail Road*, pp. 622, 623.
7. *Illustrated London News*, vol. 43, no. 1221, September 12, 1863, p. 274.

8. Lewis Tappan diary, August 14, 1856, Tappan Papers. Also William B. Gould IV, *Diary of a Contraband*, p. 35 (originally appeared in Nantucket's *Weekly Mirror*, March 13, 1858).

9. *Provincial Freeman*, September 8, 1855.

10. Minutes of Ladies Committee for Assisting Fugitives From Slavery, January 28, 1856 meeting, Rhodes House Anti-Slavery Records (microfilm at University of Michigan Graduate Library).

11. Lewis Tappan diary, January 21, 1856, Tappan Papers.

12. Henry Garnet to Gerrit Smith, March 25, 1856. Gerrit Smith Papers, Box 20, Syracuse University Library, Special Collections Research Center. Also Lewis Tappan diary, October 16, 1856, Tappan Papers.

13. RG21, Entry 20, Chancery Cases, case 1325, Rules no. 5, Box 226, NARA.

14. *National Era*, June 10, 1847, p. 2. This also appears in Harriet Beecher Stowe, *A Key to Uncle Tom's Cabin* (Bedford, MA: Applewood Books), p. 155. Reprint of original 1853 publication by John Jewett & Co.

15. Lewis Tappan diary, August 14, 1856, copies of receipts for sale of Diana by (1) J.N. Maffitt (2) Geo. W. Davis, (3) T.C. Worth, Tappan Papers.

16. Letter from E.L. Stevens to William Still, July 8, 1857 in William Still, *The Underground Rail Road*, p. 156.

17. Receipt of sale for Diana. Tappan Papers.

18. Tappan Papers.

19. *The Liberator* (Boston), Friday, April 23, 1858, p. 67, issue 17, col. D.

20. *Anti-Slavery Memoranda* by Anna Richardson. Printed by J.G. Forster, 81 Clayton Street, Newcastle. 1860 (?) Microfilm E449.R515, University of Maryland, McKeldin Library. Microfiche copied from the original in the Library of Congress.

21. *Illustrated London News*, vol. 43, no. 1221, September 12, 1863, p. 274.

22. *The Times* (London), November 5, 1858, p. 10.

23. This undated letter as well as a follow-up letter dated February 11, 1861 from Tappan to the *Evening Post* appears in the Tappan Papers.

24. James Buchanan, 15th President of the United States: 1857–1861, Second Annual Message, December 6, 1858, Message to the Senate and House of Representatives, available at http://www.presidency.ucsb.edu

CHAPTER 9

1. Lewis Tappan diary, December 26, 1856, Tappan Papers; also Tappan to Bigelow, September 9, 1856.

2. Lewis Tappan to Henry Richardson, February 12, 1856, Tappan Papers.

3. Tappan to Jacob Bigelow, January 30, September 9, 12, and October 7, 1856. These letters refer to Bigelow's letters to Tappan of September 8, 10, and 17.

4. Tappan to Mrs. S.J.I. Bennett, October 11, 1856.

5. Barbour County Land Deeds. John Cook from Alfred Green and wife on January 6, 1852; note that transaction was not registered until October 27, 1858 (microfilm

LGM8 reel 7, Book N, p. 607, at Alabama Department of Archives and History).
See also Barbour County Land Deeds Reel 6, Book N, pp. 123, 177-178, 285.

6. Robert H. Flewellen, *Along Broad Street: A History of Eufaula, Alabama 1823–1894*
(Eufaula: 1991), p. 15. Quotation by Martha Crossley Rumph, an early resident of
Eufaula. (Martha later married Dr. James D. Rumph, who owned Augustus Weems.)

7. Alrutheus A. Taylor, *The Movement of Negroes from the East to the Gulf States from 1830
to 1850*, as it appeared in *Journal of Negro History*, vol. 8, no. 4, October 1923. p. 380.

8. *Lewy Dorman Papers: History of Barbour County.* vol. 1, part 2; p. 375 (Collection at
Eufaula Public Library).

9. John C. Cook purchased a parcel of land in Eufaula from Thomas and Louisa Cargile
on March 4, 1857. Barbour County Land Records, Book N, p. 285.

10. *Spirit of the South*, August 19, 1851.

11. Eugenia Persons Smartt, *History of Eufaula, Alabama* (Birmingham: Roberts & Son,
Printers, 1930).

12. *A History of Eufaula, Alabama 1832–1882*, Master's thesis by Harry Philpot Owens,
Auburn, Alabama, 1963, pp. 36-38.

13. *National Era*, September 23, 1847, vol. I, no. 38, p. 4.

14. Ibid., August 29, 1850, vol. IV, no. 191, p. 139; October 3, 1850, p. 158; October 17,
1850, p. 166; October 24, 1850, p. 170; November 13, 1851, p. 182.

15. *Spirit of the South*, May 8, 1852.

16. *A History of Eufaula, Alabama 1832–1882*, Master's thesis by Harry Philpot Owens,
pp. 36-38. Also, Anne Kendrick Walker, *Backtracking in Barbour County: A Narrative
of the Last Alabama Frontier* (Richmond, VA: Dietz Press, 1941), pp. 177-79.

17. Barbour County Land Records. Cook registered a mortgage for fourteen-year-old
Margaret. Registered December 10, 1853, Book K, pp. 644, 645. Also, mortgage by
Cook to J.L. Hays for seventeen-year-old Susan, registered December 31, 1853,
Book K, pp. 674, 675.

18. Barbour County Land Deeds. Samuel Burnett and James Lucker to J.C. Cook and
Brother, December 20, 1853, Book L, pp. 212–13 and Alpheus Baker to John C. Cook,
p. 213. Also, Alpheus Baker and Louisa Baker to John C. Cook, December 5, 1854
(microfilm LGM8 reel 5 at Alabama Department of Archives and History).
The slaves were: Emmanuel 40, Flora 50, Abram 25, Clarisa 12, Martha 10, Hannah 8,
Nelson 25, Margaret 21, Edward 1, Hosea 30, Rose 25, Jim 6, Charlott 5, Dave 4,
Jeremiah 2, Robert 1, Dave 50, Peggy 60, Milly 18, Delia 1, Pomp 60, Lella 45,
Allen 18, Paul 16, Louis 14, Venus 12, Jimmy or Jenny 2, Chancy 45, Cella 23, Susan 5,
Laina 3, Eliza 13, Sally 11, Isaac 30, Mira 18, Mary 17, Abram 35, Dolly 30, Bella 7,
Joe 12, Becky 1, George 23, Hester 20, Georgianna 1, Richmond 40, Ben 12, Sam 10,
Pomp 7, Kate 1, and Sarah 9.

19. 1860 census for the Seventh Ward, Washington City, p. 109.

20. J.C. Cook received the following runaways: Charity on August 7, 1849; Julia on
August 19, 1849; Henry Tyler on August 19, 1849; Nancy on Howard June 3, 1852;
Sarah Panay on September 23, 1853; James Campbell on July 17, 1858; Martha on

July 26, 1858; Elizabeth Smith on February 5, 1861. Jerry M. Hynson, *District of Columbia Runaway and Fugitive Slave Cases 1848–1863*, pp. 7, 24, 23, 73 and 88. Note that on at least one occasion Hatch had also committed a runaway to the District Jail. This slave was William Hussy on August 10, 1849 (ibid., p. 7). H. Cook received the following runaways: Letty on October 19, 1850; William Doughtery on October 25, 1850; and Mary on July 5, 1851. On July 8, 1851 Hatch Cook and another District slave trader, B.O. Shekells, jointly received Henrietta (ibid., pp. 15, 16, 19).

21. Barbour County Land Deeds. William and Mary D. Smitha to J.C. Cook, January 13, 1854, Book L, pp. 210 & 211 (microfilm LGM8 reel 5 at Alabama Department of Archives and History).

22. Barbour County Land Records. Agreement between Thomas Flournoy, William Smitha and John C. Cook, February 2, 1854, Book K, pp. 681-83.

23. This advertisement was still running in the June 8, 1852 issue of *Spirit of the South*.

24. *Spirit of the South*, September 16, 1851.

25. Barbour County Land Records. John C. Cook to Willis and Julia Hughes, February 28, 1853.

26. *Spirit of the South*, June 5, 1855.

27. Barbour County Land Deeds. Amos Cory, Mary Cory, Marion Barrington and Ann Barrington to John C. Cook, March 20, 1857. Book N, p. 284 (microfilm LGM8 reel 6 at Alabama Department of Archives and History).

28. *Spirit of the South*, November 6, 1855.

29. Barbour County Land Deeds. John H. Dent and Fanny Dent to John C. Cook, February 8, 1855, Book L, p. 534 (microfilm LGM8 reel 5 at Alabama Department of Archives and History).

30. On June 13, 1854, Dent gave Cook $755.62 for "Negro C." On February 28, 1855, Dent bought from Cook "a Boy by name John" for $1,000. The previous month Dent made two separate "memorandums" to pay J.C. Cook & Co. $550 plus another $178 five days later on account "for value received." On May 28, 1857, Dent sent a $900 draft to Cook "to buy me a Negro woman."

31. January 1855 entry in John Horry Dent's Plantation Journal. Photostat copy in Auburn University Library, Special Collections. See also Ray Mathis, *John Horry Dent: South Carolina Aristocrat on the Alabama Frontier* (Under sponsorship of Historic Chattahoochee Commission: University of Alabama Press, 1979), pp. 43–44.

32. *Spirit of the South*, November 6, 1855. Microfilm at Alabama Department of Archives and History, Montgomery, Alabama.

33. Barbour County Land Deeds. Samuel Burnett to J.C. Cook and Brother, April 15, 1854, Book L, pp. 591, 592 (microfilm LGM8, reel 5, at Alabama Department of Archives and History).

34. Barbour County Land Deeds. Samuel Burnett and James Lucker to J.C. Cook and Brother, April 15, 1854, Book L, pp. 208, 209 (microfilm LGM8, reel 5, at Alabama Department of Archives and History).

35. Lewis Tappan diary.
36. Barbour County Land Records, Book M, pp. 318, 319, Microfilm LGMoo8, reel 5 at Alabama Department of Archives and History, Montgomery, Alabama.
37. Lewis Tappan diary, September 1 and 12, 1856. Also Tappan to Bigelow, September 12, 1856, Tappan Papers letter book 1852–1857, p. 130.
38. *American Slavery As It Is: Testimony of a Thousand Witnesses*, American Anti-Slavery Society, New York, 1839.
39. Lewis Tappan diary, September 6, 1856, Tappan Papers.
40. Ibid., September 27 and 28, 1856. Also mention of Tappan's trip to Niagara in the American Missionary Association papers – Canada in letter from Lewis Tappan to Bro. Jocelyn, September 28, 1856.
41. RG21, Entry 6, Circuit Court, DC, Civil Trial, May Term 1858, Box 865, *John Leslie vs. John C. Cook & Benj. O. Sheckells*. (Cook & Sheckells had stolen the slave on October 1, 1853.)
42. Lewis Tappan to Mrs. Henry Richardson, February 6, 1857, Tappan Papers.
43. Tappan to Jacob Bigelow, October 7, 1856. This page is badly torn and is missing a piece. The missing piece follows Tappan's admonition that "I would not take the security of Birch or _____(missing section)_____ like him." One wonders if the name Charles Price was written in the missing piece. It is also interesting to note that Lewis Tappan does not want Cook to know that he is involved in the transaction.
44. Tappan to Radcliffe and Kennedy, October 15, 1856, letter book 1852–1857.
45. Ibid., October 10, 1856 letter book 1852–1857, p. 146. Also Tappan to Bigelow, September 9, 1856, letter book 1852–1857, p. 130.
46. Lincoln allegedly reported wryly on the worth of one businessman: "First of all, he has a wife and a baby together they ought to be worth fifty thousand dollars to any man. Secondly, he has an office in which there is a table worth one dollar and fifty cents, and three chairs worth, say one dollar. Last of all, there is in one corner a large rat-hole which will bear looking into."
47. Marie H. Godfrey, *Early Settlers of Barbour County, Alabama*, vol. 1 (housed at the Carnegie Library in Eufaula).
48. Barbour County Land Deeds. J.C. Cook and Cecilia Cook to Hatch Cook and John Colby, Book N, pp. 146-48 (microfilm LGM8, reel 6, at Alabama Department of Archives and History).
49. Lewis Tappan to Radcliffe & Kennedy, October 15, 1856, Tappan Papers.
50. Tappan to John Smith (Glasgow), December 7, 1856.
51. *Cleveland Herald*, Monday, June 15, 1846, issue 1, col. A.
52. Tappan to E.L. Stevens, December 16, 1856; Tappan to Dr. G. Bailey, December 16, 1856; Tappan to D.A. Hall, Esquire, December 18, 1856. Tappan Papers.
53. Bigelow and French's roles as founders of the Washington Gas Light Company is described in *Washingtoniana: Records of The Columbia Historical Society of Washington DC 1948–1950*. vol. 50, ed. H. Paul Caemmerer, published by the Society

in 1952. French and Steven's role as guarantors appears in Tappan to D.A. Hall, December 18, 1856, letter book 1852–1857.

54. Lewis Tappan diary, December 30, 1856, Tappan Papers.

55. Lewis Tappan to E.L. Stevens, December 18 and December 31, 1856, Tappan Papers.

56. Tappan to Mrs. Henry Richardson, February 6, 1857.

57. Tappan to E.L. Stevens, February 6, 1857; Tappan to J. Bigelow, December 5, 1857.

58. Tappan to E.L. Stevens, undated but presumably February 1857.

59. Dorothy S. Provine, *District of Columbia Free Negro Registers, 1821–1861* (Bowie MD: Heritage Books, 1996) lists this manumission as Registration #2500, vol. 5, p. 88.

60. Manumission was registered on April 8, 1858. NARA: RG21, Entry 30, vol. 4, p. 88. Also Dorothy S. Provine, *District of Columbia Free Negro Registers 1821–1861* lists this manumission as Registration #2638, vol. 5, pp. 184-85.

61. Manumission and Emancipation Records, 1821–1862, vol. 4 E-30. p. 88, RG 21, U.S. National Archives.

62. Lewis Tappan to E.L. Stevens, July 30, 1857, Tappan Papers.

63. Ibid., April 4, 1857.

64. Tappan to Lydia Edmund Sturge, April 4, 1857, letter book 1852–1857, p. 396.

CHAPTER 10

1. 1860 slave census for Barbour County, Alabama, Beat #4, p. 34.

2. 1860 slave census for Pike County, Alabama, Eastern Division, pp. 47, 48.

3. Church of Jesus Christ of Latter Day Saints website: http://www.familysearch.org/Eng/Search/PRF/individual_record.asp?recid=180664665

4. Page 28 of Scrapbook of Martha Jane Crossley Rumph in the Rumph family papers at Alabama Department of Archives and History.

5. 1850 census of "Slave Inhabitants between Sumpter & Edisto, North of the Belville Road in the County of Orangeburg, South Carolina," p. 49.

6. *The Rumph and Frederick Families, Genealogical and Biographical*, compiled by Louise Frederick Hays (Atlanta: J.T. Hancock Publisher, 1942), pp. 97-99. (The compiler inserted "A Partial History of the Rumph Ancestors" that had been written by Dr. James D. Rumph years earlier.)

7. *The North Star* (Rochester, NY), December 1, 1848; reprinted from the *Charleston Mercury*, November 9, 1848.

8. Ibid.

9. Historical Note for the Rumph Family Collection in Alabama Department of Archives and History. Also *Memorial Record of Alabama*, vol. 1, pp. 541-43, published by Brant & Fuller, 1893. Bullock County Alabama Archives Biographies. Contributed by Ann Anderson. http://ftp.rootsweb.com/pub/usgenweb/as/bullock/bios/gbs168rumph.txt

10. Gregory A. Boyd, *Family Maps of Barbour County, Alabama: Homesteads Edition*

(Norman, OK: Arphax Publishing, 2005), p. 109, Patent Map 12, Township 11-N Range 24-E (St. Stephens).

11. September 19, 1861 entry in original journal in Rumph Family Collection, LPR 169, Alabama Department of Archives and History, Montgomery, Alabama.

12. Original journal in Rumph family collection at Alabama Department of Archives and History, Montgomery, Alabama.

13. Garnet married Julia Ward Williams (1811–1870) in 1841. She had been born in Charleston, SC, but had moved to Boston at an early age. *The Black Abolitionist Papers, Britain*, p. 499.

14. Lewis Tappan to Henry Richardson, September 30, 1857, Tappan Papers. Also E.L. Stevens to William Still, July 8, 1857 in Still's *The Underground Rail Road*.

15. Lewis Tappan to Jacob Bigelow, July 25, 1857, Tappan Papers.

16. Tappan to E.L. Stevens, July 30, 1857.

17. Tappan to J. Bigelow, July 30, 2857.

18. Tappan to J. Bigelow, August 1, 1857.

19. Tappan to E.L. Stevens, November 4, 1857.

20. Tappan to Chauncey Leonard (Providence, Rhode Island) August 4, 1855.

21. Tappan to (illegible) in Washington (presumably either Stevens or Bigelow) July 4, 1857.

22. Lewis Tappan Scrapbook No. 1 at the Moorland Spingarn Archives, Howard University. This clipping appears to have been in the *Tribune* of June 12, 1855.

23. January 17, 1855 entry in John Horry Dent Journal. Photostat in Auburn University Library Special Collection. See also Ray Mathis, *John Horry Dent: South Carolina Aristocrat on the Alabama Frontier* (University of Alabama Press, 1979), p. 90.

24. Lewis Tappan to E.L. Stevens, July 1, 1857, Tappan Papers.

25. Letter from E.L. Stevens to William Still, July 13, 1857, in Still's *The Underground Rail Road*, p. 156.

26. William Still's handwritten notes of the Philadelphia Vigilance Committee.

27. Lewis Tappan to Mrs. Maxwell, September 30, 1857, Tappan Papers.

28. Journal C of Station No. 2 of the Underground Railroad (Philadelphia, Agent William Still) 1852–1857. Historical Society of Pennsylvania, Philadelphia.

29. Lewis Tappan to Jarmain Loguen, December 9, 1857, Tappan Papers.

30. Tappan to Mrs. Maxwell, September 30, 1857; Lewis Tappan to Lydia Edmund Sturge, August 3, 1857.

31. Tappan to Friend (William) Still, undated but presumably late July, 1857; Tappan to E.L. Stevens, July (day illegible), 1857.

32. Tappan to E.L. Stevens, date illegible, 1857; July 27, 1857; July 30, 1857.

33. Ibid., July 25, 1857.

34. Ibid., July 30, 1857.

35. Tappan to Mrs. (Arabella) Weems, c/o Rev. J.W. Loguen, Syracuse, July 30, 1857, and Tappan to Lydia Edmund Sturge (Birmingham, England) August 3, 1857.

36. Tappan to Lydia Edmund Sturge (Birmingham, England) August 3, 1857.

37. Tappan to Mrs. Maxwell, September 30, 1857.

38. Tappan to Rev. J.W. Loguen, December 9, 1857.

39. Tappan to E.L. Stevens, July 30, 1857.

40. Tappan to Mrs (Arabella) Weems, c/o Rev. J.W. Loguen, Rochester [sic].
    (no doubt mistakenly written instead of intended Syracuse), August 1, 1857.

41. Lewis Tappan diary.

42. Lewis Tappan to E.L Stevens, November 4, 1857.

43. *The Southern Convention at Knoxville* Proceedings appeared on pp. 298-320 in
    *Debow's Review, Agricultural, Commercial, Industrial Progress and Resources*,
    vol. 23, issue 3, September 1857. Electronic version appears on the Making of
    America website, University of Michigan: Humanities Text Initiative
    http://www.hti.umich.edu/cache/acg1336.1-23.003/03020298tifs.gif

44. Will of John Rumph reprinted on pp. 54-55 of *The Rumph and Frederick Families,
    Genealogical and Biographical*, compiled by Louise Frederick Hays (Atlanta:
    J.T. Hancock publisher, 1942).

45. Lewis Tappan to Henry Richardson, September 30, 1857, Tappan Papers.

46. Tappan to Mrs. Weems, August 1, 1857.

47. Tappan to J. Bigelow, August 1, 1857.

48. Tappan to Lydia Edmund Sturge, August 3, 1857.

49. William Still, *The Underground Rail Road*, pp. 185, 186.

50. Tappan diary, November 9, 1857.

51. Tappan to Lydia Edmund Sturge, November 3, 1857.

52. Tappan to Henry Richardson, September 30, 1857.

53. Tappan to Jones, December 24, 1857.

54. Stevens to Tappan, February 25, 1858, *American Missionary Association Archives*, Fisk
    University microfilm, District of Columbia, No. 15828 (copy available at University
    of Maryland, McKeldin Library).

55. Manumission and Emancipation Records, 1821–1862, vol. 4 E-30, pp. 184 and
    185, RG 21, U.S. National Archives. Also: Records of the U.S. District Court
    for District of Columbia relating to slaves 1851–1863 (microfilm) M433,
    U.S. National Archives.

CHAPTER 11

1. William Still, *The Underground Rail Road*, p. 483.

2. Marriage records of St. John's Catholic Church, Forest Glen, MD. Records held at
   Montgomery County, Maryland Historical Society Library.

3. William Still, *The Underground Rail Road*, p. 485.

4. Vital Records, St. John's Church (Catholic), Forest Glen, MD, transcribed by Mabel
   Leonard Gibson and Edna Plummer Lines. Presented by the Janet Montgomery
   Chapter of Montgomery County, MD DAR.

5. Date of escape established by runaway ad in *Baltimore Sun* of July 19, 1858 for Oscar
   Payne, who accompanied Lewis Jones.

6. The stories of all of the above runaways appear in William Still, *The Underground Rail Road*, pp. 414-17 and 483-89. Captured runaways and slave dealers who acquired them in the month of July 1858 are on p. 73 of Jerry M. Hynson, *District of Columbia Runaway and Fugitive Slave Cases 1848–1863* (Westminster, MD: Willow Bend Books, 1999).

7. Moses Wood runaway ad appears in *National Intelligencer*, Saturday, July 24, 1858, p. 3, col. 7.

8. Hynson, *District of Columbia Runaway and Fugitive Slave Cases 1848–1863*, p. 31.

9. Ibid., pp. 18, 36.

10. Still, *The Underground Rail Road*, p. 415.

11. Ibid.

12. 1860 federal census for the Town of Geddes, Onondaga County, New York, p. 166.

13. Still, *The Underground Rail Road*, p. 21.

14. William Still's handwritten notes of the Philadelphia Vigilance Committee.

CHAPTER 12

1. *Frederick Douglass Paper*, Rochester, Feb. 1, 1856.

2. Sarah H. Bradford, *Scenes in the Life of Harriet Tubman* (Auburn, NY: W.J. Moses Printer, 1869).

3. Chancery Court Case, Middlesex County, Case of *Henson vs. Scoble*. Document signed by William Henry Bradley on April 27, 1863. Microfilm at Regional Collection, Weldon Library, University of Western Ontario, London.

4. 1861 Canada West census, Camden Township, County of Kent; 1871 Canada West Census, Camden township, County of Bothwell.

5. Baptismal record of Calvin, son of Lazarus and Virginia Wilson at Christ Church (Anglican) Dresden, August 11, 1861. Microfilm at Regional Collection, Weldon Library, University of Western Ontario, London.

6. *The Fugitive Slaves in Canada* (London, UK: Seeley, Jackson and Halliday, 1858), p. 7. Original held in John Rylands Library, Manchester, England; copy in the Black Abolitionist Archives, University of Detroit Mercy Campus.

7. Ibid.

8. Ibid.

9. Session Laws, 1860, vol. 588, p. 623. Archives of Maryland online.

10. *Toronto Sun*, September 17, 1847 (reprinted in Philadelphia's *The Pennsylvania Freeman*, September 30, 1847).

11. William Still, *The Underground Rail Road*, pp. 66, 67, 489. Also, 1861 census for the Town of St. Catharines, sheet 118.

12. William Still, *The Underground Rail Road*, p. 488. Also, 1861 census for Toronto, sheet 254.

13. Jerry M. Hynson, *District of Columbia Runaway and Fugitive Slave Cases 1848–1863* (Westminster, MD: Willow Bend Books, 1999) p. 72.

14. Maryland Josiah Henson from Boston bought John Henson from Jane E. Beall. Montgomery County, Maryland Circuit Court Land Records VHG7:121. Further information can be found in *Uncle Tom's Story of His Life: An Autobiography of the Rev. Josiah Henson*, Christian Age office, 89 Farrington Street, London, 1876.

15. Lewis Chambers to George Whipple AMA records (microfilm copy, mfm/F/5004/A53/1988, at Robarts Library, University of Toronto). Beginning in January, 1859 Reverend Chambers wrote to Whipple monthly with details of his missionary work in several places in Canada West.

16. William Still, *The Underground Rail Road*. Note that Still mistakenly spells the owner's name Sydan rather than Lyddan(e). Sale of slaves by Ann Lyddane to her sons is recorded in the Montgomery County Land Records at Montgomery County Courthouse, STS 4, book 42, instrument dated April 5, 1849.

17. Vital Records, St. John's Church (Catholic), Forest Glen, MD, transcribed by Mabel Leonard Gibson and Edna Plummer Lines. Presented by the Janet Montgomery Chapter, of Montgomery County, MD DAR. 1924, p. 73.

18. Roman Catholic Baptismal Records at Montgomery County, Maryland Historical Society Library, vol. 2, p. 42. The child was John Lewis Weems, who was baptized on June 3, 1849 at the age of 18 months.

19. 1861 Canada West agricultural census, Chatham Township, County of Kent.

20. Lewis Tappan to E.L. Stevens, November 4, 1857, Tappan Papers.

21. Sixteen-year-old Joseph and Mary Brown of the same age were servants of Isaac Smith and his family; 1861 census of the Town of Chatham, p. 78. Perhaps influenced by the melancholy history of Joseph Weems, Isaac Smith later became a founder of the Home of the Friendless for the poor in Chatham.

## EPILOGUE

1. Register of Baptism, Marriages & Burials, St. Josephs Church, Chatham, 1855–1867. Microfilm copy at Church of Jesus Christ of Latter Day Saints, Family History Library, Chatham, Ontario.

2. *Daily National Intelligencer* (Washington, DC), Wednesday, February 27, 1861, issue 15,147, col. E.W.B. Williams to Wilbur Siebert, March 30, 1896; Siebert Papers, Ohio Historical Society (provided courtesy of Anthony Cohen).

3. *New York Herald*, June 18, 1856. Also *National Era*, June 19, 1856 and January 22, 1857.

4. Wesley E. Pippenger, *D.C. Marriage Licenses, Register 2, 1858–1870* (courtesy of Sandy Harrelson). Also *New York Herald*, March 3, 1861.

5. *Daily National Intelligencer*, April 26, 1864.

6. *Annual Report of the National Association for the Relief of Destitute Colored Women and Children* (1864 and 1867), Samuel J. May Anti-Slavery Collection, Cornell University online.

7. Proceedings of the House of Delegates, June 18, 1861, vol. 430, pp. 270, 271, Maryland State Archives online.

8. *History of Western Maryland Including Biographical Sketches*, vol. 1, p. 668 (available at www.ancestry.com).

9. Robert J. Driver Jr., *First & Second Maryland Infantry C.S.A.* (Westminster, MD: Willow Bend Books, 2003), p. 432. For additional information on Harding's Civil War service see: permit dated May 1, 1865 from Greensboro, North Carolina from Wm, Hartsuff and M.C. Butler. John William Ward Collection, MSA SC 980, Maryland State Archives, Hall of Records, and letter dated May 22, 1865 from M. Dean to Dr. Charles A. Harding, John William Ward Collection, MSA SC 980, Maryland State Archives. Following the war, Harding returned to a much different place. His sister, Elizabeth Ann Harding, died January 14, 1862; his father, Henry Harding, died in June 1863; and the will of his mother, Catharine Harding, was probated September 29, 1863 (William Neal Hurley, Jr., Our Maryland Heritage, Book 39 (Bowie, MD: Heritage Books), *Harding Families*, pp. 12-14).

10. http://home.comcast.net/~hilld1/CWExhibit/pages/UnionArrests.htm

11. *Charleston Mercury* (article from our Montgomery Correspondent), May 14, 1861. Also, "Officers of the Navy, Natives of North Carolina, who have resigned and tendered their services" http://docsouth.unc.edu/imls/troops.html

12. *Illustrated London News*, vol. 43, no. 1221, September 12, 1863, p. 274.

13. *A History of Bullock County, Alabama*, master's thesis submitted by John Landon Rumph to the Graduate Faculty of the Alabama Polytechnic Institute, August 27, 1955, pp. 25-26 (copy in Auburn University Library). Rumph quotes this as being in the J.D. Rumph Journal held in the Rumph family in Perote, Alabama. The original (with partial page missing) is now at Alabama Department of Archives and History. Dr. Rumph could not join in any grief associated with the assassination of Lincoln, writing in his journal that ". . . a rebuke has been felt in which the fondest hopes of sycophant office seekers have been sternly blasted."

14. Dorothy S. Provine, *District of Columbia Free Negro Registers 1821–1861* (Bowie, MD: Heritage Books, 1996), Registration #2727, vol. 5, pp. 253-54.

15. *Washington* Star, July 28, 1863, p. 2. Also, Ralph Clayton, *Cash For Blood: The Baltimore to New Orleans Domestic Slave Trade* (Bowie, MD: Heritage Books, 2002), pp. 115-20.

16. Reports of the Committees of the Senate of the United States for the Second Session of the Forty-First Congress. 1869-'70, Washington Government Printing Office, 1870 (vol. no. 1409 of the U.S. Congressional Serial Set), National Archives, Washington, DC.

17. Ads appeared in *Alexandria Gazette* on November 1 and December 1, 1860 as well as on the first days of February, March, and April of 1861. Fairfield County, Virginia Library Historical Newspaper Index http://www.fairfaxcounty.gov/library/newsindex/listing.asp

18. Letter dated July 30, 1861 to "Charles" from "Ned," printed in August 1861, *Willimantic Journal;* available at http://www.geocities.com/Heartland/Fields/4791/august1861willimanticjournal.html

19. Harriet A. Jacobs to William Lloyd Garrison as printed in *The Liberator*, September 5, 1862, p. 3.

20. Deed recorded June 4, 1861, JGH8, pp. 394–95.

21. Reports of the Committees of the Senate of the United States for the Second Session of the Forty-First Congress. 1869-'70, Washington Government Printing Office, 1870 (vol. no. 1409 of the U.S. Congressional Serial Set), National Archives, Washington, DC.

22. Stephen W. Sears, ed., *The Civil War Papers of George B. McClellan: Selected Correspondence, 1860–1865* (New York: Tricknor & Fields, 1989).

23. Henry Ward Beecher to Abraham Lincoln, Scanned image of telegram appears in *Lincoln Papers*, Library of Congress American Memory website. http://memory.loc.gov/mss/mal/mal1/155/1554200/001.gif

24. Frederic Bancroft, *Slave Trading in the Old South* (Columbia: University of South Carolina Press, 1996), p. 317 (reprint from original published by J.H. Furst Company, 1931).

25. Petition for Compensation submitted by Jane E., Matilda B.L., and Margaret J. Beall, 1862, NARA N520:217 Microfilm roll 1, p. 93.

26. *An Examination of Slaves and Slavery in the Beall Family Household – A Report Prepared for the Montgomery County Historical Society* (unpublished manuscript), collected and written by Diane D. Broadhurst, September 25, 2001. Ms. Broadhurst cites information from the Petition for Compensation submitted by Jane E., Matilda B.L., and Margaret J. Beall, 1862, NARA N520:217.

27. 1868 is the first year that John Weems and Lewis Jones appear in the annual *Boyd's Directory of Washington and Georgetown*.

28. *Report to the Freedmen's Inquiry Commission, 1864: The Refugees from Slavery in Canada West* by Samuel Gridley Howe. Reprint by Arno Press and the New York Times, New York, 1969. p. 28.

29. Lewis Tappan to Mrs. Richardson, June 8, 1864, Tappan Papers.

30. Bertram Wyatt-Brown, *Lewis Tappan and the Evangelical War Against Slavery* (New York: Atheneum, 1971), pp. 337–38. Coverage of the Jubilee also appeared in the January 6, 1863 edition of *The World: New-York*. A copy of this article is in the Tappan Papers.

31. Library of Congress American Memory website http://memory.loc.gov/mss/mal/mal1/331/3316000/001.gif and http://memory.loc.gov/mss/mal/mal1/336/3369600/001.gif

32. *Daily National Intelligencer* (Washington, DC), Tuesday, April 18, 1865, issue 16, 433, col. C.

33. Ibid., Thursday, July 11, 1867, issue 17, 124, col. A. Also Charles C. Jones, Jr., *The Siege of Savannah in December, 1864 and the Confederate Operations in Georgia and the Third Military District of South Carolina During General Sherman's March from Atlanta to the Sea* (Albany, NY: Joel Munsell, 1874), p. 175.

34. 1870 census Washington DC, Ward 4, p. 237. The children in the home were

Fanny Warren, 11, from Alabama, and Charlotte Tompkins, 7, from Louisiana. Joseph Herbert, a 40-year-old coachman, and his wife, Mary, also lived in a part of the dwelling.

35. Note that Addison was listed by his Christian name Chas. A. in the 1869 *Boyd's Directory*.

36. Washington deed book D 8 at NARA. 1870 census for the 4th ward of Washington, dwelling #15.

37. *Boyd's Directory of Washington, Georgetown and Alexandria: 1871.* John's business was at 1011 Avenue Q NW.

38. *Evening Star*, October 25, 1872, p. 3, col. 1.

39. *Critic-Record*, Washington, July 9, 1872.

40. District of Columbia Land Records, book 677.

41. Records of the U.S. District Court for the District of Columbia, Equity Case Files 1900–1938. National Archives, RG21, Box 348, MLR-69a. Equity 31566, *Savoy vs. Dove.*

42. *Evening Star*, December 23, 1872.

43. *District of Columbia Interments (Index to Deaths) January 1, 1855 to July 31, 1874,* Wesley E. Pippenger, Arlington Virginia, 1999, pp. xxiv and xxv.

44. Records of the U.S. District Court for the District of Columbia, Equity Case Files 1900–1938. National Archives, RG21, Box 348, MLR-69a. Equity 31566, *Savoy vs. Dove.*

45. Marriage Record 6, Supreme Court DC 1873–1874, Mary Weems to James Savoy.

46. J.A. Tappan to Wm. Still, October 20, 1871 in response to a letter from Still to Lewis Tappan of October 11, 1871, American Negro Historical Society Collection, 1790–1905. (Correspondence of William Still are on microfilm reels 6 and 7, Library of Congress Manuscript Division.)

47. *Sketch of the Life of Rev. Charles B. Ray* (New York: Press of J.J. Little & Co., 1887), pp. 62–63.

48. *Washington Star*, May 3, 1875 and *Washington Chronicle* (undated clipping).

49. Death certificate, no. 5071, Board of Health, District of Columbia, Office of Registrar of Vital Statistics, District of Columbia Archives.

50. Baptismal records of St. Peter's Church, 313 Second Street, SE, kindly provided by Lynn Marsh Freeman, rectory manager.

51. *Boyd's Directory of the District of Columbia: 1878*, p. 710.

52. Henry Garnet to Gerrit Smith, October 23, 1865. Gerrit Smith Papers, Box 20, Syracuse University Library, Special Collections Research Center.

53. Death certificate, died May 30, 1878, 78 years old, 25 years residence in DC, gastritis cause of death (information courtesy of Charles Brewer). John is buried at Mount Olivet Cemetery, Washington, DC (information courtesy of Elisa Carbone).

54. *Washington Post*, October 13, 1983, article by Stephanie Shapiro on St. Cyprian Catholic Church history.

55. *Boyd's Directory, 1869–1882.* 1870 District of Columbia census, Series: M593, Roll 123, p. 13; 1880 District of Columbia census, subdivision 38, p. 15.

56. *One Hundred Years of Catholic Charities in the District of Columbia.* A dissertation by Louis G. Weitzman, Washington, DC, 1931, pp. 77-82, Notre Dame University Archives, Local History Collection.

57. Lewis's death certificate, no. 32697, and Mary's, no. 38962, at DC Archives. (Note that Mary's death certificate incorrectly states that she was 70.)

58. Charlotte died on April 17, 1901. Death certificate no. 136,664, DC Archives.

59. Death certificate no. 78,131, DC Archives.

60. *Evening Star,* June 13, 1891, p. 5, col. 8, and June 15, 1891, p. 5, col. 8.

61. *Dresden Times* death notice, April 24, 1913; obituary May 8, 1913. Also Ontario Vital Statistics: Death certificate, County of Kent, Division of Dresden. F-91-Dresden Co. 2 CI 7, reg. no. 017969–13.

62. *Elyria Reporter,* August 19, 1905, p. 1.

63. "Cemetery Inscriptions of Lorain County, Ohio," compiled by Genealogical Workshop of the Lorain County Historical Society, Elyria, OH, 1980, pp. 256, 257.

64. Equity Case File no. 23401, National Archives, Washington, DC, *Mary M. Savoy vs. James A. Savoy and Ossie Parker,* July 5, 1902.

65. RG 21, Records of the U.S. District Court for the District of Columbia, Equity Case Files nos. 1900-38, Box 348, MLR A1-69a (*Savoy vs. Weems and Dove*). National Archives, Washington, DC. Note that Mary won her case, and her descendants continued to own the home until 1974.

66. Relationship between Henry and Catharine Harding and Nannie C. Dove established in the series *Our Maryland Heritage, Harding Families* (Book 39), by William Neal Hurley, Jr., pp. 12, 14.

# INDEX

Tyler, John, 96
Tyler, Julia, 96

*Uncle Tom's Cabin* (Stowe), 68-71, 76, 77,
  96, 97, 199, 200
Underground Railroad, 37, 38, 43, 67, 70,
  83, 118, 120, 123, 124, 130, 131, 137, 167,
  178, 179, 180, 192, 217
*The Underground Railroad* (Still), 223
United Empire Loyalists, 21
United Presbyterian Church of Scotland, 88

Valdenar, Francis, 40
*Victorine*, 11
Virginia, 10, 21
*Voice of the Fugitive*, 124
*Voice of Liberty*, 156

War of 1812, 20-22, 164
Ward, Samuel, 62
Warren, Fannie, 219
Washington (DC), 22, 38, 103, 104-06,
  180, 217, 219, 222: Auxiliary Guard,
  158, 191, 192
Watkins, Frances Ellen, 133
Webb, Maria, 137
Weems family, vi, 107, 112, 181, 189-90,
  205, 207, 217, 220, 222, 223
  Adam (Addison), 3, 28, 31, 75, 86,
    100, 107, 112, 151, 160, 162, 165,
    167, 168, 169, 220
  Ann Maria, 3, 28, 31, 75, 88, 90, 100,
    107, 112, 114-16, 117-18, 119,
    121-23, 124, 125, 126, 127-30,
    131-33, 134-35, 138, 169-70, 199,
    200, 222
  Arabella ("Airy"), 1, 2-3, 4-5, 27, 28,
    29, 31-32, 37, 41, 42, 64, 66, 67,
    68, 72, 75, 83, 84, 85, 86, 91, 93, 95,
    97, 98, 99, 100, 112, 119, 127, 136,
    144-45, 146, 152, 169, 175, 176, 178,

  179, 180-82, 184, 185-86, 190, 198,
    205, 206, 217, 220, 224, 225, 226-27
  Augustus, 11
  Catharine, 3, 28, 31, 42-43, 71, 75, 79,
    88, 89, 90, 91, 98, 100, 112, 207,
    223, 224, 225, 227-30
  Charity, 11
  Fanny, 11
  John, 11
  John, 1, 2-3, 21, 27, 37, 41, 42, 66-68,
    72, 75, 79, 85, 88, 90, 91, 94, 95,
    97-98, 100, 101-02, 112, 145, 168,
    169, 170, 175, 176, 187-88, 204-05,
    220, 223-25
  John, Jr., 3, 31, 75, 86, 98, 100, 112,
    205, 220
  Joseph, 3, 28, 31, 75, 86, 100, 107,
    112, 151, 160, 162, 163, 165, 167,
    168, 169, 220, 221-22
  Martha, 11, 96
  Mary. *See* Savoy, Mary
    ransom fund, 85, 88, 90, 91, 98-99,
    100, 107-11, 114, 119, 130, 132, 137,
    144, 146, 151, 167, 168, 175, 176, 185,
    186
  Richard, 3, 28, 31, 42, 206
  Robert, 11
  Stella (Mary Jane), 3, 28, 31, 42, 44,
    48, 52, 53, 54, 62, 64-65, 71, 79, 82,
    87, 88, 94, 100, 112, 139-41, 206
  Sylvester, 32, 64-65, 68, 86, 98,
    100, 206
  William Augustus ("Gus"), 3, 28,
    31, 75, 86, 100, 107, 112, 169, 170,
    171, 174-75, 177, 178, 179, 180, 182,
    184, 185, 186, 187-88, 206-07
Weston, A.W., 80
White, Robert, 38
White House, 20
Whiting, William E., 99, 107, 109, 110, 119
Whittier, John Greenleaf, 19

Pierre Simon Fournier le jeune, who designed the type used in this book, was both an originator and a collector of types. His services to the art of print communication were his design of individual characters, his creation of ornaments and initials and his standardization of type sizes. Fournier types are old style in character and sharply cut. In 1764 and 1766 he published his Manuel typographique, a treatise on the history of French types and printing, on typefounding in all its details, and on what many consider his most important contributuon to the printed word – the measurement of type by the point system.